●

CONVERSATIONS

VOLUME 2

ALSO AVAILABLE

Jorge Luis Borges, Osvaldo Ferrari
CONVERSATIONS, VOLUME 1
Translated by Jason Wilson

Jorge Luis Borges

Osvaldo Ferrari

●

CONVERSATIONS

VOLUME 2

Translated by Tom Boll

LONDON NEW YORK CALCUTTA

Seagull Books, 2015

First published as *En Dialogo II* by Editorial Sudamericana in 1998/1999

© Osvaldo Ferrari, 1986 (for *En Dialogo II*)

by arrangement with Paterson Marsh Ltd.

English translation © Tom Boll, 2015

ISBN 978 0 8574 2 300 9

British Library Cataloguing-in-Publication Data

A catalogue record for this book is available from the British Library

Typeset by Seagull Books, Calcutta, India

Printed and bound by Maple Press, York, Pennsylvania, USA

CONTENTS

Jorge Luis Borges

Some 500 years before the birth of Christ, there occurred in Magna Graecia the greatest event to have been recorded by world history— the discovery of dialogue. As faith, certainty, dogmas, anathemas, prayers, prohibitions, orders, taboos, tyrannies, wars and glorious deeds astonished the world, a few Greeks acquired, how we will never know, the singular habit of conversation. They questioned, persuaded, disagreed, changed their minds, procrastinated. Perhaps their mythology helped them, which was, like Shinto, a loose collection of fables and shifting cosmogonies. Those diffuse speculations were the initial manifestation of what today we grandly call metaphysics. Without those few talkative Greeks, Western culture is inconceivable. Distant from them in space and time, this volume is a faint echo of those ancient conversations.

Like all my books, perhaps like all books, this one wrote itself. Ferrari and I tried to allow our words to flow, through us or perhaps in spite of us. We do not ever talk with a fixed purpose. People who have cast an eye over this manuscript assure us that the experience is pleasurable. One hopes that our readers will not disapprove of this generous opinion. In the prologue to one of his 'dreams', Francisco de Quevedo wrote: 'May God spare you, reader, from long prologues, and bad epithets.'

Buenos Aires, 12 October 1985

PROLOGUE

Osvaldo Ferrari

Like its predecessor, this second volume, which completes the series of well-known dialogues between Jorge Luis Borges and myself, contains 45 of the conversations that made up our public communication. Our dialogue developed during this period, aided by a growing feeling between us of friendship and of understanding or, rather, of tacit understanding.

During this period I experienced the thrill of reading his 'Conjectural Poem' out loud while he continued with the poem's conjecture. I witnessed the animation that inspired him as he talked about 'epic flavour', the mystery of language and the poet's intelligence, the unobtrusive, central place his mother occupied in his life and work; his inveterate 'cult of books', the perplexity he experienced when confronted with Buddhism, Spinoza's philosophy, the figure of Alonso Quijano, the past of the druids, Swedenborg's mysticism, Virgil's perfection, the memory and imagination of Shakespeare.

We had recorded numerous conversations and yet Borges wanted to carry on. His predisposition, his fundamental inclination was to perpetuate himself, to turn himself about, to empty himself in words. Not only was this activity undiminished as he reached 84, 85 and 86 years of age, it seemed to grow. Borges had now definitively become a form of expression—his spoken language was comparable to his writings, it seemed to come from a single foundation or space in which everything took shape.

We had two conversations about his last book of poems, *The Conspirators*, where he encapsulated his cosmopolitan ideal and explained his loyalty to the symbols that attended his poetry and his life. But we also talked about the ideas and metaphors that emerged in his later years, and his vision of happiness and beauty, of time and death, of personal destiny and writing: 'Everything is predetermined . . . and this conversation with you, Ferrari, also, without doubt. Everything has been determined.'

It was the same conviction that led him to affirm that his poems and stories were 'given' to him, that he received them from something or someone, and that the work of a writer or artist doesn't ultimately depend on that artist or writer but on something else which transcends him. In spite of his bold agnosticism, his unyielding atheism, the mystery of literary creation delivered him to a mystical perception of things. He would insistently recall two sayings: 'Art happens' by the North American painter Whistler, and 'The spirit blows where it will' from the Bible, and he was delighted to discover, at this late stage of his life, that both sayings mean the same thing.

On Argentina, he demonstrated a deep desire that ethics should come to preside over the country's life; he recalled that our whole history has been the search for a dialogue that has never come to pass, and he suggested that the other, the antagonist, the opponent, can be right, himself offering a first step in that direction; he talked affectionately about Uruguay; he reflected on the United States, recalling his classes and talks in various parts of the Union, where he passed on 'a love of Argentine literature'; and he evoked France through its literature: 'The literary country par excellence.'

On philosophy, he reiterated his permanent allegiance to idealism, the school of thought that corresponds to his vision of life as dream, or to his original poetic conception that being is dreamt being. At the same time, Buddhism and its negation of self led him to recall the affinity between that negation, the idealists and Macedonio Fernández. He maintained, on the other hand, that if he had to take one book with him to a desert island, that book would be Bertrand Russell's *History of Western Philosophy*. As for Socrates, he defended a spirit capable of 'combining reason and myth', the use of reason in tandem with intuition. Of Schopenhauer, a constant presence in his memory, he retained the saying 'To read is to think with somebody else's mind,' and this helps us to understand why Borges told me that he sometimes thought alongside Chesterton, sometimes Shaw, sometimes Schopenhauer. He assimilated into his spirit the writers and philosophers with whom he had identified over the years.

Among that company, we will find that Virgil was one of his permanent literary, epic preferences; that in Lucretius he encountered a mystic without god, as in Carlyle and our erratic Almafuerte. He viewed Quevedo as the classic man of letters, as the amanuensis who values words above all else. Flaubert's life was for him the epitome of the destiny of the man of letters. He considered Voltaire one of the major literary figures, and added that 'to not admire Voltaire is one of the many forms of stupidity.'

'The moon landing' is the only subject that Borges—who did not want to know what we were going to talk about before the recordings—proposed spontaneously, departing from custom, as he considered it 'the great achievement of our century', yet something we tend to forget.

We came to the conclusion that he had transformed the prologue into a literary, and also an affective, genre which expressed his personal attachment to specific authors. It is this, in particular, that allows Borges to reveal new aspects of many of those figures and their work, along with other questions in which attachment or affinity is the common theme of his thought.

Buenos Aires, August 1998

Socrates

●

OSVALDO FERRARI. Someone we haven't talked about before, Borges, and who at times perhaps inspires us, is Socrates. Yet in some way our conversations invoke him.

JORGE LUIS BORGES. Yes, I remember that George Bernard Shaw talks, well, about the apostolic succession of dramatists. So he begins, of course, with the Greek tragedians, and then comes to a great dramatist, Plato, who creates Socrates.

FERRARI. According to Shaw.

BORGES. According to Shaw. Then he comes to other, yet more illustrious, venerable dramatists who write the four gospels, who create Jesus. And after them we have Boswell, who creates Doctor Johnson, then the dramatists we know about, and then Shaw, who embraces the apostolic tradition and is the great dramatist of our time. . . . I think that one of the earliest was Plato, the dramatist who creates Socrates and the other characters who take part in the Socratic dialogue.

FERRARI. Consistent with a theatrical vision of the world.

BORGES. Yes, consistent with a theatrical vision of the world. And then we would have, well, the followers of Pythagoras, perhaps, since Pythagoras didn't leave anything written down, no?

FERRARI. Well, among those who didn't leave anything written down, we have what Karl Jaspers, in his own field of philosophy, describes as the greatest philosophers: Socrates, Buddha, Confucius and Jesus.

BORGES. I think that Confucius did write something . . . there are the *Analects* but he can't have written those since they are anecdotes about him. Now I'm thinking about the example of Mohammed—we have the Koran, but perhaps tradition is more important, no? So we could say that writing isn't the most important thing, what matters isn't to write but to talk and for someone to record that conversation . . . well, at the moment I'm just a modest Pythagoras (*laughs*) from the Southern Cone of South America.

FERRARI. You know that Jaspers adds that Socrates' life was a continuous conversation with everyone, that's to say, with all the citizens of Athens.

BORGES. Now, in Plato's case, I think . . . but I'd have to be a Hellenist for all this, and I can barely remember things that I read many years ago, and I can't read Greek either. It's possible that Plato, to console himself for the death of Socrates, found a way of allowing Socrates to carry on talking posthumously. And whenever he was faced with a problem, he would ask himself: 'What would Socrates have said?' Although, of course, Plato's thinking not only branches out into Socrates but also in other interlocutors—Gorgias, for example.

There are experts in philosophy who have wondered exactly what Plato's intention was in this or that dialogue. It seems to me that one could say that he has no intention, that he's allowed his thinking to branch out among various interlocutors, and that he's imagined those various opinions but without having a clear purpose in mind. That's possible, no?

FERRARI. Moreover, having captured the spirit of Socrates, he was able to perpetuate it.

BORGES. I suspect that he needed to perpetuate him, since he refused to accept the death of Socrates. Plato liked to think: 'Well, here is Socrates, who carries on thinking, carries on thinking beyond the hemlock, beyond physical death, beyond that last dialogue' in which Socrates combines reason and myth.

FERRARI. Ah, that's crucial.

BORGES. Yes, one doesn't realize that they are two different things. We seem to have lost that ability. I suppose that in the beginning, myth must have been a way of thinking. And in Christ's case, he thought in parables, that is, Christ had a special way of thinking. How strange— the person who never seems to have realized this is Milton. Because in *Paradise Lost* everything is discussed rationally, or, as Pope said, Milton makes Jesus and Satan talk like two schoolmen. How could Milton not realize that Jesus was, in addition to who he was, a style? On the other hand, Blake said that, like himself, Christ wanted salvation through ethics, through the intellect, through aesthetics as well, since those parables are aesthetic creations, and Christ's meta-phors are extraordinary. For example, anyone might have condemned funeral rites, anyone might have condemned funerals, but not Christ. He says: 'Let the dead bury their dead' and that, well, aesthetically, is a wonderful saying. One could almost write a story about that, eh? About dead people who bury the dead—a fantastic story.

FERRARI. Certainly.

BORGES. And he always talks like that. Another example is what he says about the stoning of an adulterous woman: 'Let he who is without sin cast the first stone.' They're extraordinary verbal inventions which haven't been equalled since, and each one, according to Blake, is a lesson in aesthetics. Now the example of Socrates is extraordinary because although— as far as I know—he hasn't left a single written line, we do have a sense of him as a person distinct from Plato. Plato doesn't identify with Socrates—Socrates has his own existence, and will continue to exist in people's imaginations. And then, one only has to compare this last dialogue of Socrates with the scenes from the Passion in the New Testament . . . because the scenes from the Passion are created precisely to evoke pity.

FERRARI. Confronted with hemlock and with the cross.

BORGES. Yes, confronted with hemlock and with the cross. Yet Socrates doesn't evoke pity—Socrates speaks as if this weren't his last conversation. Its power lies precisely in the contrast that we constantly feel between the wonderful reasoning and the wonderful fables that Socrates produces, and the fact that he says all that, well, on the brink of death. Besides, the problem of immortality is especially important for him, since he's dying as he discusses it. It's extraordinary, the opposite of pathetic—without any complaint he accepts his fate and carries on talking, as he had done all his life, which is much more important than the fact that he was forced to drink hemlock.

FERRARI. He would have reached that state of calm to which you say one should aspire at a certain stage of life.

BORGES. Well, that's what Spinoza wanted, of course, because when Spinoza talks about the intellectual love of God, what he means is that one must accept fate knowing that all things are, well, inherently logical, no? And we can see that in the system he employed in his *Ethics*, the 'Ordine Geometrico', since he thought that the universe was also made in that way, that the universe was also logical, that the universe was more or less made in the manner of the geometry of Euclides.

FERRARI. And he would imagine perhaps that his work was also part of that universal harmony.

BORGES. Certainly, since his life and work, well, and our lives and the lives of Spinoza's readers—they are all part of that infinite divinity.

FERRARI. Of course. Now, you say, Borges, that we've lost the capacity to use reason and myth at the same time, but you haven't personally lost it yourself, if I may say so.

BORGES. No . . . I don't know if I've ever managed to use reason at any time in my life. As far as myth is concerned, I have made modest myths, well, modest fables, let's say. In general, one assumes now that there are two types of books. Even in Aristotle's case—Aristotle had already lost the mythical capacity, although he reasoned admirably, no? Yet in Plato it's preserved, and there are whole books about Plato's myths—the myth of Atlantis, for example.

FERRARI. I think it's extremely dangerous to have lost that ability which Plato and Socrates possessed.

BORGES. For the two things to be able to exist side by side?

FERRARI. Yes, to be left with only the Aristotelian practice.

BORGES. Yes, now we either produce abstract writing or fable, metaphor which is a lesser form of myth. But, in the end, they are two different styles.

FERRARI. Of course, there's a saying in Socrates, which I think you'll like: 'I only ever address the individual.'

BORGES. The individual is the only real thing. I've used that argument to give me confidence when I'm about to give a talk. I've thought: The fact that there are 500 of my contemporaries out there isn't important, since I'm not talking to a form of many-headed monster. No, I address each one of those individuals. Even if I'm talking in front of 500 people, we are both really people—them and me. Although, of course, the individual has been rejected by Hume, has been rejected by Buddha, has been rejected among ourselves by Macedonio Fernández (*laughs*). I believe that one of the first things in the Buddhist catechism—'The dialogues of King Milinda'—that the monk teaches the king, and which will eventually become the Buddhist faith, is that the self doesn't exist. That is, the idea that would later be associated with Hume, Schopenhauer, and to which I believe by his own method Macedonio Fernández arrived.

FERRARI. Yes, well, we have a Hindu mystic, Aurobindo, who said that no revolution or evolution is possible in society if each individual doesn't change or improve.

BORGES. Yes, I think that one tends to exaggerate the State's importance now. Not only the State—everyone thinks that a country relies on its government. But governments aren't so important, perhaps the important thing is each individual, or each way of living. Well, let's take an example that occurs to me just now—let's suppose that Switzerland is a kingdom and that Sweden is a republic. Would they change in any way? I don't think so, eh?

FERRARI. It simply depends on their citizens.

BORGES. That's why I say, the other forms of government. . . . Now we tend to suppose that's all very important, but perhaps it isn't, and it also leads to the mistaken assumption that the government is to blame for everybody's ills . . . perhaps the government is as confused as the rest of us, as each one of us. That's the most likely explanation.

FERRARI. That's why, if we recall Socrates, we will see that he devoted his life to educating man as a citizen.

BORGES. Yes.

FERRARI. Because if man isn't educated as a citizen, no matter how good the government, society can't function.

BORGES. That is, in this case, each one of us would have to re-educate himself and only then would we be able to save that body of individuals we call the nation.

FERRARI. Of course.

BORGES. And hence the world—since the world is made up of individuals.

FERRARI. And perhaps the example of Socrates can help us.

BORGES. . . . Yes, in the case of Socrates one thinks in particular about that final dialogue, but one would have to think about his whole life.

47

On the United States

●

OSVALDO FERRARI. You seem, Borges, to have an extensive historical and of course literary vision of that enormous country which Argentina has engaged with and retreated from over the years. I'm talking about the United States. You know that, since the last century, the political stances of both countries have been in conflict, although at other times they have seen eye to eye.

JORGE LUIS BORGES. The political stances are the least of it. Now, what people tend to forget is that the United States are states that have been brought together, that is, they're extremely diverse. The word 'yankee' refers to whatever comes from the north. It's a rather pejorative word, and it denotes quite distinct regions. My mother and I discovered the United States through Texas—that was in 1961, and I had a chair in Argentine literature there. I told them when I started that I didn't know that literature well but that I loved certain authors, and that I was going to try to teach my students a love of some of those authors. Not all of them, of course. I had, well, a small number, that is, an adequate number, of students, and right away I realized that there was one subject that didn't interest them and that was gaucho literature. It was only natural, why would they be interested in gauchos when they were sick of cowboys (*laughs*)? And the subject, of course, of the Far West, is a subject that implies a certain nostalgia, or hope, that is experienced by the East, let's say. In Texas, they realize that is all rather artificial and they are not interested. But what interested me was the idea that, in the end, all this history is the same, in some way, as Argentine history—we also have, well, the conquest, indians, prairies, horsemen who can be called gaucho or *gaúcho*, or cowboy or *llanero*. But it made no difference—they couldn't get at all interested in that subject. I did manage to interest them in some poets who don't cultivate local colour, something which, fortunately, barely exists there. That is, I managed to get some of the students to fall in love with the sonnets of Enrique Banchs, the poems of Arturo Capdevila, also Paul Groussac's prose. And when I came back, I showed Carlos Mastronardi an analysis of that wonderful poem of his, 'Provincial Light', by a young woman from Texas, from Austin. And another woman wrote a line by line analysis of a sonnet by Banchs, and admirably, that analysis didn't use any proper names but it conveyed the metaphors, the syntax, the rhythm. . . . I thought, well, I've allowed a few people in Texas who hadn't heard of Argentina to gain some familiarity with lines of poetry written in my country. I've managed to arouse their interest. When I think about the United States, I think of so many different countries. . . . First of all, of Texas—I was told, why not mention this in passing, that the indians who gave their name to that vast territory were the Teshas indians but that *x* was used to designate the *sh* sound. And so

Cervantes talked about 'Don Quishote', about 'reloshes', about 'shaulas', about 'pásharos' and about 'Méshico'. They aren't that different—they can easily be confused. I got to know Austin, a lovely city, I have many memories of friendships there. Later on we got to know the other parts of the country. . . . Last year I discovered the 'Deep South' which sounds good in English but in Spanish . . . because if I translated it as 'profundo Sur' it wouldn't sound right. Language is so mysterious, no? 'Hondo Sur' is pleasing but 'profundo Sur' doesn't sound right. And the word 'oeste' is undistinguished in Spanish. Besides, it's difficult to pronounce 'oeste'—it's ugly. On the other hand, 'west', yes, and 'Wild West' or 'Far West' sound good.

FERRARI. Now, as for the Deep South, and the Wild West, I've noticed that, thinking in epic terms, it still suggests not only the conquest of the North American West for you but also the terrible conflict that was the American Civil War.

BORGES. Yes, that war—I was aware of it when I was there, a lot of people aren't—was the major war of the nineteenth century. The War of Independence was minor in comparison. For example, the battle of Junín—in which my great-grandfather Suárez led the Peruvian cavalry (the whole battle was commanded by Bolívar, of course)—lasted three quarters of an hour, and not a single shot was fired, all the fighting was done with sabre and lance. That is, it was a mere skirmish but with great historical consequences. And Ayacucho can't have lasted much longer. On the other hand, in the Civil War there were battles like the battle of Gettysburg that lasted three days, and it was a terrible battle because the infantry had to attack the artillery head on and, of course, it was decimated. I remember Utah, also, where I talked to the Mormons. I'd come across the Mormons for the first time in a book called *A Study in Scarlet*—a name that suggests a painting rather than a book—which was written in the last decade of the nineteenth century and which explored affinities between painting and literature. So I talked to Mormon theologians, and they told me that the Book of Mormon is so vague—naturally, one doesn't expect precision from a sacred book—that it permits an indefinite number of theological interpretations. And one of those interpretations, or ideas, was proposed by a Mormon theologian I talked to: In heaven, one carries on working and one continues to evolve. And, at the end of a certain time—I don't know if it can be calculated in centuries, or in hundreds of centuries—one can become a god. Then, being a god, one is allowed like Jehovah in Genesis to create a universe. And that universe can have (why not?) its own geology, botany, zoology, its just beings.

FERRARI. It's like the Buddhist idea of reincarnation.

BORGES. That's right, they're similar but, I don't know, it seems to offer a more attractive heaven.

FERRARI. Than nirvana.

BORGES. Or than paradise which, to judge from Dante, is a rather tedious place, a place of hymns, of exaltation, and that's it. On the other hand, the idea of an evolution that creates the soul is a lovely idea. I also know that region well, perhaps the most blessed, from the aesthetic point of view, of the whole Americas—New England. Since to talk about New England is to summon the great names of Poe, Emerson, Melville, Hawthorne, Thoreau and Emily Dickinson, and

Robert Frost who, although he was born in California, was a New England poet. That country is now part of my memory, and I believe that were it only for Poe and Whitman, and for Emerson and Melville, we would owe a great deal to the United States. And for the major feat that this century can be proud of—the fact that man has walked on the moon. Now, strangely, H. G. Wells and Jules Verne thought that this feat was impossible. And yet we've seen it happen. Carlos Mastronardi said to me that Conrado Nalé Roxlo told him, 'The moon has lost all of its allure, now that it's near.' And Mastronardi replied, 'How's that? Do trees or women lose their allure because they're near?' (*Laughs.*) Nalé Roxlo's comment was ridiculous, perhaps he said it to fill an awkward pause in the conversation. Because it seems strange to think that the moon is less mysterious simply because men have walked on it. Everything carries on being mysterious, even the men who walked there—Armstrong is no less mysterious than any of the rest of us. I taught, not Argentine literature which I don't know well—I'm certainly not Ricardo Rojas—but a love of that literature. I've taught it to young men and women in Texas, that was in 1961. And later, I taught at Harvard, Cambridge, Massachusetts. And then in a fairly indifferent city—East Lansing, in Michigan, and then in Bloomington, Indiana. I've also given talks on Argentine writers in those places.

FERRARI. And then here, in Buenos Aires, you taught a love of North American literature.

BORGES. That's right, and that's a good thing. I think I've told that story about a young man who stopped me in the street, and said: 'I'd like to thank you for something, Borges, you introduced me to Robert

Louis Stevenson.' Then I felt vindicated . . . I felt vindicated at that moment . . . one so seldom feels vindicated. To think that I'd revealed to that man the knowledge, the friendship, the love of an author like Stevenson. I thought: Well, this excuses my bad writing and my worse talks. If I've taught somebody to appreciate Stevenson, that's more important than the discovery of a continent or perhaps even the moon (*both laugh*).

FERRARI. It's strange that in the last century the United States produced two poets of such contrasting visions, so different from each other—I'm talking about Edgar Allan Poe who champions the aristocracy, and Walt Whitman who talks essentially about democracy.

BORGES. Yes, but I think that Poe was impressed by, rather than the aristocracy, let's say . . . terror, no? The supernatural.

FERRARI. But he talks about it a number of times, as Baudelaire notes. Poe had an aristocratic understanding of society whereas Whitman is at the other extreme.

BORGES. So they aren't comparable.

FERRARI. Of course.

BORGES. One doesn't have to view them in opposition. They were two men, both geniuses, and geniuses . . . well, perhaps in a way that means that the one excludes the other.

FERRARI. Great variety is extremely rewarding, as in this example.

BORGES. Yes, and it's the variety that occurs in the United States, of course, where everything is quite different. And the people. . . . When I arrived in Texas, I knew something about North American literature. However, I came to a house at night—we were staying on the fifth floor, and right away I thought: This isn't very high up. Because, of course, we were in the United States, there were skyscrapers . . . and the following morning I realized that the building was only six storeys high, and that there were no skyscrapers in Austin. I even remember going for a walk with my mother and wandering into a poor neighbourhood, and how shocked I was at those extremely poor houses, the mud and puddles. I said to my mother, 'My word, we are back in Palermo and Maldonado.' Because they were so similar. And I was shocked like that, naively, because there was poverty, because there was grass, and puddles. It's very strange, I had the idea that everything over there would be artificial, and that everything would be very tall and very imposing. When I arrived in Austin, I came across a small city, as attractive as Lomas or Androgué, for example, but completely different.

FERRARI. The United States has a great number of excellent poets, as we know . . .

BORGES. Of course, and I'd like to take this opportunity to recall Robert Frost. The example of Frost is strange—he was born in California, but he's a typical New England poet, from the north of Boston, which is precisely where I lived, in Cambridge, to the north of Boston.

FERRARI. The South, though, has stronger links with novelists than with poets. As in the case of William Faulkner, for example.

BORGES. I'd say that he's almost the only one, isn't he? The South, of course, as an aristocratic society was perhaps less propitious . . . a feudal society, as the South was, wasn't a propitious society for poetry.

FERRARI. But it was for novelists like John Steinbeck.

BORGES. Yes, but I think he's from California which isn't really the South. For example, that myth which is popular now across the world—the cowboy. It refers to the West but it didn't happen in the South, in what's called the Deep South, which is an area of cotton fields and tobacco plantations but not of prairies and horsemen. How strange to think that Mark Twain fought in the Civil War, and that his 'belligerence' (as Leopoldo Lugones would have called it) lasted for a couple of weeks. He formed a kind of regiment with his friends. I don't know how many there would have been of them . . . no, in fact, there wouldn't have been enough for a regiment. They learnt to ride a horse—they hadn't known how to until then—and they went from plantation to plantation. And they were well received—each time the enemy approached, they effected a strategic withdrawal (*laughs*). And then, one day, they were camping out in some place, and they saw a man on horseback, and they decided—since, after all, they were at war—that this horseman was an enemy fighter. So they opened fire on him, and then realized to their horror, when the man fell off his horse, that they had killed him. And then it turned out that he wasn't a soldier at all, he was a regular horseman. But they all felt the horror of having killed a man, and they disbanded. And that was the 'belligerence' of Mark Twain. It appeared in an article years later—he felt the horror. There had been a number of them all together but he'd also opened fire on that man, and it was possible that he killed him, and that seemed atrocious to him, quite reasonably, of course. And fortunately that was the end of his involvement in the war. Then he was a miner in California, he was a pilot in the

Mississippi, and he wrote his books which we all remember. And he was responsible for good works, particularly in the South. A good-natured man.

FERRARI. Perhaps the question arises whether, being so technically advanced now, that country can carry on producing such outstanding poets. If living in a technocracy will change that tradition.

BORGES. But I believe that it can. I believe that poetry survives everything, don't you think?

FERRARI. Ah, well, let's hope so.

BORGES. Yes, now one tends to exaggerate the influence of context, of political regimes. A while ago I was asked if Argentine poetry would improve after the elections (*both laugh*). It's worth remembering the North American artist, the painter Whistler. Someone was talking about these questions, and about inheritance, biological factors, and he said: 'Art happens.' That is, art is a minor miracle.

FERRARI. Yes, and that's quite right.

BORGES. I think it is, 'Art happens,' or, to put it another way, in biblical terms: 'The spirit blows where it will.' Which is the same thing, no?

FERRARI. And it's independent of historical periods and technical development.

BORGES. And the sayings are synonymous: 'Art happens' and 'The spirit blows where it will.' It's perhaps a more attractive way of saying the same thing. The meaning is the same. How strange, I've just now realized that the two expressions are identical.

FERRARI. That's right.

BORGES. I have had to live 85 years to come to the modest conclusion that both expressions are the same, and while talking to you, Ferrari.

48

The Cult of Books

●

OSVALDO FERRARI. One of your essays, Borges, is called 'On the Cult of Books'. It made me think of titles and authors you mention repeatedly.

JORGE LUIS BORGES. I don't remember anything at all about that . . . Do I talk about sacred books, about the fact that each country has a preference for a particular book?

FERRARI. You mention the former, yes, but you also refer to people who have criticized books in favour of oral language. For example, there's a passage in Plato where he says that excessive reading leads to the neglect of memory and to a dependence on symbols.

BORGES. I think that Schopenhauer said that to read is to think with somebody else's mind. Which is the same idea, no? Well no, it isn't the same idea but it is hostile to books. Did I mention that?

FERRARI. No.

BORGES. Perhaps I talked about the fact that each country chooses, prefers to be represented by a book although that book isn't usually characteristic of the country. For example, one regards Shakespeare as typically English. However, none of the typical characteristics of the English are found in Shakespeare. The English tend to be reserved, reticent, but Shakespeare flows like a great river, he abounds in hyperbole and metaphor—he's the complete opposite of an English person. Or, in Goethe's case, we have the Germans who are easily roused to fanaticism but Goethe turns out to be the very opposite—a tolerant man, a man who greets Napoleon when Napoleon invades Germany. Goethe isn't a typical German. Now, this seems to be a common occurrence, no?

FERRARI. Especially in the case of the classics.

BORGES. Especially in the case of the classics, yes. Well, and . . . the Spain of Cervantes' time is the Spain of the burnings of the Inquisition, the fanatical Spain. And Cervantes, although he's Spanish, he's a cheerful man, one imagines him as tolerant, he didn't have anything to do with all that. It's as if each country looks for a form of antidote in the author it chooses. In France's case, however, it has such a rich literary tradition that it hasn't chosen one figure, but if one goes for Hugo—clearly, Hugo isn't like the majority of French people.

FERRARI. Of course.

BORGES. And, oddly, the military here have enthusiastically welcomed the canonization of Martín Fierro, although he was a deserter, a deserter who went over to the enemy. Yet the Argentine military venerate José Hernández's *Martín Fierro*.

FERRARI. As for your personal cult of books, Borges, I recall that your favourites include *The Thousand and One Nights*, the Bible and, among many others, the *Encyclopaedia Britannica*.

BORGES. I think that the encyclopedia, for a leisurely, curious man, is the most pleasing of literary genres. And, besides, it has an illustrious forerunner in Pliny, whose *Natural History* is an encyclopedia too. There you have information on art, history—it isn't simply a natural history in the current meaning of the term—and on legends, also on myths. So that when he talks about some animal, he doesn't simply give factual information but everything recorded by legend—the magical properties attributed to it, even though Pliny probably didn't believe in them. But, in the end, he did produce that splendid encyclopedia which was also written in a baroque style.

FERRARI. Talking specifically about the *Encyclopaedia Britannica*, what have you discovered in it over the years?

BORGES. Mostly, long articles. Encyclopedias are made for reference now, so there are long articles and extremely short ones. The *Encyclopaedia Britannica*, however, was made for reading, that is, it was a series of essays—essays by Macaulay, Stevenson, Swinburne. In the later editions there were occasional essays by Shaw as well. Essays by Bertrand Russell, for example, on Zeno of Elea. I must have told you that I used to go to the National Library with my father. I was very shy—I'm still very shy—so I didn't dare request books. But there were reference works on the shelves, and I would simply take down by chance, for example, a volume of the *Encyclopaedia Britannica*. One day I was extremely fortunate, because I took down the volume D–R, and I was able to read an excellent biography of Dryden, who Eliot has written a book about. Then, a long article on the druids, and another on the Druzes of Lebanon who believe in the transmigration of souls. There are Chinese Druzes too. Yes, that day I was very lucky: Dryden, druids and Druzes, and all those things in the same volume that went from D to R. At other times, I wasn't so fortunate. I'd go with my father, my father would look up books on psychology—he was a psychology teacher—while I would read the *Encyclopaedia Britannica*. Later I'd read *Huckleberry Finn* by Mark Twain in the National Library. And it never occurred to me that, one day, in an improbable future, I'd become director of the library. If someone had told me that, I'd have thought they were joking. Yet that's what happened. And when I was director I remembered that boy who would visit with his father and timidly take down a volume of the *Encyclopaedia* from the shelf.

FERRARI. And you were director for almost two decades, I think.

BORGES. I don't know the precise dates, but they appointed me in 1955, until . . . I don't know what year Perón came back, because I couldn't rightly carry on.

FERRARI. In 1973. So 18 years in the library.

BORGES. Well, that's not bad, is it? Who's the director now?

FERRARI. Up until quite recently it was Gregorio Weinberg.

BORGES. Ah, yes. I think he resigned, didn't he?

FERRARI. He resigned, and I still don't know who replaced him.

BORGES. I remember that the budget we received was paltry. Maybe that's not changed. Perhaps that was the reason for Weinberg's resignation.

FERRARI. As usual. You'd have to manage with the bare minimum then?

BORGES. And the Ministry of Education has been the most debilitated, the most vulnerable of all. Perhaps it still is.

FERRARI. In that essay, Borges, you also refer to the eighth book of *The Odyssey*, where it says that God has given misfortune to men so that they will have something to sing about.

BORGES. Yes, I think that it says that they weave misfortunes so that men from generations to come will have something to sing about, no?

FERRARI. Yes.

BORGES. Well, that would be enough to prove that *The Odyssey* comes after *The Iliad*, because one can't imagine a reflection like that in *The Iliad*.

FERRARI. Of course, because Homer gives the idea of beginnings . . .

BORGES. Yes, and as Rubén Darío said: Doubtless Homer had his own Homer. Since literature always presupposes a precursor, or a tradition. One could say that language is itself a tradition—each language offers a range of possibilities and of impossibilities as well, or difficulties. I don't remember that essay, 'The Cult of Books'.

FERRARI. It's in *Other Inquisitions*.

BORGES. I'm sure it exists, since I don't think you've made it up to test my memory, or my lack of memory.

FERRARI (*laughs*). It exists, and it's also from 1951.

BORGES. Ah good, right, in that case I have every right to have forgotten it. It would be very sad to have remembered the year 1951.

FERRARI. But you end with that remark by Stéphane Mallarmé.

BORGES. Ah yes, that everything leads to a book, no?

FERRARI. Of course.

BORGES. Yes, because I take those lines from Homer and I say that they both say the same thing. But Homer was still thinking about song, about poetry that wells up in a surge of inspiration. In contrast, Mallarmé was already thinking about a book, and, in a sense, about a sacred book. In fact, they're the same thing—everything exists in order to end up in a book, or everything leads to a book.

FERRARI. That's to say, events are ultimately literary. But a book you always recommend, even to people who aren't literary enthusiasts, is the Bible.

BORGES. Well, because the Bible is a library. Now, how strange that idea of the Hebrews to attribute such disparate works as Genesis, the Song of Songs, the Book of Job, Ecclesiastes, to attribute all of those works to a single author—the Holy Spirit. They are clearly works that correspond to quite different minds and quite different localities and, above all, to different centuries, to diverse periods of thought.

FERRARI. Well, it must have something to do with that other saying in the Bible: 'The spirit blows where it will.'

BORGES. Yes, which is in the Gospel according to St John, I think, no? In the first verses.

FERRARI. Yes, if you compare it with that phrase from Whistler, 'Art happens,' in another of our conversations.

BORGES. I hadn't realized, but of course, that's the same idea, 'Art happens,' 'The spirit blows where it will.' That is, it's the opposite of, well, a sociology of poetry, no? Of studying poetry socially, of studying the conditions that have produced poetry. . . . That reminds me of Heine, who said that the historian is a retrospective prophet (*laughs*), someone who prophesies what has already happened. It amounts to the same idea.

FERRARI. Of course, a prophet in reverse.

BORGES. Yes, someone who prophesies what has already happened, and what one already knows has happened, no? 'The prophet who looks backwards'—the historian.

FERRARI. Who's that from, Borges?

BORGES. Heine. History would be the art of divining the past, no?

FERRARI. Yes, the art of the historian.

BORGES. Yes, once something has happened, one demonstrates that it happened inevitably. But it would be more interesting to apply that to the future (*both laugh*).

FERRARI. That's more difficult than to predict the past—it's harder to be a prophet than a historian.

BORGES. Well, that's how literary histories are written. One takes each author, then one demonstrates the influence of his background and, then, how the work must logically stem from that author. But this method doesn't apply to the future, that is, one doesn't give the names and works of twenty-first-century Argentine writers, does one?

FERRARI. But in literary histories there isn't such a demand for correctness as in history proper—one is still allowed to be literary.

BORGES. Yes, one would hope so.

FERRARI. *A*nother book that appears frequently in your library is, I think, *The Thousand and One Nights*.

BORGES. Yes, and my ignorance of Arabic has allowed me to read it in many translations, and of course I must have told you that, of all the versions I've read, perhaps the most pleasing is by Rafael Cansinos Assens. Although even more pleasing is the earliest one, the one by Antoine Galland who first presented that book to the West.

FERRARI. In your essay, there's another idea that I find interesting— you say that, for the ancients, the written word was merely a substitute for the spoken word.

BORGES. Yes, I think Plato says that books are like living things but that they are also like statues—one talks to them but they can't talk back.

FERRARI. Ah, of course.

BORGES. Then, precisely so that books could talk back, he invented the dialogue which anticipates the reader's questions and allows for explanation and a proliferation of thought.

FERRARI. Yes, that applies to oral language, but you add that, towards the fourth century, written language begins to predominate over oral language.

BORGES. Ah, and I refer to the anecdote of the person who is astonished at another person reading in silence.

FERRARI. Of course. Saint Augustine is astonished at Saint Ambrose, I think.

BORGES. Yes, he's astonished because he sees something he has never seen before—someone reading quietly to himself. Of course, he had to, because the books were written by hand. You must have experienced it many times—when you receive a letter, and the handwriting in that letter isn't faultless, let's say, you read it aloud to make sense of it, no?

FERRARI. Yes.

BORGES. And if the books were written by hand, it was only natural that they be read aloud. Aside from that point, I think that if you're reading silently, and you come to a powerful passage, a passage that moves you, then you tend to read it aloud. I think that a well-written passage demands to be read aloud. In the case of verse, it's obvious, because the music of verse needs to be expressed even if only in a murmur—it has to be heard. On the other hand, if you're reading something that's purely logical, purely abstract, it's different. In that case, you can do without reading it aloud. But you can't do without that reading if you're dealing with a poem.

FERRARI. It's part of that exaltation, however minimal, that poetry requires.

BORGES. Yes, but of course that's becoming lost now, since people no longer have an ear for it. Unfortunately, everyone is now capable of reading in silence, because they don't hear what they read—they go directly to the meaning of the text.

49

Argentina's Past, Present and Future

●

OSVALDO FERRARI. I'd like to know, Borges, how you see Argentina, or how you remember it (I'm talking about inner vision here) from the perspective of your travels—from the technocratic North American and European worlds, for example, or even from the ancient Western world: from Greece, from Sicily. In short, I'd like to know how you view Argentina from a distance.

JORGE LUIS BORGES. I always have an anachronistic memory of this country. Of course, I lost my sight a little before I was 55, more or less my reading sight. I imagine Buenos Aires in a completely anachronistic way. For example, I automatically think of Buenos Aires as a city of low houses. . . . Of course, it seems as if I've never seen that much, but when I could see, what I saw made an impression on me. Now I know that vision was false. Yet I still hold on to it, I still imagine a Buenos Aires that, of course, doesn't look like the real Buenos Aires, I keep on imagining a Buenos Aires of low houses, of flat roofs, of patios, of water tanks, of hallways. I know it's all anachronistic, I know it no longer applies. Apart from, perhaps in a rather theatrical way near the Parque Lezama, or what they now call Palermo Viejo . . . but there it's preserved in an artificial way. I still see things in this way. As for politics—the truth is that politics doesn't interest me, apart from its ethical function. That is, if I've intervened in politics, it has simply been for ethical and for no other reasons. I'm not affiliated to any party, I don't hope for or fear anything. Well, I might perhaps be afraid of something from a particular party, but I try to live at the margins of that, and I try to live in my own way, that's to say, inventing, inventing fables, thinking. . . . And, now, well, perhaps we have some right to hope. Or perhaps we have a duty to hope. I believe that an act of faith is required of each one of us if we want to save the nation. And perhaps this act of faith isn't difficult, although its consequences are . . . and they're still rather remote. But we have to think, not about what will happen this year or the next but about, well, what things will be like in five years, and perhaps in that way we can work together. An act of faith, yes.

FERRARI. Of course. This anachronism that you talk about is related to a wider anachronism. You know that there's the suspicion that there is something in us, in the Argentines, that's reluctant to adapt itself unconditionally to technology as a way of life. Taiwan or Brazil, say, and of course Canada, adopt technology as something beneficial and use it productively. In Canada, they claim that by 2000 they will have created what they call 'the technocratic society'. While we seem to be resisting that line.

BORGES. Yet I don't know if we have any other choice. Well, the practice of ethics is always open to us, and that's something individual. I don't know if I'm capable of thinking in a general way. I can think about my behaviour, about the behaviour of the people I love, about my friends. But something as vague as the future of history, I don't know if I'm capable of thinking like that. . . . Of course I've spent my life rereading Schopenhauer, and Schopenhauer said that to look for a purpose in history is to look for bays, rivers or lions in the clouds—one finds them because one is looking for them. He thought that history has no purpose. However, it seems extremely sad to think that. We must believe that history has a purpose, at least an ethical purpose, perhaps, an aesthetic purpose as well. Otherwise, we would live in a chaotic world, which perhaps we do but that isn't comforting. But . . . our dreams are also a part of reality, and can have an effect on it, no? So that even looking for lions counts for something (*both laugh*).

FERRARI. This reluctance that I'm talking about, towards the fashion for technology, seems to have something to do with a form of root-edness, and that rootedness, that difficulty in changing the way that the West is changing, well, my question is: Can it help us? Can it harm us? What do you think?

BORGES. I would say that it harms us, but I don't know if my opinion is worth anything. Besides, I don't know if we have an existence outside the West—we're part of the West.

FERRARI. Let's suppose that, from our limited cultural perspective, we suspect that the West is wrong in its current path of development. In that case . . .

BORGES. What other possible path is there? Would you suggest humanism? But we practise that as well, as does the West.

FERRARI. Yes, that's exactly what I'm talking about.

BORGES. But that isn't an Argentine invention either—that would be most strange. We haven't invented anything, as far as I know.

FERRARI. No, the invention would be the sense of rootedness in what went before. Another thing that doesn't change with the Argentines— this is probably a negative thing—is the lack of an inclination to belong to a community. To act in a community for the common good.

BORGES. That's a serious failing, of course. I think that it's due to the fact that one thinks, well, in terms of such and such a party, of personal gain—one doesn't think about the country. And that seems to me a serious failing, and I think that you'll agree with me, and everyone will agree with me, in theory. But in practice, they act in a different way. There's no question about that, no?

FERRARI. Since the last century, it seems, one of the things that we've steadily perfected among ourselves is sectarianism . . . Unitarians and Federalists, etcetera, etcetera, etcetera.

BORGES. Yes, but they also correspond to genuine differences. The fact of being Unitarian or Federalist isn't meaningless, I think that it's something real. Besides, now it seems to me that it's fairly clear-cut, well, to be or not to be a supporter of a certain dictator whose name I don't wish to recall. All this relates to a particular ethical position and to particular people, or at least I hope that it relates to them.

FERRARI. But sectarianism persists in relation to questions surrounding the common good, where one assumes that a sensible country would behave differently.

BORGES. In relation to what, for example?

FERRARI. For example, in relation to the economy.

BORGES. Yes, of course, but the result has been ruinous. Of course, a country like ours, made up entirely of schemers, would inevitably end in ruin, no?

FERRARI. It's clear that countries which make economic progress share a sense of community in economic affairs.

BORGES. Yes, and here, unfortunately, it seems that we don't. Each person thinks about personal gain and personal destiny. The result is generalized ruin.

FERRARI. It's the triumph of the psychology of drowning over the psychology of community.

BORGES. Yes, that metaphor is very good, it's spot on.

FERRARI. Every man for himself.

BORGES. Yes, and with that one ends up with a situation where no one is saved. That's the end result.

FERRARI. No one is saved. Only recently I saw a reader's letter in a newspaper which said: 'I would like to explain one thing to my compatriots: no one will be saved if we cannot save every one of us.'

BORGES. That's very good, that's true.

FERRARI. I hope that, in time, we'll come to grasp that idea and put it into practice. What do you think? Will we get there some day?

BORGES. You . . . certainly, will get there, you're a young man. Myself no, I expect to die at any moment. Of course I won't live that long, I don't know if I'll live 10 more years. Certainly not. Besides, it would be a calamity for me to do so. I've left the term, well, the reasonable term of life behind. Scripture fixes it at 70 years, I'm 84. Now, Schopenhauer—he prefers the Hindu calculation which says that in human life the norm is a hundred years, that if a person dies before they reach a hundred, they die as the result of illness or an accident, like falling in a river or being eaten by a tiger. So that figure of a hundred would be right, since only after a hundred years will a person die without suffering, spontaneously, that is, he will cease to be, all of a sudden. Before that is a different matter. Before that, something as random as, well, an illness or an accident is needed to kill him.

FERRARI. But you know, Borges, that miracles can defy time.

BORGES. Yes, and then?

FERRARI. Then, you might suddenly see the country that we wish for.

BORGES. Ah! It's possible. There's also another possibility, which Shaw suggests—that a generation appears among us of immortals or people who live an extremely long time (*both laugh*). Perhaps we'll be the first people to live for an extremely long time, the first immortals, as in that splendid comedy *Back to Methuselah*, in which people suddenly appear who live to 300 years. They have to hide, of course, so as not to draw attention to themselves, because if they draw attention to themselves they might be punished or persecuted. But a generation appears in which, according to Shaw, there are no adults. He thought that in the East there could be adults but not in the West. In the West, says Shaw, a man dies at 90 with a golf club in his hand, that is, he dies at 90 but he's still a child (*laughs*).

FERRARI. Either of those two possibilities—a miracle among us, or longevity, would be an extremely good thing in any case.

BORGES. Yes, but rather painful. One gets tired of life, no?

FERRARI. Yes, but there's a permanent renovation, we see it in your own case, in your travels, in your . . .

BORGES. Well, I try to provide whatever variety I can.

FERRARI. And you're successful.

BORGES. How?

FERRARI. You're frequently successful.

BORGES. I don't know if I'm successful. It seems to me that I'm always writing the same story, I'm discovering the same metaphor, I'm writing the same poems . . . but with slight variations which may be worth something.

FERRARI. Those variations could prove, all of a sudden, that man is capable of perfection, if only for a brief period . . .

BORGES. I don't know if that's true, but one needs to believe in it. If not, what reason would I have to carry on living?

FERRARI. Reading your work, Borges, allows us to believe in that possibility.

BORGES. Well, thank you very much.

FERRARI. We must say goodbye once again. Until next week.

BORGES. Until next week, yes.

50

On Philosophy

●

OSVALDO FERRARI. Just as in literature you regard the fantastic as real, Borges, so in philosophy I believe that, for you, idealism is reality.

JORGE LUIS BORGES. Yes, that is, the conception of life as one long dream, perhaps without a dreamer, no? A dream that dreams itself, a dream without a subject. In the same way that one says, 'It snows, it rains,' one could say that, 'It thinks, it imagines, it feels,' without there necessarily being a subject behind those verbs.

FERRARI. Yes. Alicia Jurado observes that your stories are frequently inspired by philosophical doctrine, that they frequently spring from a metaphysical concept.

BORGES. Yes, in certain cases, especially in the case of 'The Aleph' which is perhaps the most famous of all. There I thought that in the same way that one arrives at the concept of eternity, that is, all the yesterdays, all the presents, all the futures—all that in just one instant—so one could arrive. . . . We can apply that idea to a more modest category, the category of space, and imagine all the points of space in a single point. And from that abstract thought a concrete story emerged, in any case, a story that I tried to imagine coherently. Another obvious example would be 'The Circular Ruins'—the idea of the dreamer dreamed. After having written that, I forgot about it and went on to write two sonnets about chess, which is the same theme—the pieces assume that they enjoy free will, the player who moves them assumes that he enjoys free will. The god who moves the player assumes that he enjoys free will. And then, I imagine—for literary reasons, clearly, without thinking about verisimilitude—a chain with infinite links, and each link is a god who moves the next one, or a man who moves the pieces. I use that idea many times, which is perhaps not rationally plausible but which offers the writer pleasing, momentary possibilities.

FERRARI. Of course. But with idealist philosophy, it seems to me that the philosophers who have been closest to you over the years are George Berkeley, David Hume, Arthur Schopenhauer . . .

BORGES. Precisely. I will also have had India in mind, since I read Paul Deussen's three volumes about Indian philosophy, Max Müller's *The Six Systems of Indian Philosophy*. And I came to the conclusion that everything has already been thought in India, as far as philosophical thought is concerned, of course. Yes, everything has been thought of, but it has been worked out in a way that corresponds to a mentality fundamentally different from our own. So I don't know how much that philosophy can help us, even though it may be interesting to study, since we come, perhaps belatedly, to the same conclusions but by means of simpler routes, or routes that appear simpler to us. Perhaps they're more complicated for somebody from Asia.

FERRARI. Well, we have, for example, the Hindu idea that the universe is almost a cosmic illusion.

BORGES. A cosmic illusion, yes, and then we come to the idea of cycles. Now, strangely, during those eclipses that occur between the end of one universe and the beginning of another, there are periods, well, that last for what the Hindus call 'kalpas', that last . . . eternities. But during all that time, although I don't know how, the Vedas persist, and they become archetypes for the creation of the following cycle.

FERRARI. Yes, but Mahayana Buddhism goes even further, because it also denies the existence of the self, the existence of a subject who perceives reality. That is, it denies reality and the subject who perceives it.

BORGES. Yes, in such a way that it's wrong to say that a person, in this life, well, receives the rewards or suffers the punishments of a previous life, because it's not a matter of a particular person, since the self doesn't exist. But one assumes that, throughout life, through acts, through words, through dreams, through visions, we are creating that form of mental construct that is called karma. And that karma is inherited by someone else, although I don't know if we have the right to use the expression 'someone else' since the expression 'someone else' presupposes a self. I don't know how far orthodox Buddhism permits the use of 'self'. In any case, one creates a karma, and that karma, well, it produces an end or a future. And that end, in its turn, will generate another destiny, and so on into infinity, since the process is infinite. Unless one achieves nirvana. Then one falls from the wheel of life. And once nirvana is achieved, the acts that one commits don't give rise to any karma, that is, a person could, well, commit crimes but they wouldn't matter, apart from the fact that one supposes that if he has reached nirvana he won't commit crimes. But his acts won't now engender karma, that is, he lives with impunity; and that impunity, of course, isn't subject to judgement—he isn't punished, nor is he rewarded. Nor do those acts give rise to a future destiny. Now, we could suppose that each individual—if the word 'individual' is legitimate—at the end of a perhaps infinite number of generations reaches nirvana. Then, what happens to the universe? I suppose it ends. I suppose that each of us is destined for salvation, but a salvation that's infinitely distant. That is, you and I, Ferrari, we are Bodhisattvas in disguise, or, rather, future Buddhas, but not in this life, nor in the next, nor in the one after that, nor the one after that, but, certainly, at the end of an infinite number of lives, one day we will reach salvation, we will fall from the wheel of life one by one, and a moment will come when that wheel will be uninhabited. I haven't thought about this until this moment, as I talk to you—that there will be a time when the wheel of life no longer exists, because there will be no more life. Then that infinite dream will end. In any case, that dream is a dream without beginning, because in Buddhism everyone can be granted salvation. In the case of Buddha, he is saved immediately, during his life, but that same Buddha had an infinite number of reincarnations in the past, and one supposes that the past is rigorously infinite. And it has to be like that, because if each destiny presupposes a previous destiny, there can't be a first destiny, since that initial destiny would be arbitrary and its fortunes or its misfortunes would be undeserved.

FERRARI. So that we'll be 'samsaric' or illusory until we reach nirvana.

BORGES. Yes, we'll be samsaric, and we have been so for a strictly infinite number of . . .

FERRARI. Of incarnations.

BORGES. Of 'kalpas', yes, of eternities.

FERRARI. Now, with regard to idealist philosophy, Borges, I think that an essential work for you was *The World as Will and Representation* by Schopenhauer.

BORGES. Yes, I taught myself German precisely so that I could read that book, and also because I'd read, when I was a boy, the poem 'The Light of Asia' by Sir Edwin Arnold, a poem about the legend of Buddha. Well, that reading . . . one could call it childish . . . no, I would have been ten years old, and the discovery of *The World as Will and Representation*, those two things led me to study Buddhism. And, oddly, I got hold of a copy in Buenos Aires of the book that Schopenhauer read and which made him declare himself a Buddhist— the two volumes by Karl Friedrich Köppen, a German orientalist who studied all those things but studied them ironically, as if he were studying the Christian faith. He makes comparisons between the doctrine of Buddha and the Christian faith. It's an attractively written book which I got hold of here, in Buenos Aires, and it's one of the many books that I read and used for a project in collaboration with Alicia Jurado, called *What is Buddhism?* for the guides published by Columba.

FERRARI. And that book, written by you and Alicia Jurado, was translated into Japanese.

BORGES. Yes, oddly, given that the translator must have known more than we did.

FERRARI. About Buddhism.

BORGES. It's one of the two official religions of Japan. The emperor is Shinto and also observes Buddhist doctrine. I say Buddhist doctrine because the word 'Buddhism' isn't used. One says 'Buddhist doctrine', and that's consistent with what Buddha wanted, because when he dies his disciples weep, but he doesn't tell them, like Christ, that they will meet in the future. He tells them, rather, that he has left them his doctrine. He doesn't ask them to see him personally, because personality and the self are illusory. Now, Macedonio Fernández, of course, partly through the work of Hume and Schopenhauer, but more than anything through his own meditation, had reached the same conclusion, which I expressed, repeating Hume and Macedonio's concepts, in an article called 'The Insignificance of the Self'. I think it was published in the magazine *Nosotros*, but I'm not sure—all that belongs to a fairly distant past. Unfortunately for me, I make use of a distant past—after 85 years one makes use of a distant past or, rather, that past makes use of one, no? Because one is controlled by those yesterdays which are now forgotten but which still have an effect, which still project their karma onto our life.

FERRARI. Certainly, and with regard to your interest in the idealism of Berkeley and Hume?

BORGES. Well, in Berkeley's case, he was a devout idealist, since he supposed that God was a continuous dreamer. Someone asked him: 'But if a room is closed, what happens to forms and colours?' And he replied that God perceived them.

FERRARI. That God was there?

BORGES. Perceiving them, yes, that is, an eternal and ubiquitous spectator of everything from every angle. Because one wouldn't miss many things. But, in the end, those infinite attributes don't trouble God. Now, in Hume's case, no—Hume came to the conclusion that materialism and idealism are equally flawed, and that led him to a form of idealism beyond the various orthodoxies, even beyond religion.

FERRARI. Yes, well, he was also the philosopher . . .

BORGES. He denied the self, because he said: 'Each time that I want to examine my self, it turns out that nobody is at home' (*both laugh*). Of course. 'Nobody is at home,' he said. That's to say, there's no self beyond emotion and perception, but a self that exists outside those activities that are attributed to it . . .

FERRARI. . . . He didn't believe in that.

BORGES. It doesn't exist, or Hume couldn't find it. I don't know if he found it later on . . . possibly not.

FERRARI. In any case, Borges, we can see that your work has benefited from your contact with philosophy.

BORGES. Yes, it has been beneficial, and I owe all that to my father, who taught me the form of doubt that we call philosophy, but without using the word 'philosophy'. He asked me straightforward questions, he invited me to share perplexities with him. In the beginning I didn't realize what he was doing, but he was teaching me philosophy, metaphysics, psychology, and all those things orally, affectionately, without my suspecting a didactic intention at any time. The most intelligent way of doing things. Of course, my father was a psychology teacher and he knew how to do that, how to get people interested in the subject without them thinking that they were learning a discipline.

FERRARI. One of the strangest things in philosophy is Plato's idea that to learn to philosophize is, in some way, to learn how to die.

BORGES. To gradually perfect ourselves towards death.

FERRARI. Yes, and that was a form of wisdom, well, the wisdom of philosophy, let's say.

BORGES. Yes. On the other hand, Spinoza said that he didn't teach an *Ars moriendi* but its opposite.

FERRARI. An *Ars vivendi*?

BORGES. Yes, he taught how to live—his philosophy wasn't directed towards a future life but towards, let's say, using life ascetically, at least, and enjoying the pleasures of thought, which are perhaps the most intense, or no less intense than other pleasures.

FERRARI. He would perhaps have agreed with Epicurus.

BORGES. He would perhaps have agreed with Epicurus, except that his practice would be different, no?

FERRARI. Of course, and talking of Epicurus: Santayana says that in spite of what is generally believed, Epicurus was a saint . . .

BORGES. I didn't know that Santayana had said that. . . . Of course, as Epicurus has been so denigrated. But how sad to think that we know about so many philosophers through their adversaries' refutations. For example, in the case of the pre-Socratics, we generally know them through Aristotle who was hostile to them. In Zeno of

Elea's case, we know what his detractors said about him. So all that comes down to us, well, rather like the historical vision we have. I think that we've talked about this before, of Carthage, which we know from the Romans who were their enemies, so much so that they destroyed them. Who knows what vision we'd have of Rome if the Carthaginians had won the Punic Wars? We would have a partial and probably unjust vision.

FERRARI. Probably. We will return then, to philosophy, Borges, but without using the word 'philosophy', on another occasion.

BORGES. Yes, I think so. That's an excellent idea.

On Borges' Mother, Leonor Acevedo Suárez

●

OSVALDO FERRARI. A figure who seems to me a decisive presence in your literary life, Borges, and who we haven't talked about directly before, is your mother, Leonor Acevedo Suárez.

JORGE LUIS BORGES. Yes, I owe so much to my mother . . . her indulgence, and later, her help with my my literary work. She discouraged me from writing a book about Evaristo Carriego, and she suggested two others that she thought were much better—a book on Lugones, and another, perhaps even more interesting, on Pedro Palacios Almafuerte. I told her, feebly, that Carriego had been our neighbour in Palermo, and she said to me, quite rightly: 'Well, now the whole world is someone's neighbour'—of course, unless one is in a wasteland, in a wilderness, no? But I don't know, I wrote that book . . . I'd become excited about that, more or less apocryphal, mythology of Palermo. I received second prize in a local competition, a significant sum of money—three thousand pesos. They gave the third prize to Gigena Sánchez, I don't know who got the first prize. In the end, those prizes afforded me—I put some of the money aside—let's say, a year of leisure. Though I misspent the year writing that book which I sorely regret, as with almost everything I've written, titled *Evaristo Carriego* which Don Manuel Gleiser published for Villa Crespo. The book is illustrated with two photographs by Horacio Cóppola, of old houses in Palermo. It took me more or less a year to write and involved a certain amount of research which led me to become acquainted with Don Nicolás Paredes, who'd been the *caudillo* of Palermo in Carriego's time and who taught me, or told me, so many things—not all of them apocryphal—about the area's rough past. He also taught me. . . . I didn't know how to play the card game Truco (*laughs*), he introduced me to the gaucho singer Luis García. . . . I'd like to write something about Paredes one day. Certainly, he's a more interesting figure than Carriego. Yet Carriego discovered the literary possibilities of the slums. Well, I wrote that book in spite of the opposition, or, rather, the resignation of my mother. Later on my mother helped me a lot, she would read long works aloud though her voice was already faltering, and her eyesight was failing, she kept on reading to me, and I wasn't always as patient with her as I should have been . . . and . . . she came up with the end of one of my most famous stories, 'The Intruder'. That was thanks to her. Now, my mother knew very little English. When my father died, in 1938, she wasn't able to read—she would read something and then forget it, as if she'd been reading a blank page. Then she set herself a task that forced her to concentrate, which was to translate. She translated a book by William Saroyan, *The Human Comedy*. She showed it to my brother-in-law, Guillermo de Torre, who published it. On another occasion, the

Armenians arranged a small function for her at the Argentine Society of Writers, on the calle México, that great run-down old house close to the National Library. I remember that I went with her, and how, to my great surprise, she stood up and gave a short speech, for about 10 minutes. I think it was the first time in her life that she'd spoken, let's say, in public. Well, it wasn't a very large audience, a group of gentleman with surnames that ended in *ian*—no doubt inhabitants of that Retiro neighbourhood, where I live, which is essentially an Armenian neighbourhood. In any case, there are more Armenians here than people from elsewhere. And close by, there's an Arabic neighbourhood. Unfortunately those neighbourhoods have disappeared, or they don't have their own architecture—one has to pay attention to the names, and here, no doubt, there are many Toppolians, Mamulians, Saroians.

FERRARI. But other translations by your mother also come to mind, which were exceptional, like the one of D. H. Lawrence's stories.

BORGES. Yes, the story that gives the book its title is 'The Woman who Rode Away' and she translated it, accurately I think, as 'La mujer que se fue a caballo'. And then (why not admit it) she translated, and I later revised—I barely altered anything—that novel, *The Wild Palms*, by William Faulkner. She also translated other books from French, from English, and they were excellent translations.

FERRARI. Yes, but perhaps you didn't agree with her taste for D. H. Lawrence? I've never heard you talk about D. H. Lawrence.

BORGES. . . . No. She liked D. H. Lawrence but I, in the end, I haven't had much luck with him. Well, when my father died, she started translating, and then she thought of a way of getting closer to him, or of seeming to get closer to him, which was to acquire a deeper knowledge of English.

FERRARI. Ah, what a lovely story.

BORGES. Yes, and in the end she enjoyed it so much that she couldn't read Spanish any more, and she was one of the many people here who reads English. . . . There was a time when all society women read English, and as they read a lot, and read good authors, it meant that they could be witty in English. Spanish, for them, was rather, I don't know, what Guaraní would be for a woman in Corrientes or Paraguay, no? A household language. So that I've known a lot of women here who were effortlessly witty in English but dreadfully banal in Spanish. Of course, the English that they'd read was a literary English while the Spanish they knew was only a household Spanish.

FERRARI. I always thought, Borges, that being witty in English was one of your best-kept secrets.

BORGES. No. Goethe said that one shouldn't admire French writers too much because 'The language writes poetry for them.' He thought that the French language was immensely resourceful. But I think that if someone writes a good page of French or English, that doesn't permit any judgement on them—they're languages that are so refined that they almost write themselves. On the other hand, if someone manages to write a good page of Spanish, they've had to get around so many problems, so many forced rhymes, so many *ento* sounds which combine with *ente*, so many unaccented compound words. . . .

To write a good page of Spanish, some literary ability is essential. In English or in French that's not the case, they're languages that have been so well crafted that they almost write themselves.

FERRARI. Another characteristic that you seem to share with your mother is a capacious memory. I've heard that she was able to remember her childhood and what she'd seen of the past of Buenos Aires.

BORGES. Yes, she's told me so many things, and in such a vivid way, that I think they are now my own memories, when in fact they're memories of things she has told me. I suppose that happens to everyone at some stage, especially when it concerns things from the distant past . . . the confusion of what one has heard with what one has perceived. And, besides, to hear is a mode of perception as well. So that my personal memories of . . . the *mazorca* political group, of the oxcarts, of the Plaza de las Carretas, in the Once neighbourhood, of the 'Tercero' del Norte—I don't know if it went along the calle Viamonte, or the calle Córdoba—of the 'Tercero' del Sur which went along the calle Independencia, of the houses of the Barracas neighbourhood.

FERRARI. What was the 'Tercero'?

BORGES. A stream, I think. I have personal memories that I couldn't have experienced for chronological reasons. My sister would sometimes remember things, but my mother would say, 'That's not possible, you hadn't been born.' And my sister would reply, 'Well, I was already walking around there' (*laughs*). Which leads us to the theory that children choose their parents—that's what is assumed about

Buddha, that from his lofty paradise he chooses a particular region of India, chooses to belong to such and such a caste or parents.

FERRARI. And that memory is also hereditary.

BORGES. And that memory is hereditary, like anything else. One of my mother's admirable features was, I think, never having had a single enemy—everybody loved her. She had the most varied friends. She would receive an important lady in the same way as the old black woman, a great-granddaughter of her family's slaves, who used to come to see her. When that woman died, my mother went to the poor tenement where they had the vigil, and one of the black women got up onto a bench and said that the dead woman had been my mother's wet nurse. My mother was there, surrounded by black people, and she did it just like that, entirely naturally. I don't think she had a single enemy. Well, she was a prisoner, a venerable prisoner, at the beginning of the dictatorship. And once she was praying when the woman from Corrientes who served us at that time, asked her what she was doing. And she replied, 'I'm praying for Perón,' who had died, 'I'm praying for him, because he really needs someone to pray for him.' She hadn't harboured any resentment whatsoever.

FERRARI. Talking about that—courage seems to be another of her characteristics. One has to remember the telephone calls!

BORGES. Yes, she once received a telephone call and a duly coarse, menacing voice said to her, 'I'm going to kill you and your son.' 'Why señor?' my mother asked with a rather surprising courtesy. 'Because I'm a Peronist.' 'Well,' my mother said, 'as far as my son is concerned, he leaves the house at 10 every morning. All you have to do is wait for him and kill him. As for me, I'm now (I don't remember what age she was) 80-something years old—I would advise you not to waste your time talking on the telephone! Because if you don't hurry, I'll die before you get to me.' Then the voice put the phone down. I asked her the day after, 'Did someone call last night?' 'Yes,' she said, 'some fool called me at two in the morning,' and then she repeated the conversation. After that there were no more calls. Of course, that nuisance-caller terrorist must have been so shocked that he didn't dare repeat his offence.

FERRARI. That's a wonderful story. Now, she came from a family of many distinguished military figures.

BORGES. Well, yes, she was the granddaughter of Colonel Suárez and the great-niece of General Soler. I was once leafing through some history books . . . I was a child, and it was one of those books with lots of pictures of eminent people. My mother showed me one of them and she said, 'That's your great-great-uncle, General Soler.' And I asked how it was that I'd never heard of him. And my mother said, 'Well, he was a scoundrel who was on Rosas' side.' So he was the black sheep of the family.

FERRARI (*laughs*). He was a Federalist.

BORGES. He was a Federalist, yes. Later, I was approached to sign a petition to raise a statue of Soler on horseback. The last thing our unfortunate country needed was more equestrian statues. We already had too many—you can barely move without bumping into one, so of course I didn't sign it. Besides, almost all of them are dreadful— why encourage that statuary? But I've been told that there's now a statue of Don Quixote which has surpassed all the others in ugliness.

FERRARI. That's right, it has. But some of those outstanding military figures have inspired you. In the case of Francisco Narciso de Laprida . . .

BORGES. Yes, except Laprida wasn't a military figure . . .

FERRARI. But he fought . . .

BORGES. Well, he fought, but at that time even the military fought (*laughs*), however unlikely that may seem. I know, but my grandfather fought, he was a civilian . . . first, in 1853, he was shot as a soldier— as the soldier Isidoro Acevedo—on the corner of Europa (which was Carlos Calvo) and I don't recall which other street. Then he fought in Cepeda, in Pavón, on the Puente Alsina, and in the revolution of '90, which can't have been too bloody a revolution since he was living in the house where my mother was born and where I was born, on Tucumán and Suipacha. Every morning, at seven or eight, he would go out to fight in the revolution—he was known in every neighbour- hood in the plaza Lavalle—in the Revolución del Parque. And he would come back in the evening from the revolution to eat at home, at about half past seven. And the following day he would go out again to the revolution. And that lasted, well, until Leandro Alem surren- dered—at least a week. So he would go out to fight in the revolution, and he would come back from the revolution, and he did all that without running into any great danger, so it can't have been that ter- rible. Although some people must have died, and once a single person dies that's a terrible thing.

FERRARI. Yes. There's something that moves you, it seems to me, in epic destinies, even in the epic destinies of some of your family.

BORGES. That's right. In any case, they've served me for elegiac ends and for poems. Yesterday, I came across a poem that I'd forgotten in which I say:

> I am not the Oriental Francisco Borges
> who died with two bullets in his chest
> in the stench of a bloody hospital.

FERRARI. Francisco Borges, who always reminds you of the battle of 'La verde'. Now, in this country, where there are a lot of people who are inaccurately described as Christian, I think that your mother's Christianity was genuine.

BORGES. Yes, she was deeply religious. Like my English grandmother also, because my grandmother was Anglican but from a Methodist tradition, that is, the older men travelled around England with their wives and their Bibles. And my grandmother spent almost four years in Junín. She married Colonel Francisco Borges, who we've just mentioned, and she was very happy—she said so to my mother—since she had her husband, her son, the Bible and Dickens, and that was enough for her. She didn't have anyone to talk to—she was among soldiers and beyond that, the plain with nomadic indians, and beyond that, the settlements of Coliqueo, who was a friendly indian, and of Pincén, who was a warlike indian, an indian raider.

FERRARI. And tell me, do you think that your preoccupation over the years with ethics, with morality, could have been passed on to you by your mother in particular?

BORGES. And . . . I'd like to think so. I think that my father was also an ethical man.

FERRARI. Both of them, of course.

BORGES. And they're disciplines that have been lost in this country, no? I'm proud of not being a *criollo* schemer—I'm *criollo*, but the most credulous *criollo*, it's easy to fool me, I allow myself to be fooled. . . . Of course, every person who allows himself to be fooled is in some way an accomplice of the people doing the fooling.

FERRARI. That's entirely possible. As for your mother's familiarity with literature . . .

BORGES. Yes, the love that she had for literature is remarkable. And then, her literary intuition. More or less around the years of the centenary celebrations of independence, she read Queirós' novel *The Illustrious House of Ramires*. Queirós was unknown at that time, at least here, because he died in the last year of the century. And she said to my father, 'It's the best novel I have read in my life.' 'And who's it by?' my father asked. And she said, 'It's by a Portuguese author, who is called Eça de Queirós.' And she's been proved right, it seems.

FERRARI. Of course. Well, I'm delighted that we've created some sort of a portrait of her.

BORGES. I think so, an imperfect portrait, of course.

FERRARI. Like all portraits, but the best that we could manage.

BORGES. Yes, and I thank you for having talked to me about her.

Prologues

●

OSVALDO FERRARI. I have noticed that you express your love of literature, your love of writers, much more in the prologues for writers and books that you have admired over the years than in your essays.

JORGE LUIS BORGES. Well, of course, the prologue is an intermediate genre somewhere between the critical study and the panegyric, let's say. That is, one assumes that a prologue will involve moderately excessive praise, so the reader discounts it. At the same time, a prologue has to be generous, and after so many years, after too many years, I've come to the conclusion that one should only write about what one likes. I think that adverse criticism is pointless. For example, Schopenhauer thought that Hegel was a fraud or an imbecile, or both things at once. Well, now they coexist peacefully in the histories of German philosophy. Novalis thought that Goethe was a superficial, a merely correct, merely elegant writer . . . he compared Goethe's work to the production of English furniture. . . . Well, now Novalis and Goethe are both classics. So what one writes in criticism of someone doesn't harm them, although I don't know if what one writes in praise elevates them either. But for quite a while now I've only written about what I like, since I think that if I don't like something it's rather because of my incapacity or slow-wittedness, and I have no reason to try to convince other people. I've taught English and North American literature for 20 years, I've taught—I won't say the love of those literatures, because that's too general and too vague—certainly the love of certain writers or, more specifically, the love of certain books or, more specifically, the love of certain paragraphs, or certain lines, or certain storylines. Well, and I have managed to do that. It seems to me that to write disparagingly serves no purpose. Now, of course, if one writes wittily, then the remark sticks. For example, I remember that remark by Byron, following Horace. Horace had said that the good Homer sometimes nods, sometimes falls asleep. Byron added that Wordsworth sometimes wakes (*laughs*). His remark is witty but it doesn't do Wordsworth any harm, because if a remark is witty it exists in its own right, and it doesn't matter if it refers to this or that person. That remark, 'Wordsworth sometimes wakes,' lives alongside Wordsworth's admirable work.

FERRARI. Of course.

BORGES. And it doesn't do him any harm. For example, when Groussac said: 'The History of Spanish philosophy by Menéndez y Pelayo'— a somewhat imposing title—he added: 'The seriousness, or the solemnity of the noun "philosophy" is undermined by the mirth that the epithet "Spanish" provokes.' Now, that does no harm to Spanish philosophy, if there is such a thing, because the remark exists in its own right. As for myself, I've written many prologues, I've written prologues for authors who were unknown at the time—well, so was I—and I have been generous in all those prologues.

FERRARI. But of course. Some of your prologues which express your greatest admirations, your greatest literary affections, have been collected in a book.

BORGES. Yes, that selection was made by a nephew of mine, Miguel de Torre. I didn't want to make an enemy of anyone, and sometimes, well, those prologues were products of circumstance, no? Prologues written out of courtesy. Or, otherwise, simply honest prologues, although not that well written or not that reflective—simply, praise of a book. So I let my nephew choose the texts.

FERRARI. Nevertheless, one can say that no one has been as generous as you in writing prologues for young or unknown writers.

BORGES. I wrote the prologue, for example, to Norah Lange's first book. I don't know if her first book deserves to be reread, but later on, she published *Childhood Notebooks* which is a beautiful memoir about her childhood in Mendoza.

FERRARI. In the selection of your prologues, there is the one that you wrote for Pedro Henríquez Ureña, for example, in which all your affection for him is visible, all your admiration and all the things that your affection reveals.

BORGES. Yes, I have the happiest memories of Henríquez Ureña and, well, the same thing happens to me with Macedonio Fernández— perhaps I remember their conversation, or their presence, which is a form of dialogue, more than what they wrote, no? But the great teachers of humanity have been oral teachers.

FERRARI. As you say, those who expressed themselves in conversation.

BORGES. Yes, Pythagoras purposefully didn't write anything down, because he wanted, I suppose, for his thought to continue branching out through his followers. Well, that phrase—I have the Greek expression in Latin—I quote it in Latin: *Magister dixit* ('the teacher said it') doesn't imply a rigid authority. On the contrary, when Pythagoras' disciples modified his teachings or, rather, they extended that thought beyond the physical death of Pythagoras, they would say, in order to justify themselves: 'The teacher said it.' But it was understood that the teacher hadn't said it textually, that it was, well, as if they were continuing the original thought of Pythagoras textually, which is what someone does in life—one isn't simply faithful to what one has said or written but to what one carries on thinking, and one can even change one's mind. Well, the example among us would be Lugones, who was an anarchist, a socialist, a supporter of the allies, that is, a democrat, during the First World War but later on he preached the hour of the sword, that is, fascism. Then lots of people said: 'He's a weathercock.' No, he wasn't a weathercock—he was a man who was very interested in politics, and who in different periods of his life came to different conclusions but without ever benefiting from any of them. On the contrary, making himself unpopular each time he said: 'I was wrong, now I think this.'

FERRARI. In many cases, Borges, it will probably be said that you invented an author through the prologue that you wrote about them.

For example, there's a prologue of yours for Almafuerte, which expresses your abiding admiration for him and where you praise him in a way that is revealing, let's say.

BORGES. Well, I can certainly call on a great example: When Shaw published his *Quintessence of Ibsenism*, he was told that there were a lot of things in that book that weren't there in Ibsen. And he said, 'If I repeated everything that Ibsen said, the work would be worthless.' Then he added, 'What I say here is perhaps an abstract version,' or, rather, the hidden intention behind what Ibsen wrote. That is, he was continuing Ibsen in some way. Besides, as he said, 'If my study were limited to saying what Ibsen has already written, it would be worthless.' So in that book he was a follower or disseminator of Ibsen, and what Ibsen said in fiction, fables, dramas, Shaw said in an abstract way. It's as if Ibsen provided the fable, and Shaw drew a moral which may or may not be the same as Ibsen's. I came across that book by Shaw—I was relatively young, I would have been 11 when I read it, then I read Ibsen's work. And I could see that the summaries that Shaw gives weren't perhaps the summaries that Ibsen would have given, since they're no less inventive than what the inventive capacity of Ibsen was capable of. That seems to me a good thing. Certainly, a work as complex as the one that includes Macbeth and Hamlet, has been modified by . . . Goethe, by Coleridge, by Bradley, and, well, by other Shakespearean critics. That is, each critic renews the work they are criticizing in some way, and they continue it also. And that coincides with the understanding I have of tradition—a tradition that doesn't have to be an imitation of something but a continuation, a branching out more than anything. One would have to conceive of tradition as something living, something that's continually changing and enriching itself through that change, of course.

FERRARI. So that when an author writes about another author, we can assume that he discovers those profound things for which he himself has a propensity.

BORGES. Yes, and that's Shaw's idea too. Well, we could say that theology, or the various theologies, Catholic and otherwise, do the same thing with Holy Scripture, since theology is an intellectual construction which is based, well, on the fairly heterogeneous books of the Bible. But, certainly, Holy Scripture is one thing and the *Summa Theologicae* another. And they don't contradict each other, of course.

FERRARI. However, it has been said that theology must have arisen from a lack of faith, that is, when a religion has to explain itself . . .

BORGES. Well, that has been said, especially . . . the fact that there are various proofs for the existence of God means that we aren't entirely certain of that existence. On the other hand, in Indian philosophy, which is so various, there doesn't seem to be a single proof for the transmigration of the soul, because it's something that's taken for granted. That is, there is a genuine faith in it.

FERRARI. Without theology.

BORGES. Of course. Nobody needs to be convinced, nor has it occurred to anyone to rationalize that belief. It's a natural belief for them. For us, it's not—one can believe it or not. Personally, I don't believe in the transmigration of the soul, but in India they do, it's something that they believe instinctively.

FERRARI. Of course. Now, to come back to your prologues—a lot of them are dedicated to your favourite authors.

BORGES. That's true, I don't think anybody has written as many prologues as I have.

FERRARI. Yes, you've turned it into a genre and, moreover, into an affective genre.

BORGES. Yes, and I've aimed in those prologues to include not only praise of the book I was writing about but also, well, my personal ideas with which the reader can agree or disagree.

FERRARI. Your personal discoveries.

BORGES. Yes, because I think that if one reads those prologues—of course, I never reread what I've written . . . but I think that my opinions on aesthetic matters are there as well.

Flaubert

●

OSVALDO FERRARI. There's a particular form of destiny, Borges, which emerges from a vocation and the choice of the man who embodies that vocation—I'm talking about the writer's destiny, which you see, above all, in the life of Gustave Flaubert.

JORGE LUIS BORGES. Yes. In the end, I always thought, modestly, that I'd be a writer. Now, in Flaubert's case, well, he was a writer, and he practised that vocation like a priest, no?

FERRARI. Of course.

BORGES. There's a lovely remark by him: 'Je refuse d'hâter ma sentence' or, rather, 'I refuse to hurry my sentence.' That is, he would work on a sentence, and he wouldn't go on until it was perfect.

FERRARI. Yes.

BORGES. He constrained himself with that attitude which he said suited his nature—he would read and reread each sentence aloud, he dedicated his life to that. Now, he didn't do it out of vanity—he wrote that a genius has licence to commit great errors, and I think that he referred to Shakespeare, Cervantes and Hugo, but since he didn't regard himself as a genius, he felt he couldn't commit great errors, so he had to take extreme care over what he wrote.

FERRARI. Ah, of course, the responsibility we were talking about . . .

BORGES. Yes, besides, when Flaubert talks about the *mot juste*, he doesn't necessarily, inevitably, mean the surprising word. No, the right word can often be banal or a cliché but it's the precise word. Well, he imposed on himself the search for the *mot juste*. So that the excessive care he exercised isn't due to vanity—on the contrary, it's a form of modesty. Well there's a word that's commonly used, and it was coined, I think, by the Flemish painters—the word 'perfectionism'. Now, perfectionism doesn't necessarily mean vanity—one looks for perfection, well, because one can't look for anything else. Flaubert more than anybody, whose idea of style was to a large extent phonetic, he wanted each of his sentences to read effortlessly and pleasingly. He said that the right word is always the most harmonious word. Although that seems odd . . . well, perhaps the *mot juste* in French isn't 'the right word' in Spanish or German, possibly not. Then one would have to think that, depending on the language being used, the right words will vary, since sound is different in each language, and for Flaubert sound is extremely important. Now, I believe that we're wrong, for example, to think that a sentence in Spanish shouldn't have three words ending in *ión* because they clash. I think this applies, rather, to the visual aspect of the page, because

I've discovered—after all, I have given a lot of talks—that orally it doesn't matter, orally we can say: *tristemente, alegremente* and then *descubrimiento*. They clash to the eye but that doesn't matter for the ear.

FERRARI. That's right.

BORGES. So that someone talking in public can make those errors, and, as what they say is auditory, one doesn't notice but, of course, once it's printed on the page . . .

FERRARI. It changes.

BORGES. But it doesn't matter when one is talking. Unless someone is translating everything that he hears into writing, but that doesn't happen. Rather, one moves from sound to sense.

FERRARI. Yes, and it's the visual effect that changes that. But we could say that Flaubert's search for the right word might also have been a veiled attempt to make himself ready for the right word. That is, all that effort and work were preparing him for the appearance of what you call . . .

BORGES. The aesthetic object.

FERRARI. So that the word could be revealed to him at some time.

BORGES. Yes, I hadn't thought about it like that, but it's possible . . .

FERRARI. Another route . . .

BORGES. Now, to think that one can write well simply by producing numerous drafts seems mistaken to me. The word comes to one or it doesn't, there's always—well, as I've said many times—an element of chance, there's a gift, that one receives or one doesn't. And one probably makes oneself ready for that gift. Now, the question is, how to make oneself ready for that gift. T. S. Eliot said that he wrote many works that, of course, weren't poetry but were verse. And he talked as well about the occasional visit of the muse, that is, of inspiration.

FERRARI. Of course.

BORGES. And he said that one has to practise the habit of writing to be ready for that occasional or eventual visit by the muse, because if someone never writes, and they feel inspired, they might not be ready for their inspiration or they might not know how to carry it out. But if they write every day, if they are continually writing verse, that gives them the habit, and they can write verse that is not only verse but also genuine poetry.

FERRARI. They have made themselves ready in anticipation.

BORGES. They have made themselves ready in anticipation, yes. I think that's good advice. Besides . . . it seems good to me, it's important to practise something, no?

FERRARI. Of course. On the other hand, one assumes that sometimes the poet or the writer is in the hands of the spirit that blows where it will.

BORGES. Of course, as St John says, yes.

FERRARI. Yet it seems to me that in your own literary life, you've behaved as if your writing depended on nobody but you.

BORGES. This morning I was asked if I write for the many or for the few. And I replied, as I've replied so many times, that even if I were Robinson Crusoe on a desert island, I'd keep on writing. That is, I don't write for anybody—I write because I feel an inner need to do it. That doesn't mean that I approve of everything I write—I may not, but I still have to write it, at that particular time. And if I don't, I feel . . . worthless, unhappy, yes, miserable. On the other hand, if I write, what I write may be worthless but while I'm writing I feel worthwhile, I think: I am fulfilling my destiny as a writer, regardless of whatever value my writing may have. And if somebody told me that everything I write will be forgotten, I don't think that I'd greet that news with happiness, with satisfaction, but I'd keep on writing. Who for? For no one, for myself—it doesn't matter. I fulfil my purpose.

FERRARI. Your destiny.

BORGES. Yes, and my destiny is, clearly . . . a literary destiny. It would have been wiser to have confined myself to reading and not to writing. But that seems difficult, no? It seems that reading leads to writing or, as Emerson said: 'Poetry is born of poetry,' a statement that Walt Whitman would have rejected, since he talked contemptuously of 'Books distilled from other books.' However, language is a tradition, all past literature is a tradition, and perhaps we are barely able to try out some moderate, extremely modest variations on what has already been written—we have to tell the same story but in a slightly different way, changing some emphases perhaps, no more. But that need not dismay us.

FERRARI. I think that Flaubert would have approved of that. Now, you were saying about Flaubert . . .

BORGES. Flaubert did a lot of research, as you know.

FERRARI. Yes.

BORGES. And oddly, that led him to errors. For example, before writing *Salammbo* he went to Carthage and saw cactus there. That's why there are cactus in *Salammbo*, but he didn't know that those cactus had been imported from Mexico (*both laugh*). So that the observation was good, but those cactus were, well, futuristic, let's say.

FERRARI. An enhancing variation.

BORGES. Yes (*laughs*).

FERRARI. You said the type of writer's destiny that he embodied would have been inconceivable in antiquity, since in antiquity the poet was regarded as an instrument, let's say, of the divinity.

BORGES. Yes, by contrast, in Flaubert's time, the author was already thought about in terms of his name. I think that I once told you that with a cousin of mine, Guillermo Juan Borges, and Eduardo González Lanuza and Francisco Piñero, we thought about founding an anonymous magazine, a magazine whose editor wouldn't be named and whose contributors wouldn't sign their works. But we couldn't do it, because everybody thought that their name mattered, and that to do it would be to compromise oneself . . . and, well, to condemn oneself to obscurity.

FERRARI. And they didn't go through with it.

BORGES. No, they didn't. I remember George Moore said that a friend was telling him an outline, the outline of, I don't know, a story or a poem that he was going to write. Then Moore suggested an alteration that would improve the work but the friend said no, he couldn't use that because it was Moore's idea and not his—he wasn't going to use someone else's idea. And Moore said: 'I realized that he wasn't an artist, because what matters to an artist is the perfection of his work and not whether that work comes from him or from someone else.'

FERRARI. And so, in some way, we all participate in the writing of a work.

BORGES. Yes. Of course, that can be used as a justification for plagiarism (*both laugh*), but that doesn't matter. If the work is improved, why not, why can't everyone take part in it? In any case, it's a lovely observation by Moore, no?

FERRARI. But what Moore says is quite right.

BORGES. Yes. At the same time it's a strange idea. I don't remember ever having heard it, no? The idea that the perfection of a work doesn't exclude the participation of others.

FERRARI. Of course, you will recall that Flaubert was associated with that notorious idea of his time, the idea of art for art's sake to which Baudelaire and Gautier also subscribed, for example.

BORGES. Perhaps because it's a good idea. In any case, art benefits from being its own end and not a mere instrument, let's say, of ethics or politics or, currently, of sociology. It's good, 'Art for art's sake'—it has a meaning, no?

FERRARI. It has a meaning that should perhaps be remembered at the present time in particular.

BORGES. Yes, now of course that can lead to a *précieux* art, as the French say, a vain art, a decorative art. But that isn't the idea—the idea is that a poem, for example, is something no less real that any other object in the universe, than any other thing. Then, why not seek beauty in a poem, in a story, in a painting, or in a musical score—it's the same thing, no?

FERRARI. No less real than life itself. Besides, what we call life is itself, in large part, made of art.

BORGES. No less real than life itself.

FERRARI. Naturally.

BORGES. And language is an essential part of life, yes, language—as Croce was perhaps the first to assert—is an aesthetic object, that is, each language is a literary tradition and corresponds to a certain way of perceiving the universe. I think we've said at some time that there are no exact synonyms. Well, there would be synonyms in abstract discussion but not in art, since each word has distinct connotations, a distinct atmosphere, a distinct magic, and I don't know how far that can be translated. The example that I always recall—that we have doubtless recalled here more than once—is the English word 'moon'. The English word 'moon' forces the voice to slow down, which doesn't happen with other words. For example, if you say moon for 'luna', they're different. First, the word 'luna' is made up of two syllables rather than one, and, besides, it can be spoken rapidly. On the other hand, 'moon' forces you to slow down, which in some inexplicable way is appropriate to the object it describes. A few days ago . . . yes, we were glancing through an edition of *Las mil y una noches* (*The Thousand and One Nights*), and there was a glossary at the end, and I came across the name 'Aro de la luna' ('Ring of the moon') which is lovely but which doesn't have anything to do with the moon, 'kamar'. 'Kamar' is a lovely word, no? 'Silene', on the other hand, in spite of evoking a divinity, seems too long for the moon, it seems that the moon, that simple, round thing needs . . .

FERRARI. Two syllables.

BORGES. Or one syllable—moon. Well, 'lune' as well, no? Because *lune* is as light as 'moon'. On the other hand—a piece of bad news, at least for me, as I love Old English so much—in Old English, one said *mona*, and it was masculine as well (*both laugh*). Sun is different—'sunne', but 'sun' is much better, which is one syllable.

FERRARI. Certainly, 'sun'.

BORGES. Yes, a long word doesn't seem appropriate for something as immediate as the moon, for example, no? 'Luna', 'sol', they should be . . .

FERRARI. Short.

BORGES. Monosyllabic, yes.

FERRARI. I think, Borges, that Flaubert would have been satisfied today with the way that we have evoked words, and evoked him.

BORGES. I like Flaubert a lot, and more than anything his *Bouvard and Pécuchet*. I have a first edition, which cost me 300 pesos, of *The Temptation of Saint Anthony*, one of the most extraordinary and perhaps least read of Flaubert's books. I think also, a first edition of *Salammbo*, a less successful work. In short, I have all of Flaubert's work, and I think especially about the first chapter of *Bouvard and Pécuchet* . . . tender, ironic, and so moving, because of that theme of the start of a friendship. And one comes across that seldom enough, no? The theme is that, of course there are friendships in every literary tradition but, more than anything, friendship is an essentially Argentine theme, I'd say, since I think that we feel friendship more deeply than other passions. When Eduardo Mallea published *History of an Argentine Passion*, I thought: What precisely would a specifically Argentine passion be? It has to be friendship.

FERRARI. It's strange, Borges, that you've paid such attention to a novelist, in this case Flaubert.

BORGES. You're right, because I'm not a reader of novels. But not to have read Flaubert would have been a mistake, I would have been the poorer for not having read him.

54

On Uruguay

●

OSVALDO FERRARI. You talk with particular affection about Uruguay, Borges. I've always thought that there must be literary but also historical and family reasons for that affection.

JORGE LUIS BORGES. Well, family reasons, of course—my grandfather, Colonel Borges, was Uruguayan. His father was Portuguese, his mother was from Punta del Este, Carmen Lafinur Juan Crisóstomo's sister. My grandfather first took up arms in the siege of Montevideo, during the Guerra Grande, as they still call it in Uruguay. He defended the besieged Plaza de Montevideo as an artilleryman. He was 'colorado', that is, Unitarian, and the square was besieged by the 'blancos', that is, the Federalists, Oribe's men. Incidentally, I think that Oribe was the great-grandfather, or something like that, of Ulises Petit de Murat. He was 14 years old, and later on, when he was 18, he fought in the Oriental Division under César Díaz, the division whose actions were decisive in the battle of Caseros. And later, in the end, he was involved in the civil wars here, the Paraguayan war. He went to lift the siege of Paraná by López Jordán's forces . . . their commander was a gaucho called 'el Chumbeao' because he'd been wounded. I had a photograph of 'el Chumbeao' and I gave it to Carlos Mastronardi, thinking that, as he was from Entre Ríos, he would appreciate it. In the picture 'el Chumbeao' was, well, a gaucho, wearing a kepi, with a military jacket and *chiripá*, his hand resting on the back of his horse, with his rifle across his saddle.

FERRARI. And there are other reasons for your affection towards Uruguay.

BORGES. Yes, of course, I think about my uncle, the historian Luis Melián Lafinur, I'm called Luis after him. Luis Melián Lafinur became very well known in Uruguay because he attacked, well, two Uruguayan idols, let's say. He said that José Gervasio Artigas was an extremely cruel *caudillo*, he talked about the continual defeats of Artigas who was defeated in Entre Ríos by Francisco Ramírez. Later he fled to Paraguay, and Doctor Francia granted him asylum but wouldn't let him leave, because he thought that he was dangerous. So Artigas ended up dying in Paraguay. And later on, there was a questionnaire about the gaucho, and my uncle replied, well, in a fairly derogatory way, saying, 'Our rustic'—a derogatory term—'lacks any distinctive characteristics apart, of course, from incest.' And they wouldn't forgive him for that, because they revere the gaucho over there.

FERRARI. That was in Uruguay.

BORGES. Yes, that was in Montevideo. I've thought, well, my childhood is divided between memories of the old city of Montevideo—my uncle's house was in the calle Buenos Aires—and Francisco

Haedo's estate in el Paso del Molino. Now, Luis Melián Lafinur suffered a terrible fate, because he wanted to write an impartial history of Uruguay, independent of what were called the factions, the *blancos* and the *colorados*. He lived in a house in the old part of Montevideo, it had rooms and rooms full of books, I remember, and collections of newspapers up to the ceiling. All for that great history of Uruguay that he was going to write. I think that he had some diplomatic post in Washington, though later on he said that diplomats are no use now that people can communicate directly by telephone or telegraph. Then he resigned his post, which didn't go down well with his colleagues, and he went back to open his lawyer's office in Montevideo. But he always had that project to write the history. Besides, he'd written a book, *Sonetería*, works by a resident of Montevideo, novice rhymester (*laughs*). And another, *Tabaricidio*, attacking the *Tabaré* by Zorilla de San Martín. Well, he'd gathered all that material I've mentioned to write his history, and around that time he travelled to Barcelona. He had surgery there—I don't know what operation, one assumes to treat a cataract. But they took out his whole eye without telling him. And when he tried to look at his eye on the journey back, he found he'd been left without an eye. As he was blind in the other eye, he could never write that great history, and he spent the last years of his life surrounded by those books he couldn't read, thinking about the great book that he would have loved to write, that he'd dreamt about all his life, and then he died. And I'm called Luis after him. I also remember Fray Bentos. . . . Now, how strange memory is—I thought I'd lived at least a couple of months in Fray Bentos, I talked about this with my mother later on but she said that we'd spent barely a week there. But, of course, for a young boy, a day lasts a long time . . . I'm living proof, since now that I've reached my 85th birthday, I get distracted. I remember that, when I was a boy, I was extremely scared (as I have been since) of the dentist. I was also aware that I'd once had a molar removed without anaesthetic—the pain was atrocious. Well, I was told, 'They are going to take out a molar.' I said, 'When?' They replied, 'Well, tomorrow afternoon.' I thought, 'But tomorrow afternoon is ages away, it's as if it were next year!'—I felt that instinctively. Now it's different, now I get distracted and . . . well, I have become distracted and I have reached my 85th birthday. As we talk, I'm on my way to my 86th, since time passes so quickly for old people (*both laugh*).

FERRARI. Successive distractions.

BORGES. They say that it's due to the fact that one measures time according to the length of time that one has lived. For a boy who has only lived a short time, it seems long. By contrast, as one lives longer, it seems as if time passes more quickly.

FERRARI. I see.

BORGES. Well, in the same way that with inactivity time passes slowly, the time of any activity goes quickly. That's one of the reasons to keep on working. Shaw said that the current system, capitalism, condemns many people, poor people, well, it condemns them to that— to poverty, destitution. And it condemns the rich to something even worse—it condemns them to boredom, to having to fill their lives in a contrived way with parties or whatever. That is, it's a system which ends up being harmful for both, for rich and poor. Then he added something that I don't think is very likely—that the rich, because they were fed up with being rich, would eventually lead the social revolution.

FERRARI. Fed up with the boredom.

BORGES. Yes (*laughs*), fed up with the boredom, they were going to lead the social revolution. But I don't think. . . . In the end, it was possibly a joke that Shaw added to an idea that is, of course, plausible. And then I have excellent memories of Uruguayan friendships. I was friends with Emilio Orbe, I always remember those lines of his, that start off in a thoroughly mediocre way:

> I was born in Melo
> city of houses colonial

Of course, 'houses colonial' is colonial houses lightly dressed up, no? And then: 'In the middle of the fearful endless plain.' Which is geographically incorrect if poetically appropriate, since there are a lot of hills in those parts:

> I was born in Melo
> city of houses colonial
> in the middle of the fearful endless plain
> and close to Brazil.

That is, the last word inflates the whole stanza, annexing an empire, no? Annexing that vast territory, well, in which there are still unexplored regions, which makes it vaster still, and 130 million people and numerous races. Then I was friends with Fernán Silva Valdés, and I'd like to recall a poem here in which he talks about the night before a battle, a battle between the *blancos* and the *colorados*. He talks about the bugle call, and says that when the bugle call sounded:

> Fire ran through the veins of some
> cold ran through the throats of others.

That directly refers to slitting their throats, no?

FERRARI. The cutlass, yes.

BORGES. Of course, that's the power of metaphor, to say things in an indirect way which is the most powerful way, because that's much more powerful than if one used the words 'to slit their throats' or 'cutlass'—it suggests them, the reader gets it immediately. I was also friends with Pedro Leandro Ipuche. This morning I received a copy of the poetic works of Ipuche, author of a book whose title is already a poem, it's called *Rejoicing and Fear*. And I still have a postcard somewhere around here that he sent me at the Hotel Cervantes in Montevideo. The card says, 'I will expect you at such and such a time for lunch at my house,' and then, 'If you don't come, I'll kill you' (*laughs*), a joke, yes, a very *criollo* joke.

FERRARI. And what other memories do you have of Uruguay?

BORGES. Well, as a child I would listen endlessly to my cousin Melián Lafinur as well. He would play 'The Abandoned Village' by Doctor Elías Regules on the guitar, and 'The Gaucho', which were very popular at that time but which are now forgotten:

> A sad abandoned village is
> resting on the hillside.

And there's a poem by Silva Valdés in which he talks about the abandoned village, and says:

> It doesn't soar into the air, it stoops on the low ridge
> like a large, despondent bird.

'It doesn't soar into the air, it stoops' is good. We can forget the bit about the large bird, no?

FERRARI. In recent years, a number of books have appeared that bring both literatures together, including one that's called *Stories from Both Sides of the River*, to which the Uruguayans Onetti and Benedetti contribute as well as yourself, Bioy Casares and Silvina Ocampo.

BORGES. Yes. I don't know either of them. I also remember Ema Risso Platero, who had the great fortune of being cultural attaché in the Uruguayan embassy. That allowed her to stay in Buenos Aires for three years, which seems to be the most difficult post to secure, because, of course, it suits the Uruguayans—they're in Buenos Aires, and they're right next door to their country. It seems much easier to become cultural attaché in Europe. Well, she did that too—three years in London, where she received me. She had a painting by Xul Solar there, who had been a friend of hers. And then three years in Japan, thanks to which she was able to spot a number of errors in my story 'The Universal History of Infamy'. I didn't have the slightest idea about Japan at that time, I made mistakes, I talked, for example, about the dining room, the bedroom, the sheets, all those things alien to the Japanese since they set up the table or futon in any part of the house.

FERRARI. I see, Borges, that the simple word Uruguay has evoked many memories.

BORGES. I've also written a milonga for the Uruguayans, I remember some lines—it refers specifically to slitting throats. It seems that they slit throats in Uruguay's last revolution, the one in 1905 with Aparicio Saravia. And that revolution—why not say it now—was financed by my uncle, Francisco Haedo, who ordered his farmhands to the revolution, which was fairly common at that time. My song goes:

> Milonga of the forgotten one
> who dies and does not complain
> milonga of the throat
> slit from ear to ear.

And then:

> Milonga of the gauchos
> who sick of dust and the road
> were smoking black tobacco
> in el Paso del Molino.

FERRARI. That's lovely.

BORGES. Milonga of the first tango
> that burst forth, it makes no difference to us
> whether in the houses of Junín
> or in the houses of Yerbal.

That is, the brothels of Buenos Aires, on Junín and Lavalle, or on the calle Yerbal, in the south of the peninsular, in Montevideo. There are other lines, well, perhaps even less worth remembering than the ones I've just quoted. In short, that milonga was written out of affection.

FERRARI. Of course.

BORGES. I also met Juana de Ibarbourou, yes, and I have personal memories of Montevideo, of el Cerro. El Cerro made a greater impression on me than the Alps, greater than the Rocky Mountains because, of course, I come from here, from Buenos Aires, a city built on the plain.

FERRARI. On level ground.

BORGES. On level ground, where the highest slopes, what were they? The Barrancas of Belgrano Park, the incline of the calle Belgrano, no? That was it.

FERRARI. And then, el Cerro.

BORGES. And then, el Cerro impressed me more than Mont Blanc, for example. And if I ever get to see the Himalayas—well, I won't get to see them now—they would impress me less than el Cerro, since that was my first mountain.

FERRARI. Well, I think that Uruguay deserves another hearing in the future, Borges.

BORGES. Well, and why not? Why not talk about the Uruguayans?

55

Poetic Intelligence

●

OSVALDO FERRARI. You made an important observation, Borges, when you said that every intelligent poet is also a good writer of prose.

JORGE LUIS BORGES. Yes, my starting point was Stevenson, who said that prose was the most difficult form of poetry. And proof of that is the fact that there are whole literatures that have never come to terms with prose. For example, in five centuries, the Anglo-Saxons produced wonderful elegiac and epic poetry, but the prose they have left us is truly awful, it's very poor quality. And that would support Mallarmé's point that the moment one is at all careful about what one writes, one is writing verse. So they are the same thing.

FERRARI. You conclude that the opposite doesn't always apply, that is, that an intelligent writer of prose can be a good poet.

BORGES. Well, prose doesn't necessarily exclude poetry, because I suppose that in order to write a good sentence in prose, one has to have a good ear, and without a good ear one can't write verse, particularly free verse which requires constant rhythmical invention.

FERRARI. Of course. Now you end up saying that good prose is incompatible, however, with those mysterious poets who can do without the intellect.

BORGES (*laughs*). I said that?

FERRARI. Yes (*laughs*).

BORGES. Well, I agree with the comment, even though I said it myself, or even though it's a gift that you've presented to me just now.

FERRARI. I'm particularly interested in this idea of yours about the poet's intelligence when it's applied to prose, because the most, let's say, interesting essays that I've read were written by poets. And the same thing has happened to me with short stories, although not with the novel, of course.

BORGES. No, not with the novel—the novel seems to require that the narrator be invisible, let's say, or hidden, no? In a good novel, it's the characters who are real and not the author, or the author less so. It's a genre I've never attempted and that I have no intention of attempting, since to be a good novelist I'd need to have been a good reader of novels, and I think that, apart from Conrad, apart from Dickens, apart from the second part of *Don Quixote*, I haven't read any novel that didn't involve an effort, a sort of learning process. And that seems to me a bad thing, since the aim of reading must be—I wouldn't say pleasure, but—certainly to produce an emotion in the reader.

FERRARI. Of course. But to come back to the poet's intelligence—that type of intelligence seems to be designed to see reality, or what we call reality, in a particular light. It's different from the philosophical or scientific intelligence.

BORGES. Yes, I suppose that it's completely different. . . . For example, I think that everything that happens to me ends up being a form of material for my work, that I don't try to look for words that are, let's say, a mirror of reality. I need to modify that reality in some way, and those various modifications are called fable, story, tale, and poem. I'd say that everything I write is autobiographical. But never in a direct way—rather, in an indirect way, which can be more effective. Besides, if one uses metaphor, metaphor is an indirect way of saying things. And verse as well, the rhythm of verse is different from oral rhythm.

FERRARI. The poetic intelligence seems to have a closer relation to intuition than to formal logic. You'll remember, by the way, that Zen Buddhism insists that one shouldn't be governed by logic—that one should allow room for intuition.

BORGES. Yes, it's assumed that intuition is essential, and in every situation.

FERRARI. That's in the East. In the West we don't seem to have discovered the importance of intuition—we carry on thinking that logic is the only way of arriving at truth. But with regard to intuition, poets can be linked to mystics. Or we can speak of mystical poets, of which we have many examples.

BORGES. Yes, because both categories occur. I think that one is constantly intuiting things. I don't know if I've said that, for me, the transmission of thought isn't an irregular phenomenon which is open to debate, let's say, but something that happens constantly. That is, I'm always receiving messages, and I'm also, I think, sending messages. And from that exchange what we call, well, friendship, love, also enmity and hate arise. All that doesn't arise from what one says but from what one feels.

FERRARI. Yet you've said to me that you've never experienced hate in your life.

BORGES. Yes, although Xul Solar told me that anger and hate are useful, because one releases emotion. In contrast, in my case, well, if someone harms me. . . . The truth is that people have been very good to me, they haven't, in the end, deliberately done me any harm. I'm led, rather, to sadness. And perhaps sadness isn't useful. Spinoza said that neither is remorse, because remorse is a form of sadness. He thought that to do wrong is ethically blameworthy, but to regret having done wrong is to add a further sadness to the initial one. And he believed that all men should seek calm. And that if they're thinking about their sins, they are tormenting themselves, and they are contributing to their own misfortune. Now, in my case, I find it easy to forget, since my memory—as Henri Bergson said of memory in general—is selective. If I think about the many, about the too many years of my life, I only remember the happy times. For example, I've undergone many operations, on my eyes in particular, I've spent a large part of my life in sanatoriums. But now I've forgotten all that. I could think about many days, about many nights in the sanatorium, but I condense them into a single instant—a small inconvenient eternity. And yet, they have lasted long days in succession, and, more importantly, long nights in succession, filled with exhaustive detail, no doubt. But all that has been forgotten.

FERRARI. Yes, and then we come to the calm of recent years.

BORGES. Yes, the day before yesterday I wrote a sonnet. I can't read it out yet because I have to work on it but its subject is this—that these years of my life are perhaps the best. These years, I say so in the poem, of having accepted my blindness.

FERRARI. . . . Yes.

BORGES. Accepting my blindness, not complaining or mourning. I have accepted blindness, well, as I have accepted growing old. . . . And, of course, to accept life, that's quite an achievement, no? Blindness is one of the accidents of life. Someone told Shaw not to do this or that because it was unwise. And Shaw said, 'Well, it's unwise to be born, it's unwise to carry on living.' Everything is unwise, but it's a fine adventure.

FERRARI (*laughs*). You remind me of two lines by a Chilean poet who said: 'I don't have any problem with / putting on an eleven-yard shirt.'

BORGES. Ah, that's good, yes. But how odd. How do you picture an 11-yard shirt? I think of it as 11 yards wide . . .

FERRARI. For years I've tried to picture it and I can't.

BORGES. Cunninghame Graham says that it means 11 yards wide. I don't think so, I think it's more like an 11 yard–long shirt, like a tunnel, no?

FERRARI. Yes . . .

BORGES. That is, one puts the shirt on and, well, one disappears in a tunnel of fabric.

FERRARI (*laughs*). Yes, there's another poet, this time an Argentine, Alberto Girri, who told me that, for him, the one constant human truth was 'Know thyself.' And that poetry can lead the reader to a better understanding of himself.

BORGES. Well, Walt Whitman read a famous biography, and he thought for a while and then he said, 'And is this what you call a man's life? These dates? These names? Is that what they are going to write about me when I am dead?' Then he added in brackets—of course, to emphasize the remark—that he knows very little or nothing about himself. But so that he could find something out, he has written his poetry. In a grander vein, Victor Hugo said, 'Je suis un homme voilé pour moi même' and 'Dieu seul sait mon vrai nom.' 'I am a man veiled by myself' and 'Only God knows my true name.' It's the idea, of course, that the thing resides in the name.

FERRARI. And that the name is secret.

BORGES. And that the name is secret, yes.

FERRARI. And if the poet reveals himself and comes to know himself through writing, that helps to awaken the reader's intuition and allows him to know himself better.

BORGES. Of course, because the reader is in some way a poet. I wrote some time ago that when we read Shakespeare, we become Shakespeare, if only for a moment.

FERRARI. That's right, that's a very characteristic idea of yours.

BORGES. I think it's true. Although, perhaps in some cases, we can prolong Shakespeare even further, since Shakespeare's text has been enhanced not only by his commentators but also by history, by those repeated experiences that we call history, no?

FERRARI. Yes, but that's all related once more to those great lines of philosophical thought that we've talked about before—the line of Plato, which incorporates intuition or myth or poetry, and the line of Aristotle, which is that of logic.

BORGES. Yes.

FERRARI. But since the line of Aristotle has prevailed, it seems to me that the poet's mission, let's say, is to recreate the Platonic line.

BORGES. Yes, that is, to think in terms of myth or in terms of fable as well.

FERRARI. Or to help one think in a way that incorporates those things, and without excluding logic either, is that not so?

BORGES. That's right, since they're equally valuable tools.

FERRARI. And complementary tools.

BORGES. Now, of course, myth comes earlier—cosmogony predates astronomy, also astrology, and myth predates the syllogism.

FERRARI. That's right.

BORGES. It's the oldest form of thought, and we return to that ancient form of thought when we dream.

FERRARI. Of course.

BORGES. Because when we dream, well, it can be confusing, because it seems rather like a fiction, a theatrical fiction rather than a logical treatise.

FERRARI. Naturally. But of course our age is the one that perhaps, of all the ages, least accepts the reality of myth.

BORGES. And yet we're creating them continually, eh? Let's say, the different countries are different myths. And the act of talking, well, one talks so much about national identity, one seeks it in every part of the world . . . one assumes that there's a particular virtue in having been born in this or that place, no? And of course, that's quite dangerous because it leads to conflict, to war and to hostile acts, in short, to so many ills. But it also corresponds to beautiful dreams, it can have a value which is aesthetic, even ethical, since people die for those concepts.

FERRARI. So that myth sometimes occurs without our meaning it to.

BORGES. Yes, and we must try to be sensible, eh? Since we have a tendency to produce fables and myths. . . . But that doesn't depend on us.

FERRARI. But being sensible involves accepting the reality of intuition and of poetry, I think, together with logic.

BORGES. Yes. And there we have again those two opposing forces which are reconciled and which complement each other.

56

Almafuerte

●

OSVALDO FERRARI. You said recently, Borges, that this country has produced two men of genius. The first, who we've already talked about, is Sarmiento. The other is Almafuerte. I thought that we couldn't overlook him, given his importance for you. Besides, you have a theory about Almafuerte.

JORGE LUIS BORGES. Yes, I think that Almafuerte has revitalized ethics and taken Christianity beyond Christ. He's been compared to Nietzsche, but it's hard to find two people more different. Nietzsche, like Gibbon, opposed Christianity because he thought that it was a slave religion, and that forgiveness was a form of cowardice, while Almafuerte condemned forgiveness, but he didn't condemn it for being a form of humility, or an *aflojada*, to put it in *criollo* terms, no? He condemned forgiveness because it seemed to him a form of pride. I don't remember how the lines go . . . yes:

> When the son of God, the Ineffable,
> Forgave from Golgotha the sinner . . .
> He hurled in the face of the Universe
> The most terrible insult imaginable!

That is, Almafuerte thought or, rather, Almafuerte felt that we are all contemptible, and that we don't have the right to be forgiven. He condemned forgiveness because it seemed to him a form of pride, since the person who forgives considers himself superior to the person who is forgiven.

FERRARI. A form of presumption.

BORGES. A form of presumption. And then he adds that he doesn't believe in free will, and in another poem he says that since the first instant of Creation, the Judases, the Pilates and the Christs were already foreseen. Now, if one denies free will, as I tend to, then forgiveness and vengeance make no sense, since each individual has acted as he had to act. That is, if we deny free will, well, we can't punish anyone, nor can we reward anyone, given that everyone has acted in accordance with fate. And Almafuerte was an atheist, so I suppose that when he understood . . . when he talked about acting in accordance with fate, he wasn't thinking about a God who had ordered things. He was thinking, rather, about effects and causes which were like a tree, branching out infinitely across time, each instant brought about by a previous instant, and that instant by an earlier one, and so on into infinity . . . So we have here a new ethics, an ethics that condemns forgiveness, because forgiveness is seen as a form of pride. Nietzsche condemns Christianity too, but for different reasons, and as a pagan might condemn it. But in Almafuerte's case, well, we could regard Almafuerte as the ultimate consequence of Christianity, as an ultimate form of Christianity, since Christ doesn't only forgive but goes beyond forgiveness.

FERRARI. Of course.

BORGES. Well, his is an ethical revitalization, and it was put into words at the beginning of the century by a poet who not only wrote the best but also the worst poems in the Spanish language. He said it in an environment that was completely undeserving of all that, since if there's one thing that doesn't interest Argentines, I think it's ethics. Perhaps because of the influence of Catholicism we have the idea of confession—confession absolves one of sin. . . . Also the idea of salvation through works . . . well, and those works are interspersed with the Holy Mass which corresponds, let's say, to the most commercial, mercenary aspect of the Church. That is, one gains salvation by works, one gains salvation by confession, and, no, the truth is that I don't know if anyone can be saved by what they've done. Almafuerte was a mystical thinker about those ethical questions. Almafuerte was that terrible thing, as Carlyle was too—a mystic without God.

FERRARI. A mystic without God and without hope, you say.

BORGES. Without hope, well, also without fear. As Caesar says, I remember, in *Caesar and Cleopatra* by Shaw, when they say to him: 'Caesar, do you despair?' Caesar replies: 'He who has never hoped cannot despair.'

FERRARI. Of course. Now, the way that you view Almafuerte, as a mystic without God and without hope, reminds me of the vision that

Claudel had of Rimbaud, describing him as 'a mystic in the savage state'.

BORGES. Yes, except that in a savage state means that he would later arrive at a civilized state.

FERRARI. Well, not necessarily.

BORGES. In Almafuerte's case, and in Carlyle's case, they didn't believe in a God—they viewed the world as a sort of inexorable machine of effects and causes. I say effects first, and then causes, because if I begin with effects I imply that the cosmic process is infinite, since each effect arises from a cause and that cause from another one. That is, we go backwards into infinity.

FERRARI. I understand that your first contact with Almafuerte was through reading Evaristo Carriego.

BORGES. No, not reading.

FERRARI. Through Evaristo Carriego's memory.

BORGES. Carriego knew Almafuerte's 'The Missionary' by heart.

FERRARI. Yes . . .

BORGES. I remember, it was a Sunday evening. Carriego was a short man, a slight man, he had a glow in his eyes as if he were . . . consumptive, and a rather sonorous voice, and he read it aloud—I don't know how old I would have been at the time . . . I'm looking at him and listening to him, reciting that long poem 'The Missionary'. And I didn't understand it, but I did something better—I felt it, I felt the power of Almafuerte, through Carriego. Carriego started to imitate Almafuerte when he wrote. For example, that poem, 'The Wolves':

A winter night so harsh
that poverty came out of the doorway,
and in their hospital beds
sick women wept for the lost son
with the cold of Evil in their soul
and absinthe burning in their veins,
through a gloomy anguished silence
a poor drunk man sang in the tavern.

Then he says:

Friend: don't go out, I have a foreboding.

. . . and then one of his visions, when he imagines that the street is
full of wolves:

and in horrible hours they scratch the door

And the end of the poem, well, it's more muted:

And for that reason the mad, the strange
half of that song, remained in the bottle.

Carriego was proud of that poem. Then he abandoned it, when he
devoted his attention to singing for the *barrio*, for the poor neighbourhoods. The poor neighbourhoods, in Carriego's case, were, well, the
calle Honduras and the avenida Coronel Díaz, no? (*Laughs.*)

FERRARI. In Palermo.

BORGES. Yes, but at that time they were the poor neighbourhoods.

FERRARI. At that time, as a very young man, you felt what you call
'the inexplicable poetic power of Almafuerte'.

BORGES. Yes, Almafuerte was one of the people who introduced me to poetry.

FERRARI. Of course.

BORGES. And then, the voice of my father reciting poems . . . particularly Swinburne and Shelley. I still like Swinburne a lot—I never really liked Shelley. . . . My mother told me that when I recite poems by Swinburne, by Shelley, by Keats, by Byron, by Wordsworth, I do it, or I used to do it, with my father's voice. I hadn't noticed that. But in fact when I read poems aloud in English, I do read them with my father's voice.

FERRARI. Because he provided your initiation in them.

BORGES. Yes, he provided my initiation. And the revelation of poetry in Spanish was provided for me, well, in an admirable way by 'The Missionary', perhaps Almafuerte's greatest poem.

FERRARI. It's magnificent.

BORGES. Read aloud by a fervent disciple of his, Evaristo Carriego.

FERRARI. So you experienced it in a more direct form. But that mysticism of Almafuerte, as well as being . . .

BORGES. It's a mysticism without hope, because it's a mysticism that doesn't expect any reward but which isn't afraid of punishment either.

FERRARI. Of course.

BORGES. Or, rather, I think that he must have experienced life as something terrible, since he was a neurotic man, he must have experienced life as a form of long illness. He was insensitive to many things. For example, he said that he didn't have any feeling for landscape. 'I am like Dante,' he said. Well, one shouldn't censure him for saying that about Dante, since Lugones also talked about Dante in the same way. Almafuerte said, 'The only life I feel is that of man.' The rest—the landscape, the beauty of the sky, of the earth—all that left him cold. Possibly music too, although not verbal music because he had an excellent ear.

FERRARI. Another very strange aspect of Almafuerte's mysticism, aside from being, let's say, an agnostic mysticism, because he wasn't a believer, is that it's a mysticism of failure as well.

BORGES. Yes.

FERRARI. Like T. E. Lawrence, that is, he saw failure as the fate of every human path, of every human destiny.

BORGES. Yes, and he says that, I don't know if it's in 'The Missionary' or in 'Confiteor Deo': 'I think that defeat deserves its laurels and triumphal arches.' He appreciated the dignity of defeat.

FERRARI. Precisely.

BORGES. And Stevenson said: 'I do not know for what we are intended, certainly not to succeed.'

FERRARI. Of course.

BORGES. He accepted that, but he said it with a smile. In contrast, Almafuerte was thunderous, no? With a great fluency.

FERRARI. Now, you've also said that since 1932, the idea or the outline of a book on Almafuerte has been with you.

BORGES. Yes, I have around here somewhere a theory about Almafuerte, it's only five or six pages long. I'll have to find examples . . . but perhaps those five or six pages could be a starting point for someone doing research on Almafuerte, although now it seems that it's impossible to do research on poets, since we have structuralism (*laughs*) which seems to prevent any research on a poet, which staunchly refuses to feel beauty and which prefers, well, to judge poetry in terms of syntax. Which seems rather sad to me, no? I mean, to refuse to feel emotion and to concentrate on the construction of the sentence seems miserable to me. Miserable not only from the critic's point of view but also the writer's. Because, of course, structuralism, which has been so damaging for criticism, will give us poets who write according to the theory. And those works will be completely devoid of emotion, completely meaningless, but they will contain the forms—the syntagmas I think they're called or whatever—that they think are necessary. So structuralism poses a double threat. Now we've experienced the beginning of that threat—the fact that criticism has become restricted to syntactic minutiae. Oddly, Almafuerte talked about 'Your minutiae, your terrible minutiae' (*both laugh*), as if he foresaw what was going to happen. And now we will no doubt have poets who write so that they can be praised by the structuralists.

FERRARI. And those structuralist minutiae seemed to be a sure way of not understanding poetry.

BORGES. Not only not understanding but also not feeling, which is even more serious. They are created by insensitive people, no? Of course they're untroubled, because the universe doesn't astound them, poetry doesn't move them. They can devote themselves to those small formal, merely formal, miseries.

FERRARI. Well, let's hope, Borges, that the memory of Almafuerte saves us from that other paltry, insignificant memory.

BORGES. Yes, we can hope so.

57

Buddhism

●

OSVALDO FERRARI. In a number of our conversations, Borges, you've touched on, or have demonstrated without setting out to, a particular understanding of Oriental philosophies and religions, especially Buddhism.

JORGE LUIS BORGES. Yes, that's right. Well, I came to Buddhism . . . I was a boy and I read a poem by a fairly mediocre English poet, Sir Edwin Arnold, titled 'The Light of Asia', where he recounts in fairly unremarkable verse the legend of Buddha. I remember the last lines: 'The dew is on the lotus / Rise, great sun!' and then, 'The dewdrop slips into the shining sea!' that is, the individual soul is lost in the whole. I read that poem—it was quite an effort—but those lines which I must have read around 1906 (*laughs*) have been with me ever since. I've never tried to learn anything by heart, I've never imposed that chore on myself, but there are lines, good or bad, that have stuck, and my memory, my memory . . . how sad, is made of quotes, mostly . . . like Alonso Quijano, I remember more of the books I've read than the things that have happened to me. So, I read that poem which gave a more or less general idea about the legend of Buddha. I'd heard the word 'nirvana' which is such a . . . I don't know, such a suggestive word, it seems inexhaustible, no? Nirvana which is called 'nehana' in Japanese, which is less attractive, and there's 'nivana' which isn't attractive either. On the other hand, 'nirvana' seems perfect, I don't know why. Then I read Schopenhauer . . . I must have been 16 years old . . . Schopenhauer talks about Buddhism, he says that he is a Buddhist and that led me . . . I don't know how a copy of the book by Köppen fell into my hands, a now forgotten book in two volumes and the one that Schopenhauer had read, the one that introduced him to Buddhism. That book caught my interest straight away, and then I read the book by Max Müller, *Six Systems of Indian Philosophy*, and I read—much later on in Buenos Aires—the philosophical history by Deussen, Schopenhauer's disciple, who begins his *History of Philosophy* with three sizeable volumes about India, and only later gets around to Greece. Usually, one would begin with Greece, but not him—he begins with India. And reading those books, the one by Müller and the one by Deussen, I came to the conclusion that everything has been thought in India and in China—all the possible philosophies, from materialism to the most extreme forms of idealism, everything has been thought by them and in a distinctive way. Since then, we've been engaged in rethinking what has already been thought over there. I've read two histories of Chinese philosophy. Japan, on the other hand, hasn't produced philosophers, as far as I know. Well, the occasional admirer of Buddhism, but that's all. But in China and India there have always been philosophical schools, there have been philosophers who are very different from one another. For example, in Zeno of Elea's famous paradox, an object is at a starting point, and it has to reach the finishing line. My father explained this to me with a chess board. First, let's suppose that one has a rook. Before that rook can get to the other rook's square, it has to pass over the king's. And before it can pass over the king's square, it has to pass over the bishop's, and then over the knight's. Now, if a line is made up of an infinite number of points . . . let's say, the line that describes this table, or the line that goes from here to the moon . . . any line is made up of an infinite number of points, space is infinitely divisible, and the moving object doesn't reach its destination because there's always an intermediate point. Well, regarding this, I was reading the English version by Herbert Allen Giles of a book that is attributed to Chuang-Tzu and in which he talks about the philosopher Hui-Tzu's story about a dynasty. The king of that dynasty has a sceptre. When he dies, he leaves the sceptre to his son— he cuts it in half and leaves a half to his son. The son cuts off half again and leaves it to his son. And as the sceptre is, in theory, infinitely divisible, the dynasty is infinite. That is, it's precisely the paradox of Achilles and the tortoise, the paradox of motion, the paradox of Zeno's arrow but with rather a different intention. I learnt that by reading two histories of Chinese philosophy, bought, oddly, in the same place—the Fray Mocho bookshop, in the calle Sarmiento, between Riobamba and Callao. There I found, within a year of each other, a history of Chinese philosophy written in English and another written in German. And I read them and I discovered that everything is there, but in a slightly different form. And I've observed the same thing about India—they have thought of everything, but in a way that's rather laborious for us. For example, the Hindus have the syllogism—ours generally consist of three parts, while I think theirs consist of five or six, but it's the same thing, it's a sequence of propositions. As for one of the essential ideas, the doctrine of the transmigration of souls—in Hinduism and Buddhism it's taken for granted, that is, people accept it immediately, they don't need proof, in the same way that we don't need proof that three and four are seven, because we feel that it's true. Well, they feel that there is an infinite, a rigorously infinite, number of incarnations before this one, and that this will carry on into the future unless we reach salvation in nirvana. I have the greatest respect and the greatest love for Indian philosophy, in particular, and for Chinese philosophy. If I have appreciated so many things studying those philosophies, guided by some knowledge of Western philosophy, it means that there are many other things that I haven't appreciated because they haven't yet occurred in the West, but they will. That's why those Eastern philosophies are, in fact, inexhaustible.

FERRARI. I also thought that perhaps you've had some contact with Shinto through your travels to Japan.

BORGES. With Shinto and with Buddhism. I talked with a Buddhist monk, he wasn't yet 30, and he told me that he'd reached nirvana twice. That he didn't know how long that mystical experience had lasted but he'd reached it and it was something completely new. And I said to him, 'And then?' 'Well,' he said, 'since then I've carried on living, since then I've known physical pain, physical pleasure, various tastes, various colours, friendship, loneliness, nostalgia, happiness, sadness, but I feel all those things in a different, better way, because I've had the experience of nirvana.' He also told me, 'There's another monk I can talk to about this, because he's had that experience. But I can't say anything to you.' Of course, I understood—every word presupposes a shared experience. If you're in Canada and you talk about the taste of *mate*, no one is going to know precisely what that is. On the other hand, if you talk, well, to someone from around here, he will immediately know what you're talking about. That is, every word presupposes a shared experience, and as I haven't had, as far as I know, the experience of nirvana, he couldn't talk to me about that.

FERRARI. Of course.

BORGES. So I hope I can go back to read those three volumes by Deussen again, I hope I can go back to study the *Six Systems of Indian Philosophy* by Max Müller, and then . . . But I'm not so sure about Eastern texts, because Eastern texts aren't written to explain anything—they're created to suggest things. That's why I've read the Kabbalah—it has interested me a lot—I've read the English and German versions of the *Zohar* (The Book of Splendour), of other Kabbalist books. None of them are written to be understood, they're written to suggest something or to recall an experience—not to explain it. The best book on the Kabbalah is the one by Gershom Scholem, where he explains things. If you look at the Oriental texts, or texts taken from those texts, they simply declare, for example: 'The En Soph exists, the En Soph has six emanations,' but one doesn't really know what En Soph means, or what emanations means. Scholem, on the other hand, explains it.

FERRARI. I hope, Borges, that we can go back to talk about the East in other conversations.

BORGES. Yes, I like to go back to the East physically and mentally. There's not a day goes by without my remembering my travels to Japan, which were one of the most lovely experiences of my life.

FERRARI. We will travel with you, then.

BORGES. But of course.

58

'Epic Flavour'

●

OSVALDO FERRARI. In one of your essays, Borges, you say that there's a flavour that our age doesn't commonly perceive—the elemental flavour of the heroic.

JORGE LUIS BORGES. Yes, oddly, poetry began with the epic, that is, poets didn't start off singing about their sorrows, or their occasional personal good fortune—rather, they took themes from the epic. And it has been said that the novel is a degraded form of the epic. Now, the word 'degraded' is pejorative, I wouldn't use it—but why not suppose that it began with verse, more memorable, of course, more easy to remember than prose, and that this verse was . . . heroic, epic . . .

FERRARI. Yes.

BORGES. Strangely, the epic moves me more than lyric, or even elegiac poetry. Sometimes—why not admit it, since we are both alone here—sometimes I've cried while I was reading . . . I've always cried when I was reading something epic, not when I was reading something which was moving in another, elegiac, or sentimental, way. But my preference for epic is so great that I judge novelists in epic terms, which is clearly illogical. Perhaps that's why I'd say that, for me, the ultimate novelist—although there's no reason to choose one, as there are so many—would be Joseph Conrad. In Conrad, there's clearly the epic element. And we have the theme of the sea with him, which is epic, since it's the theme of adventure, of heroic navigation. So in Conrad one senses that difficult, that now inaccessible epic flavour. And as we're talking about the epic, I'd like to recall something in passing that no doubt I've already recalled, and it's that when poets had forgotten their epic origin—and, why not—their duty to be epic, Hollywood took responsibility, on behalf of the world, for that duty. And now the West, the Far West, is all over the world, since in every corner of the world, the myth—now we can call it a myth—of the prairie and the man on his horse, the myth of the cowboy, takes place. All over the world there are people coming out of the cinema surprised to find themselves back in . . . well, wherever it may be, in Bucharest, in Moscow, in Buenos Aires, in London, in Montreal. They come out into those cities, which are their cities, but they seem to have stepped out of the West. And not from the West as it is but the mythical West, the West of the cowboy.

FERRARI. That is, Hollywood has made the epic universal in our time.

BORGES. Yes, and the fact that it has done so for commercial reasons doesn't matter—the important thing is the epic flavour. I don't know if I've told you—why not talk about it now—about an episode in the 'Grettir Saga', the saga of the powerful Grettir, that goes like this: A man has a farm on top of a hill. He hears someone approaching and he calls out, but he calls out weakly and no one replies. So he calls out louder. Then he goes outside, but he's unsettled because it's drizzling. A man has come, and that man is his enemy, and that enemy is waiting, at that moment, around the side of the house. Suddenly he throws himself on the man and stabs him to death. And the man, as he is dying—of course, they must have liked knives a lot—says, 'Yes, now they use such wide blades.' And one can see that he's a very brave man, who forgets his own death, who doesn't say anything pathetic but focuses on the detail—that at that time they used such wide blades, that a wide blade has killed him.

FERRARI. That has the epic flavour.

BORGES. Yes, and when I read that for the first time, I cried. Now I've told you this so many times that I can repeat it with dry eyes, but I think that it has the epic flavour. Any other writer, whether it be Euripides or Shakespeare, would have made the man say something about that moment. But precisely because the man is brave, he forgets that he's dying and he makes that observation. I'm going to give you some bad news now, which is that the German translator was a good Scandinavian scholar but he had no artistic sense. So he didn't trans-late it using the expression that he should have: 'Now they use such wide blades.' He translated it as something like, 'These blades are in fashion.' The whole thing is ruined.

FERRARI. He spoils the whole thing.

BORGES. He's spoilt the whole thing, eh? Which shows that in order to translate a book it's not enough to have academic knowledge—one has to feel it as well. That passage is one of the most moving in literature for me, but its unquestionable epic flavour is ruined by the word 'fashion'. How strange, because the translator's an excellent Scandinavian scholar—I think he's also the editor of a series of Scandinavian sagas, books of Scandinavian mythology, studies on the culture of Iceland . . . and yet, he's committed that gaffe, let's say, which disqualifies him as a translator. Well, there would be other examples of epic. . . . For example, I remember that stanza in *Martín Fierro* although I don't know if that's epic or if it can be classed as epic:

> One moves as if asleep
> when one comes back from the desert,
> I will see if I can explain myself
> among such brave people
> and if on hearing the guitar
> I awake from my dream.

I think that 'One travels as if asleep / when one comes back from the desert' makes one feel the vastness and monotony of the desert, no?

FERRARI. Exactly.

BORGES. Because in some way the desert is compared to a dream, and in an indirect way, which is the most effective way. But even in contemporary literature one comes across literary qualities. Talking of recent books, I would say . . . I can think of two: *The Seven Pillars of Wisdom* by Colonel T. E. Lawrence which has two passages that I remember as epic. Both occur after a victory, perhaps the same victory, a victory for the Arabs under his command, against the Turks. In one of them, Lawrence says (as he's mounting a camel), that he felt 'the physical shame of success', the physical shame of victory. The other passage is finer still—it's about a regiment of Germans and Austrians who are fighting, naturally, on the side of the Turks. Now, those men, the Turks, they flee, but the other men stand firm, and . . . well, of course, they were Europeans, so Lawrence might have felt an affinity with them. But it's better not to pay any attention to that. . . . Then he writes, unforgettably: 'For the first time in that campaign I felt proud of the men who had killed my brothers.' And that act of feeling proud of the enemy's bravery is epic.

FERRARI. And it reveals a particular greatness.

BORGES. Of course, I don't think that's a common attitude. Generally, one supposes that in order to fight one has to hate one's enemies. Governments know it full well, who incite hatred, because if it weren't for hate, for that passion which is unfortunately so strong, people would understand that to kill a man is senseless and criminal. On the other hand, driven by hate a man can do it. But Lawrence, certainly, didn't feel hatred for those enemies, he was proud—I think that is unique in literature or history, that he was proud of the bravery of his enemies. An extremely noble sentiment. And those two remarks are enough to prove something that doesn't need to be proved—that Lawrence was a man of genius, and an exceptional man. To feel victory or success as shame, and to feel that shame physically, to feel proud of the bravery of one's enemies—as far as I know, these sentiments can't be found anywhere else. And I've spent a large part of my life reading, or, rather, rereading, since I think that to reread is as pleasurable as to read—as to discover—for the first time. Besides, when one rereads one knows that what one is rereading is good, since one has chosen it for rereading. Here I'm reminded of Schopenhauer who said that one didn't have to read any book that was less than a hundred years old, because if a book has lasted a hundred years, there must be something in it. On the other hand, if one reads a book that has just come out, one is exposed to not always pleasant surprises. So that would be the virtue of the classics—the fact of having been endorsed, of course, often through superstition, at other times because of patriotism . . . ultimately, for various reasons. But, in the end, the fact that a book has lasted shows that there's something in it that people have found, and that they want to return to. I think that the theory that literature started with the epic is generally accepted. The novel comes along later, and becomes a form of prose epic. Although the sagas, many of which are heroic, are written in prose. So that isn't the most important thing.

FERRARI. But that flavour, that epic flavour, which has undoubtedly inspired much of your writing . . .

BORGES. Well, if only, but I don't know if I am . . . I think that I'm a better reader than a writer (*laughs*).

FERRARI (*laughs*). You found it among our writers, I remember now, in Ascasubi, the joy, one could almost say, of the epic.

BORGES. Yes, and it's something that one doesn't find in *Martín Fierro*, for example, because Martín Fierro is a brave man, he's a brave, sad man who is quick to feel sorry for himself—but not for other people. On the other hand, in Ascasubi there's a sort of—I once wrote the expression, why not repeat it, since no one remembers it—'florid courage', that is, the idea of courage, and of courage blooming like a flower.

FERRARI. 'Singing and fighting.'

BORGES. Yes, the book's subtitle, which is delightful and which is perhaps superior to many of the pages in the book: *The Gauchos of the Argentine and Oriental Uruguayan Republics Singing and Fighting until They Defeat the Tyrant Don Juan Manuel de Rosas and His Henchmen.*' 'Henchmen' isn't very fortunate, but it doesn't matter . . . the idea of 'singing and fighting'. . . . Talking of that, a few days ago I was glancing through the voyages of Marco Polo, and it says there—I recalled this in a recent poem—that the Tartars sang in battle. Doubtless, they would be epic songs, but they sang those songs. I think that up until recently it was common for battles to be accompanied by music.

FERRARI. You also say that you've discerned the heroic flavour, unmistakably, in *The Iliad*.

BORGES. In *The Iliad*, yes, but not in *The Odyssey*, where there's a rather romantic flavour of adventure, of travel. . . . One feels that when Hector says goodbye to his wife, and one realizes they know that they won't see each other again—Hector is, after all, about to go out to fight, well, with a demigod, with Achilles, the son of a god and a woman. And as for Achilles' birth, I recall a phrase from the poet Lycophron, known as 'the Obscure', who calls Hercules 'Lion sprung from Triple Night'. Now, why 'sprung from triple night'? Because Zeus, so that his pleasure would last longer, made the night in which he conceived Hercules last for three nights. And 'lion' is readily synonymous with hero. So that phrase—obscure, of course, at first glance—refers to the triple night of Hercules' conception. Now, I'd like to make another observation, and it's this: I have explained the phrase, and it's the explanation that the commentators give, but I think that, even if one didn't know the explanation, it would still be a lovely phrase, no?

FERRARI. It's very beautiful.

BORGES. The aesthetic effect precedes the logical explanation.

FERRARI. Of course.

BORGES. One hears the phrase.

FERRARI. And that's enough.

BORGES. And that's enough, and perhaps it's a shame to explain it, no? Not in this case, as the explanation justifies it. But perhaps the aesthetic object always precedes the explanation, that is, if a phrase sounds good, it is good. It's important for it to have an explanation, naturally, it's important that it isn't nonsense because that could disturb the aesthetic pleasure. If it can be explained, all the better. The explanation, though, is secondary, I think that one immediately feels the aesthetic emotion when one hears 'Lion sprung from Triple Night'.

FERRARI. The effect is, as the Greeks said, apparent, created by what is apparent, what is immediate.

BORGES. Yes, it's immediate, and it occurs, well, with so many epic flavours. For example, something that I've recalled many times—when the Anglo-Saxon king promises the Norwegian king 'six feet of land'. Then, as the Norwegian king is so tall, he offers 'one more foot'. Now, this works because the threat is more like an offering, like a gift, no? Of course, the other one wants land, and he is offered 'six feet of land'.

FERRARI. Which implies the grave.

BORGES. It implies the grave, which is more forceful than if he'd said, six feet to bury him.

FERRARI. Of course, it's implicit.

BORGES. And now that we're talking about land, I remember General Patton . . . the French accused him, most ungratefully, of some imperialist designs. The United States had sent at least a million men, I think, to the war. When many of them died to liberate France, Patton said that he was only requesting the land necessary to bury his dead. So he reminded them of what he'd done for them but he did it in an indirect way, which is more powerful than a direct statement. If he'd said, 'I only need the land necessary to bury the soldiers who died for you.'—no, it wouldn't have had the same power.

59

Virginia Woolf, Victoria Ocampo and Feminism

●

OSVALDO FERRARI. There's a female literary figure, Borges, who has written two books that you've translated, and who we haven't mentioned before . . .

JORGE LUIS BORGES. Virginia Woolf.

FERRARI. Yes, the English writer.

BORGES. I thought that I didn't like Virginia Woolf, or, rather, I wasn't interested in her, but the magazine *Sur* commissioned me to translate *Orlando*. I agreed, and as I translated, I read, and I was surprised to find my interest growing. Now, that book is a great book, and its theme is a strange one—the Sackville family.

FERRARI. Sackville-West.

BORGES. Yes. The novel is dedicated not to a specific individual in that family—apart from her friend, Victoria Sackville-West—but, let's say, to an idea, to that family as a Platonic archetype, as a universal form which is the name that the scholastics gave to archetypes. And to realize that aim, Virginia Woolf imagines an individual who lives in the seventeenth century and who later comes to our time. Wells had also employed that device in one of his novels—I don't remember which—where the individuals, for the novelist's convenience, so that he could place them historically in different periods, live to be 300 years old. Shaw had also played with this idea of immortality.

FERRARI. In *Back to Methuselah*.

BORGES. Yes. There are some individuals who live a long time and some whose lives last a normal span . . . well, now I'm running the risk of becoming one of those long-lived people . . . my reaching 85 is dangerous—I could become 86 at any moment. In the end, let's hope not, let's hope I don't become one of those people who are miserably privileged or miserably worn out by time, by so much time, by too much time. Now, in the illustrations for that book, *Orlando*, there are portraits of the family, and one realizes that they're all Orlando. *Orlando* also serves to provide a panorama of different periods, of different literary fashions. All that, in prospect, suggests a book that's unreadable but, no, it's extremely interesting.

FERRARI. Another thing that's also real is the house of the Sackville-Wests, which serves as the background of the book and which, according to Victoria Ocampo, had 365 rooms.

BORGES. Of course, so it's an astrological house, because 365 suggests astrology and, naturally, the calendar year.

FERRARI. That's right. You've translated *A Room of One's Own* too, I gather, which is also by Virginia Woolf.

BORGES. Yes, but now, since it's just the two of us here, I'm going to let you into a secret—that it was really my mother who translated that book. I edited the translation a little, in the same way that she edited my translation of *Orlando*. The truth is that we worked together. *A Room of One's Own* interested me less . . . well, the theme is, let's say, a plain argument in favour of women and feminism. But as I'm a feminist, I don't need arguments to convince me—I'm already convinced. Virginia Woolf became a missionary for that cause. But as I support that cause already, I can do without missionaries. That other book, *Orlando*, is truly admirable. And it's a shame that in the last pages it tails off, although that often happens with books. For example, with *One Hundred Years of Solitude*—it seems that the solitude shouldn't have lasted a hundred years but eighty, no? But, for the sake of the title, it had to be one hundred years of solitude. The author gets tired, and the reader feels that tiredness, and . . . shares it. And the end of *Orlando*, it seems to me that there's something, I don't know, there's a vague link with diamonds, but those diamonds have faded rather from my memory—I see only their sparkle . . . but it's a very, very lovely book. I remember a chapter, a page in which Shakespeare appears. His name isn't mentioned but every reader realizes that it's Shakespeare. He's watching a theatrical production but he's thinking about something else in the middle of the production—thinking about productions of comedy or tragedy perhaps. One gathers that it's Shakespeare. But if we had been told it was Shakespeare, then everything would have been lost.

FERRARI. Precisely. *Orlando* goes back to different periods and, at times, it's an excellent example of fantastic literature.

BORGES. Without doubt. It's also unparalleled, since I don't remember any other book written like that. I think that at the beginning one doesn't realize that Orlando is still alive, no? That Orlando will be, well, if not immortal, then almost immortal.

FERRARI. Immortal and ubiquitous.

BORGES. Yes, immortal and ubiquitous. Virginia Woolf's critical works satisfy me less. In a discussion of writers from a particular generation, she took Arnold Bennett as her example. . . . It's strange that she chose Arnold Bennett when she could have chosen two men of genius like George Bernard Shaw and H. G. Wells. She said that Bennett had failed in what she thought was essential for a novelist—the creation of character. But I don't think that's true applied to Bennett, and I'm not sure either that the creation of character is the most important consideration for a novelist. We could say that, in the end, Charlie Chaplin and Mickey Mouse (*laughs*), and Laurel and Hardy, are characters. So it doesn't seem too difficult to create characters, no? They're created constantly—a cartoonist can create a character.

FERRARI. You know that Silvina and Victoria Ocampo have also been very interested in, and preoccupied with, Virginia Woolf. Victoria Ocampo wrote . . .

BORGES. Yes, Victoria knew her personally, but perhaps in a rather submissive way. I remember that Victoria talked to me about a number of *Sur* dedicated to English literature. So Bioy Casares and I gathered a series of texts, and then it turned out that Victoria had agreed to publish a selection by Victoria Sackville-West and Virginia Woolf in England. I didn't much want to publish many of those poems because I didn't like them, but Victoria told me, no, the number had been arranged. So then it came out like that. Later, I went about publishing the texts that we'd chosen, by authors who had been arbitrarily excluded by Virginia Woolf and Victoria Sackville-West. I think that those two wanted writers from their group to appear. In contrast, I'd planned an anthology that would represent the whole of contemporary English literature. I remember that when Victoria Ocampo said to Virginia Woolf that she came from the Argentine Republic, Virginia Woolf said that she thought she could picture the country— she could picture a scene with people in a garden, or on a lawn, drinking cordial at night, somewhere with trees and fireflies. And Victoria replied, politely, that was exactly what the Argentine Republic was like (*laughs*).

FERARRI. When Victoria Ocampo writes about Virginia Woolf, she talks extensively about the condition of women at the end of the Victorian period, in England and even in Argentina. And, really, Borges, feminism and its claims are understandable after reading that.

BORGES. But of course. But before reading it I thought the same thing, yes.

FERARRI. One of the victims of those Victorian attitudes to women— although she was able to overcome them—was Virginia Woolf.

BORGES. Ah, I didn't know that.

FERARRI. She experienced them in her father's attitude, who ordered her, 'No writing, no books.'

BORGES. I think that her father was the editor of *English Men of Letters*, but I didn't know that . . .

FERARRI. He objected to his daughter reading and writing.

BORGES. Some of the biographies in the collection that he edited were excellent, for example, one by Harold Nicholson, on Charles Swinburne, another on Edward FitzGerald, then a study by J. B. Priestley on George Meredith, which was extraordinary.

FERARRI. There are some strange lines, written by Virginia Woolf to Victoria Ocampo, where she says: 'Like most uneducated English women, I like to read, I like to read books constantly.'

BORGES (*laughs*). Well, that bit about being uneducated is a sort of joke on her part, no? But, maybe not, perhaps for a scientist or a philosopher a writer is uneducated . . .

FERARRI. And the other way round, of course.

BORGES. And the other way round, but perhaps we writers, whether literary or historical, are completely uneducated. I know that, well, compared with 'the man in the street' I'm ignorant. Because, doubtless, I will use the telephone many times, so many times, and I still won't know what a telephone is, and even less what a computer is. I've barely managed to understand what a barometer or a thermometer are, and perhaps I've already forgotten what I knew.

FERARRI. Of course, as I've said, between Victoria Ocampo and Virginia Woolf, there seem to have been a series of discussions. In a letter, Victoria Ocampo quotes a passage from *Jane Eyre*, and says: 'Charlotte Brontë's breathing can be heard, an oppressed and laboured breathing.' And she adds that this oppression was the oppression that the age imposed on her, in her condition as woman.

BORGES. Yes, well, now it seems that we all have the right to oppression and laboured breath, no? Men too (*both laugh*). Unfortunately, we can experience that sad privilege which previously belonged exclusively to women.

60

The Conspirators

●

OSVALDO FERRARI. Even if you think that books by contemporary authors should be read in the future, Borges, rather than in the present, your last book of poems, *The Conspirators*, seems already to have the necessary maturity to be read and appreciated.

JORGE LUIS BORGES. I don't know—I wrote that book, I didn't correct the proofs, I have a rather vague idea of its contents, I know that they asked for 30 poems and I produced 40, and I tried to order them in a particular way. . . . For example, I put similar poems side by side so that their alarming affinity to my previous work wouldn't be exposed. But I suppose one book of mine can't be that different from another. I suppose that at my age certain themes are expected, a certain syntax. And perhaps a certain monotony is expected as well—if I'm not monotonous, I don't provide satisfaction. Perhaps an author, at a certain age, has to repeat himself. According to Chesterton, every author—or every poet, in particular—ends up involuntarily becoming their own best parodist. Swinburne's last poems sound like parodies of Swinburne, because he has certain habits and he ends up exaggerating them. In my case, I think that my most conspicuous habit is enumeration, no? Sometimes it has turned out well for me, and at other times, let's say, a little less well. Doubtless there will also be syntactic habits that I don't know about . . . probably every writer's vocabulary, as time goes on, becomes progressively impoverished, or simplified.

FERRARI. Rather, it's simplified around the essential things.

BORGES. Yes, but there are certain themes that recur, certain metaphors that recur. And in my case, since I haven't been able to read what I write since '55 or '56, perhaps I think I'm writing a new poem but what I'm writing is an echo or a poor imitation of what I wrote some time before. I have the impression that each day is different, but I don't know if I can reflect the novelty of each day in what I write, since I'm tied, as I say, to a particular vocabulary, a particular syntax, to particular rhetorical figures. . . . I hope it isn't too obvious. Have you read the book?

FERRARI. Yes, and I have certain opinions which I'll share with you presently . . .

BORGES. But, of course, we're going to talk about the book. Doubtless you know it better than I do, because you'll have read it, let's say, a couple of times while I've written it only once (*both laugh*). So the book belongs less to me than to you. Besides, you've just read the book, it's a fresh experience—I wrote it a year ago, and it's an experience which is already in the past, already spent, and which, besides, I've tried to forget, since I try to forget what I write. And for that very reason I often rewrite what I've already written, without realizing it. I'm writing a story at the moment whose protagonist is Dante, and it seems to me that this story isn't going to be like any of my others. Well, I'm going to try not to make it erudite—my Dantescan erudition is slight, in any case. I'll look for facts about the last days of Dante's life, that is, the last days he spent in Venice, before going back to Ravenna, where he died, no? I'm going to see if I can refrain from landscapes. The story is going to begin in Venice. . . . It seems to me that Venetian landscapes have been attempted so many times, and with such good fortune, that I have no reason to get involved in them, or to attempt them again.

FERRARI. I remember that when we talked about Dante, you wondered what Dante would have felt about being in Venice.

BORGES. Yes, well, I began with that question, and then I came to others, and now I have enough questions. . . . But I think that I'm going to write that story.

FERRARI. Now, as for *The Conspirators*, I think that the title is surprising, given that it's a book of poems. However, the idea of 'conspirators' who act with a good intention, and to call people conspirators who propose a good intention, has been with you since at least 1936.

BORGES. I didn't know that. Why 1936?

FERRARI. Because in the speech that you gave to celebrate the quatercentenary of the foundation of Buenos Aires, in 1936, you said: 'In this American home, men from the nations of the world have conspired to disappear in the new man who is not yet any one of us but who we predict will be Argentine, so carrying us steadily towards hope.'

BORGES. I said that?

FERRARI. Yes.

BORGES. A rather pompous statement, but perhaps pompous phrases were what was expected at that event, no? (*Laughs.*)

FERRARI (*laughs*). And later you added that 'The *criollo* is one of those conspirators.'

BORGES. If only.

FERRARI. 'That having made up the whole nation, he has chosen to be one of many, now.' That is, he also chose to disappear, let's say, in the new man.

BORGES. Yes, I did have that idea. But in those nationalist times, I thought: How strange, this country which is singularly dedicated to immigration, that is, which has devoted itself, in a certain sense, to disappearing. But I had that idea a long time ago, and in a book, well, whose title I don't wish to recall, since I want the book to be forgotten, there's an article about this. It's as if failure were our destiny, and wilful failure . . .

FERRARI. But now, in this case, the people who give the book its title are conspirators found in central Europe.

BORGES. Yes, the Swiss. They're my compatriots, let's say. How strange, I'm one of the first people to dedicate a poem to Switzerland . . . The hotel-owners of Switzerland owe part of their prosperity to Lord Byron, for example, no? And to the people who paid homage to the Alps, among them Schiller. But I think that the idea of writing a poem dedicated to Switzerland, and of proposing Switzerland as an ideal, is a new idea. In Switzerland the perfect type of confederation occurs, since we have the German Swiss, the French Swiss, the

Italian Swiss. People of different races, of different languages, of different religions, of different atheisms, and all of them have decided to become Swiss—which is a little puzzling, no?

FERRARI. Yes, that's why you refer to Paracelcus, Amiel, Jung and Klee.

BORGES. Yes, who are quite different. I could also have referred to an architect whose architecture I don't like, who is Swiss—Le Corbusier. And I could have talked about the founders of the Dada movement (there were some Swiss people involved). But as I'm not interested in either Le Corbusier's cubes, or Dada's literature of incoherence, I haven't referred to them. And then it produced a great poet, Keller, but . . .

FERRARI. Gottfried Keller.

BORGES. Yes, but I suppose that if I included him, the reader would think that I wanted to pad the list out, and that I was including obscure names.

FERRARI. In any case, they all share two essential characteristics—they're men who are capable of reason and faith.

BORGES. Yes, that's right.

FERRARI. And that reason and that faith carry the hope of a new wisdom, it seems to me.

BORGES. And the wisdom encapsulated by the word 'cosmopolitan'.

FERRARI. Of course.

BORGES. It would be that, simply. How strange that after so many centuries, it seems that it's still rather distant that ancient . . .

FERRARI. That Greek ideal.

BORGES. The ideal that the Greek Stoics had, yes. Perhaps the people who suggested it didn't see it clearly either. Doubtless they would have thought that they were Greeks, and that everyone else was a barbarian, no?

FERRARI. That's possible.

BORGES. Although, who knows, if by the word 'cosmos' they meant not only Greece but also the world . . . possibly the world for them was Greece.

FERRARI. Of course, that is the question.

BORGES. However, they must have felt a sort of gravitation to what we call the East, without doubt. . . . Well, Egypt, to judge by Herodotus, made a great impression on the Greeks. And I think it's Herodotus who writes that for the Egyptians, the Greeks are children. That is, they must have felt that there was something more ancient than them, no? That's what we feel now when we think about Greece. And strangely, it's what they think in Japan when they talk about China.

FERRARI. To get back to *The Conspirators*.

BORGES. Ah yes, let's get back to *The Conspirators*.

FERRARI (*laughs*). In the prologue, you suggest new ideas which are related to recent discoveries of yours, such as the idea that beauty, like happiness, is an everyday occurrence.

BORGES. Yes, but I think that, to get to that idea, one has to have lived a long time, eh? Because young people, well, perhaps they expect too much of life, and concentrate primarily on the disappointments, more than anything they feel let down. On the other hand, in the case of old people, what they feel, above all, is gratitude. In my case especially, since beyond my blindness, beyond that physical accident is, well, hospitality, that open hospitality of people with me, that I've experienced in so many countries, honours that I've received . . . even people stopping me in the street and talking to me about what I've written. It has all seemed so amazing to me. I'm 85 years old, any moment now I become 86 . . . and I am overwhelmed with gratitude for everybody's indulgence.

FERRARI. I see that you talk in your book with the greatest naturalness about death, with the greatest calm, and that naturalness and that calm are communicated to us all.

BORGES. Let's hope that's what happens. I've been invited to a conference—I think that there will be a lot of medics there—on death. And I'm going to say that I wait for it not with impatience but with hope, no? Well, not with great impatience, of course.

FERRARI. That calm is close to what you attribute to Socrates in his last dialogue.

BORGES. It's extraordinary that dialogue, yes. There's a remark which is so ambiguous, or so knowingly ambiguous, when Socrates says to one of his followers: 'Remember that we owe a cock to Asclepius.' And that has been interpreted to mean that Asclepius has cured him of the worst illness, which is life. Otherwise, the fact that he should owe a cock to Asclepius isn't that interesting, no?

FERRARI. Precisely at that moment.

BORGES. Yes, but at that moment he says: 'Remember that we owe a cock to Asclepius,' and death was so close that it was impossible for him to think about anything else, or to talk about anything that didn't refer to death.

FERRARI. Yes, another thing that I would like to point out in your book . . .

BORGES. I'm looking for digressions so as not to talk about my book (*laughs*).

FERRARI (*laughs*). Nevertheless, I want us to talk about *The Conspirators*.

BORGES. But of course.

FERRARI. The other thing is that, having completed, I would say, an almost circular poetic path, you return, in a certain sense, to the beginning—the poems of *The Conspirators* have a cosmogonical tone which suggests the beginning, or beginning once again.

BORGES. Well, I thought that they had the tone of *Fervour of Buenos Aires* when you said the beginning—I think not, eh? I thought that you were talking about my literary beginnings.

FERRARI. No, I was talking about a Borgesian creation in this case, but a new one.

BORGES. No, I don't think so. Let's hope that it's something more far-reaching.

FERRARI. They're far-reaching, but they return, I would say, to the elemental—to marble, to stone, to fire, to wood, to foundational attitudes of men, Caesar, Christ . . .

BORGES. I think those are words that have more power.

61

Teaching

●

OSVALDO FERRARI. A paradox, Borges, which I've thought about a lot, is that, although you were a teacher for many years, you've always had a stronger vocation as a pupil than as a teacher, or a stronger vocation to learn than to teach.

JORGE LUIS BORGES. I have the impression that my students have taught me a lot. My father used to say that children educate their parents, which is the same idea. Of course, I would always have preferred to teach seminars—I don't know how some teachers can be happy teaching a lot of students, because, well, a lot of students are difficult to manage.

FERRARI. And one can't hold their attention.

BORGES. Yes, precisely. I was a teacher for a year in the Catholic University on the calle Córdoba, and eventually I resigned because I had about, let's say, 80 English literature students, and only 40 minutes for the class. I couldn't do anything at all. For them to come in, for them to leave—the 40 minutes have gone and nobody's done anything. The ideal would be a seminar with a maximum of six people, even better if there were five, and better still four. And two hours. Then one could do something. I think I did a lot when we were studying Anglo-Saxon in the National Library, when I was director. I think that there were five of us, occasionally six, but never any more than that, and we didn't have to measure the time at our disposal—it flowed past generously, and we made the most of that. Then I had a chair in philosophy and literature, first in Viamonte, then in Independencia.

FERRARI. And then followed, I think, four four-month periods teaching Argentine literature in the United States, and a series of lectures.

BORGES. Yes, in four different universities, and lectures on Argentine writers in various states of the Union. And I enjoyed doing that a lot. But now I've learnt that I don't know how to teach, I don't know how to give lectures, and that I prefer dialogue. The night before last, I was in a woman's house—she runs a literary workshop in Villa Crespo—and I answered questions, very sympathetic and interesting questions, on literary subjects. They say that it lasted two hours and five minutes, but I would have reckoned that time as half an hour since it flowed by so generously.

FERRARI. With the questions they were asking.

BORGES. With the questions, yes, and now I realize, well, that dialogue is the best method for me. I hope that it will be for our listeners and our readers as well (*laughs*).

FERRARI. It seems to me that over the years you've consistently rejected pontifical behaviour.

BORGES. 'Pontifical' in its most overbearing sense, yes. A friend of mine, Emilio Oribe, the Uruguayan poet, taught philosophy in the Faculty of Philosophy and Literature at the University of Montevideo. He was a forbidding man. He was also deaf which made him, in some sense, invulnerable since he couldn't hear what he didn't want to hear. And he'd managed to establish this strange ritual—about 10 minutes before the bell sounded, that forbidding man, who looked a bit like Almafuerte or Sarmiento, would close his eyes. Then the students knew that they had to leave, that the class was going to finish 10 minutes early. He'd established that ritual—the students understood it, and they respected that forbidding man who had, well, pretended to fall asleep. His students told me that they didn't think any less of him for it—they realized that it was only natural that after talking for, I don't know, 40 minutes, he was rather tired, no?

FERRARI. Of course. As far as your lectures go, I don't know if my chronology is right—first you delivered several, I think, in the Colegio Libre de Estudios Superiores.

BORGES. Yes, of course. When I had to resign from that minor post as an inspector for the sale of poultry and eggs, they sent me to the Colegio Libre de Estudios Superiores, and I gave a series of lectures. The first on classic American literature, and I talked, obviously, about Ralph Waldo Emerson, about Hermann Melville, Nathaniel Hawthorne, Emily Dickinson, about Henry David Thoreau, Henry James, Walt Whitman, about Edgar Allan Poe. And the second series was classes on Buddhism.

FERRARI. Later I think that you carried on teaching at the Argentine Association of English Culture.

BORGES. Yes, I also taught classes there, and a lot of lectures. Later on, I taught classes in various universities. In La Plata I taught a lot, at the Catholic University of La Plata also, in spite of the fact that everybody knows that I'm not a Catholic. In the end, for 45 minutes, I'm forgiven for not being Catholic (*laughs*), and I can talk with complete freedom. I try to do it respectfully, of course.

FERRARI. Then, the Faculty of Philosophy and Literature.

BORGES. Yes, I taught classes exclusively on English and American literature there. And my assistant was Jaime Rest, who is dead now. He was in charge of American literature and I was in charge of English. It was taught in four-month-long terms, and it included some, let's say, inevitable names, well, Chaucer, Doctor Johnson, Shakespeare, Shaw—I tried to change the authors around. That is, if my students knew something about Chesterton but didn't know anything about Shaw, or if they knew something about Stevenson but didn't know anything about Meredith. For example, I alternated between Tennyson and Browning, but then I realized that the students weren't interested in Tennyson while Browning interested them a lot, which is only natural, as Tennyson's appeal is primarily auditory, no? I mean, his verse is very pleasing to the ear. Browning is a different matter—each poem is a technical surprise, not to mention his invention of characters, of quite believable, extremely vivid characters. And then, what he invented, and which was later imitated—the same story recounted by various protagonists. Well, Wilkie Collins had done it earlier, in 'The Moonstone', where various characters recount the story and so we get to know what one character thinks about another. Of course, that will all have come from the epistolary novel, perhaps, the epistolary novel which is now unreadable for us but which gave rise to that type of literature, to the idea of a fiction in which one can experience the point of view of each of the characters and participate in their 'sympathies and differences', as Alfonso Reyes would say. Yes, I feel nostalgia for those years of teaching, although I've been told that I was a terrible teacher. But that doesn't matter. If I've managed to convert the odd student to a love, I wouldn't say of literature, which is too great, but, yes, to the love of an author, or to a particular book by an author . . .

FERRARI. That's enough for you.

BORGES. I won't have lived in vain, I won't have taught in vain.

FERRARI. As for your 18 years as director of the National Library, Borges, is there a way of synthesizing the experience of those years in your memory?

BORGES. It would have to be an extremely vivid memory, because wherever I am in the world I dream of the Montserrat neighbourhood, more specifically about the National library, on the calle México, between Perú and Bolívar. Yes, it's strange, in my dreams I'm always there. So that something has remained of that old building. Although I don't have the right to call it old—the building dates from 1901 while unfortunately I date from 1899. So for me it's a young building, a younger brother with 900,000 volumes. And I—I don't know if I have read even 900 volumes in my life (*laughs*), perhaps not. But I've studied many books. . . . Now that it's just us two, I can tell you that I think I haven't read any book from beginning to end, apart from a few novels and the *History of Western Philosophy* by Russell. I've enjoyed browsing, which means that I always had the idea of being a hedonistic reader—I've never read out of a sense of duty. I remember what

Carlyle said: That a European could only read the Koran from beginning to end if he were moved by a sense of duty.

FERRARI. Perhaps you always went back to the indexes of the books with which you were familiar but whose entire contents you hadn't read.

BORGES. I'm not so sure, eh? (*Both laugh.*) I don't want to boast, but there's always a pleasure in rereading that isn't there in reading . . . For example, I always say that my favourite author is Thomas de Quincey. Well, here I have the 14 volumes that I bought some time ago. When I die, it will probably be revealed that many pages are still uncut in that favourite book of mine. But that doesn't mean that it isn't my favourite—my memory comes back to it, and I've returned to it many times.

FERRARI. Or that you've read them in a fragmentary way so that you have something left to enjoy.

BORGES. Possibly, but perhaps without having been ready for those pages, perhaps the ones I would have liked the most. Yesterday somebody read me something that I liked a lot, it's called I think *The Maker*, and at the end I remembered that I'd written it. So many years have passed, and I experienced it now with surprise, with gratitude and with a certain envy, thinking: My word, Borges—in those days, what a good writer he was! Now he's declined markedly. . . . Now I couldn't write paragraphs like that. Of course, I was able to write them when I had my sight, more or less. I wrote, I edited drafts, I reread, and that meant that I was capable of long, not cacophonous sentences. Now it's different, now I have to hold everything in my memory. I try to salvage what I can.

FERRARI. Yet your readers' opinion doesn't agree with your own.

BORGES. Readers are very inventive. Stevenson said that the reader is always much more intelligent than we are, eh? (*Laughs.*) And it's true.

FERRARI. One can't do without them.

BORGES. No, but if one keeps a manuscript, if one leaves it in a box, and one comes back to look at it three months later, in a way one is that reader who is more intelligent than the author. I remember reading in Kipling's autobiography that he would write a story and then he would leave it. Then he would reread it, and he'd always find basic errors, really, really stupid errors. Before publishing anything he would allow at least a year to pass, so that it could have time to mature. Sometimes I write something, I make a clumsy error which seems impossible to correct, and then, suddenly, walking in the street, the solution comes to me, which is always extremely simple—it's so obvious that it's invisible, like Poe's 'Purloined Letter'.

FERRARI. So yesterday you were the reader of *The Maker*.

BORGES. Yes, it was a nice surprise for me, as I'd forgotten about it. That book is made up of small pieces, and it works because none of them was written to form part of a book—each one of them responded to a necessity that I felt at the time of writing. So it's impossible for the book to be too bad, although doubtless there will be errors and erroneous moments.

FERRARI. It was written out of necessity.

BORGES. Yes.

62

Bertrand Russell

●

OSVALDO FERRARI. A contemporary thinker who I think has accompanied you, Borges, in your contemplation of our age is Bertrand Russell.

JORGE LUIS BORGES. Yes, of course, I read and reread his book, *Introduction to Mathematical Philosophy*, and I lent it to Alfonso Reyes. It's a simple book, very pleasing to read, like everything that Russell writes. It was the first place I read an explanation, well, which for me is the best, the most accessible explanation, of set theory by the German mathematician Cantor. Reyes read the book and he also found it very interesting. At times I've been asked that question about which book I'd take to a desert island . . . a journalistic cliché. Well, I used to answer that I'd take an encyclopedia, but I don't know if I'm allowed to take 10 or 12 volumes, I think not (*laughs*). Then I chose the *History of Western Philosophy* by Bertrand Russell . . . but, of course, I don't have the island for that, and I don't have my sight either, no? (*Both laugh.*) I do have the book, but that's not enough.

FERRARI. Unless you take a reader with you.

BORGES. In that case, yes, that changes everything. And, besides, the memory of books. . . . I'd like to study that book for, well, what I've read and forgotten.

FERRARI. That is, to recover the memory of the book.

BORGES. Yes, the memory of the book that I'd like to have. In a perfect world, I'd also have the book to hand. I'm thinking that there was a time . . . well, among Muslims I think that it's quite common for people to know the Koran by heart. There's the word 'hafiz' which means just that—memorious, memorious with regard to the Koran in particular. I think that there are current systems of teaching in which one doesn't ask the student—who can be a child—to understand the book. Rather, they have to learn it by heart. I would have been fortunate if I'd been able to benefit from that system, since I would know lots of books by heart and I would be able to understand and read them now. That would be the best part. For example, if I'd been able to read the *History of Western Philosophy* by Russell when I was a boy, as part of that system, I would have understood very little, but I could consult that book now . . .

FERRARI. You could read it in your memory.

BORGES. Yes, I could read it in my memory. So that system, for people who will eventually go blind, would have been an excellent system for me. Unfortunately I didn't have such luck—I was asked to read and understand. On the other hand, if they'd asked me to perform a mere exercise in learning by rote, well, I could be reading so many books now that remain extremely distant. That's why I referred to the example of several books by Bertrand Russell. Later I read other books by him, in which he develops his personal system of philosophy, but I've always felt excluded from that system, that is, I understood each page as I read it but later on, when I tried to organize it all in my mind, I failed, and I failed spectacularly.

FERRARI. But what idea did you form of Russell's system?

BORGES. That it's an extremely rigorous system, that it's a logical system. But, for some reason, if I try to imagine it now, I can't.

FERRARI. I think you've been particularly interested in the originality of Russell's view of contemporary social and political events . . .

BORGES. Yes, and, besides, I think that he's a singularly free person, free of the popular superstitions of our time. For example, the superstition of nationalities—I think that he's free of that. Then he has another book, *Why I Am Not a Christian*, but, as I'm not a Christian, I began reading that book but didn't finish it—I felt that it was unnecessary. I didn't need arguments to not be a Christian.

FERRARI. You also agree with his vision of the State.

BORGES. Also with his vision of the State, yes, but I think that is due to English individualism more than anything. Since we have. . . . One of the fathers of anarchism would be Spencer, yes, of course.

FERRARI. Well, you've written about that collection of essays by Russell, *Let the People Think*, I don't know if you remember . . .

BORGES. Ah, yes, I've written about it . . . and some time ago, eh?

FERRARI. Yes, one of those essays is called 'Free Thought and Official Propaganda', the other is 'The Ancestry of Fascism'.

BORGES. I fully agree with Russell. I suppose that Fichte and Carlyle appear in that ancestry, no?

FERRARI. Exactly.

BORGES. Yes, because I remember an article by Chesterton in which he talked about how old-fashioned Hitler's doctrine was, which corresponded more or less with, or which was, in fact, Victorian.

FERRARI. Here we come to the idea that current events spring from the theories of earlier periods.

BORGES. Yes, I would say that politicians are the ultimate plagiarists, the ultimate writers' disciples. But, usually, trailing a century behind, or a bit more even, yes. Because everything that's called the contemporary world is really . . . it's a museum which is usually antiquated. Now, for example, we're all entranced by democracy—well, all that brings us to Paine, to Jefferson (*laughs*), all those things which could provoke excitement when Walt Whitman wrote his *Leaves of Grass* in 1855. All that is the contemporary world. So that politicians would be backward readers, no? Old-fashioned readers, readers of old libraries. Well, as I am too now, in fact.

FERRARI. Perhaps, Borges, they led to the invention of that phrase: 'Reality is always anachronistic.'

BORGES. Who said that?

FERRARI. You did (*laughs*).

BORGES. I think that you've just made a gift of it to me.

FERRARI. No, no.

BORGES. I agree with it, but I agree with it so much, that it seems strange, no? I generally agree with what I read, and not with what I think. How does the phrase go?

FERRARI. 'Reality is always anachronistic.'

BORGES. And I must have said that to you, no?

FERRARI. It appears in the discussion of that article from Russell's book, 'The Ancestry of Fascism', which is included in your book *Other Inquisitions*.

BORGES. Ah well, there yes, the truth is that book is full of surprises for me (*laughs*). I wrote it so long ago that it's new to me now.

FERRARI. You talk about a book by Wells there, and you talk about the book by Russell.

BORGES. But of course, and it was published in *La Nación*, naturally, and there Russell said that one has to teach people the art of reading newspapers.

FERRARI. Precisely.

BORGES. Well, that was changed, because it could apply to *La Nación* itself. So they put 'The Art of Reading Certain Newspapers', to exclude themselves (*laughs*). Yes, I remember, during the First World War—which we were hoping would be the last—the Germans began an offensive and took the town of Aix. Then they announced that they'd taken that town, or that city. Whereas the Allies, two or three days later, said that the German offensive had failed, that they'd got no further than the town they had taken. They were two ways of saying the same thing.

FERRARI. Of course.

BORGES. And Russell wanted to warn the reader about precisely that kind of error.

FERRARI. That's why he said 'Free Thought and Official Propaganda', of course. Now, he . . .

BORGES. Well, I think we've come across something of that in this country, no? Perhaps too much, perhaps everything there is to know! And no doubt we'll continue to be at the mercy of propaganda.

FERRARI. Russell comes to a strange conclusion—that the eighteenth century was rational but our own age is irrational. Of course, he was confronted with Fascism and Nazism at that time, wasn't he?

BORGES. He was confronted with so many things—confronted with Surrealism, confronted with the cult of disorder, confronted with the disappearance, well, of certain forms of verse, or even of prose, confronted with the disappearance of punctuation marks which was an extremely interesting innovation, no? (*Both laugh.*)

FERRARI. He also added that the threat to individual freedom is greater in our time than at any time since 1600. But, once again, we have to remember that he said it when Nazism and Fascism were at their peak, no?

BORGES. Yes, but that peak hasn't subsided.

FERRARI. You see it like that?

BORGES. I would say that one of its most extreme forms is what is called communism in the Soviet Union, no? It's the most extreme form of fascism, of State intervention. I mean, in that suffering proposed by

Spencer in 'The Man versus the State'. . . . Well, it's clear that the State is now ubiquitous in the Soviet Union.

FERRARI. Although in Western countries also the State threatens us, as you constantly remind us.

BORGES. Perhaps it's threatening us right now (*laughs*), as we speak, perhaps while we're both talking here.

FERRARI. Another of Russell's particular characteristics is his stance towards religions, not only towards Christianity but also the phenomenon of religion. You remember that book of his, *Religion and Science*.

BORGES. Yes, I read it a while ago but I remember it, and the opposition seems obvious to me. Of course, in the long term it's religion that gives way. For example, when Hilaire Belloc replies to H. G. Wells, he doesn't cast doubt on evolution, etcetera, except that he says that it's all already there in Saint Thomas Aquinas, in the *Summa Theologicae*. But it certainly wasn't there in the *Pentateuch*. Yes, religion, of course, is always becoming more subtle, it continually interprets science, it tries to reconcile science, if not with Holy Scripture then certainly with theology, with the various theologies. But, in the end, it's science that triumphs, not religion.

FERRARI. It has been said that we live in an age without faith, or, in any case, that ours is a scientific age.

BORGES. In Iran, they're apologists for Islam, but one feels that, really, they have more faith in the machine gun than in miracles, that is, they believe in a technological war, not in scimitars and camels. And here we've suffered a war, or a small war, which was terrible, like all wars are, even if they last for just a few minutes. I'd like to recall here that, as far as I know, there were two people who spoke out in print against that war which I hope will have been completely forgotten very soon—Silvina Bullrich and myself. I don't remember anybody else—either they kept quiet, or they applauded the regime. Of course, many people thought the same way as us but they didn't publish what they were thinking.

FERRARI. In any case, another of your points of agreement with Bertrand Russell is your attitude to war.

BORGES. Yes, of course.

63

The 'Conjectural Poem'

●

OSVALDO FERRARI. I have resisted the temptation, Borges, of reading and discussing a poem with you that appears in your *Personal Anthology*, an inclusion which indicates that you like it too.

JORGE LUIS BORGES. Or that I'm resigned to it, no? Because from the moment that one agrees to compile an anthology, it has to be a certain length . . . so that, in any case, I've become resigned to that poem. I hope that it isn't too long.

FERRARI. Your poem has the virtue of offering such a concrete vision of history that it seems as though it's not you speaking but history speaking through you. I'm talking, of course, about the 'Conjectural Poem'.

BORGES. Ah, well, yes, it begins: 'Bullets whine in the afternoon's finale'. Of course, that 'afternoon's finale' is deliberately ambiguous, since it could be the end of the afternoon or the last afternoon of the protagonist, my distant relative Laprida.

FERRARI. The epigraph says, 'Doctor Francisco Laprida, killed on 22nd September 1829 by Aldao's gaucho militia, reflects before he dies.'

BORGES. Yes, of course. When I wrote that poem, I knew that it was historically impossible. But if one views Laprida symbolically, the poem becomes possible. Of course, his thoughts must have been quite varied, more fragmentary, and perhaps without learned references to Dante, no?

FERRARI. Nevertheless, there's a historical coherence throughout the poem.

> The bullets whine in the afternoon's finale.
> There is wind and there is ash on the wind.

BORGES. I don't know if that can be justified, but it sounds good—aesthetically, it's justified. Whether there really was ash, I don't know, it's possible that something was burnt. But that doesn't matter. I think that the reader's imagination accepts that improbable ash, no?

FERRARI (*laughs*). Yes.

> . . . The day and the mangled battle are scattered,
> and the other side is victorious.

BORGES. 'Mangled' sounds strange alongside 'battle' but 'the day and the battle are scattered' is well put, I think.

FERRARI. Excellent.

> . . . The barbarians have won, the gauchos have won . . .

BORGES. Yes, I wanted those two words to be completely synonymous as there's a cult of the gaucho, unfortunately.

FERRARI. Laprida then moves into speculation:

> . . . I who studied canon and civil law,
> I, Francisco Narciso de Laprida,
> whose voice declared the independence
> of these cruel regions, defeated,
> my face stained with blood and sweat,
> without hope or fear, lost,
> I flee towards the South through far-flung backlands.

BORGES. Yes, I think that fortunately he went towards the south, since *sur* is such a resonant word. On the other hand, *oeste* and *este* don't have any resonance in Spanish, *norte* is a little better, but *este* and *oeste* . . . we could disguise them as *oriente* and *occidente* which sound better.

FERRARI. . . . Like that captain in Purgatorio

> who, fleeing on foot, bloodying the plain . . .

BORGES. That line is good because it's not mine—it's by Dante: 'Sfuggendo a piede e insanguinando il piano.' I translated it directly, of course, without any great difficulties.

FERRARI. . . . he was blind and laid low by death

> where a dark river loses its name,
> thus I will have to fall. Today is the end.
> The flanking night of the marshes
> lies in wait, holding me back. I hear the hooves
> of my own hot death, which seeks me
> with horsemen, with swollen lips and with lances.
> I who longed to be someone different, to be a man
> of judgements, of books, of laws,

in the open air I will lie amid swamps;
but a secret joy inexplicably
swells my chest. In the end I am
confronted with my South American destiny . . .

BORGES. Well, that's the best line. When I published that poem, it wasn't just historical—it referred not only to the past but also to the present. A certain dictator had just seized power and we were all confronted with our South American destiny. We, who were playing at being Paris, but who were, well, South American, no? At the time those who read it understood it as a contemporary statement: 'In the end I am confronted with my South American destiny . . . '. South American in the most mournful sense of the word . . . or the most tragic.

FERRARI. But with those two lines you've established a metaphysical understanding of our destiny, because now we all know that at some point we are going to be confronted with our South American destiny.

BORGES. I would say that we've already been confronted with it, and excessively so, no? (*Laughs.*) The strange thing is that one gravitates towards it, eh? Because before, one thought of South America, the America of the South, as a very distant place, with a certain exotic charm. But now it's different, now we're South Americans—we have to resign ourselves to that, and to be equal to that destiny which ultimately is our own.

FERRARI. Of course. The poem continues:

. . . I was led to this ruinous afternoon
by the manifold labyrinth of steps

that my days had woven ever since
childhood. In the end I have discovered
the hidden key to my years,
the fate of Francisco de Laprida,
the missing letter, the perfect
pattern that God knew from the beginning.
In this night's mirror I see
my eternal face revealed. The circle
is about to close. I wait for it.

BORGES. It's good this poem, eh? Even though I wrote it, it's good.

FERRARI. It gets better (*laughs*).

BORGES. Improved by you at this moment, yes, who read it with such conviction.

FERRARI. It ends:

My feet tread the shadow of the lances
that pursue me. The taunts of my death,
the horsemen, the manes, the horses,
lie ready to attack . . . Now the first blow,
now the hard steel that rends my chest,
the intimate knife at my throat.

BORGES. Well, I'd been reading Browning's dramatic monologues, and I thought: I'm going to try something similar. But there's something here . . . which isn't in Browning, and it's that the poem follows Laprida's consciousness and it ends when that consciousness ends. That is, the poem ends because the person who is doing the thinking and feeling dies. 'The intimate knife at my throat' is the final moment of his consciousness as well as the final line. That gives the poem its power, it seems to me, no?

FERRARI. Yes, without doubt.

BORGES. Although, of course, it's completely unbelievable. Pursued by the people who were going to kill him, those final moments of Laprida must have been less rational, more fragmentary, more erratic. He must have had visual perceptions, auditory perceptions, wondering if they were going to catch up with him. But I don't know if that would have worked in a poem. It's better to imagine that he can see all this from the relative tranquillity of poetry, and with more or less well-constructed sentences. I think that if the poem had been a realist one, if it had been what Joyce calls an interior monologue, it would have lost a lot. And it's better for it to be untrue, that is, for it to be literary.

FERRARI. In spite of that, there are aspects of the poem that are true for everyone. You suggest that 'the manifold labyrinth of steps' that he crossed in his life was 'weaving' that destiny . . .

BORGES. Of course, and I have travelled in so many countries, I have taken so many steps, and those steps lead me to the final one, which is still unknown to me, and which will be revealed to me in good time—which could be very soon, since once one reaches a certain age one might die at any moment. Or one hopes to die at any moment.

FERRARI. Or one can keep on travelling.

BORGES. Yes, or one can keep on travelling, yes, one never knows. I should be tired of life, and yet I'm still curious, particularly when I think about two countries—China and India. I feel a duty to get to know them.

FERRARI. For some years I've wanted to discuss at least two possible deductions from the 'Conjectural Poem' with you.

BORGES. What are they?

FERRARI. The poem implies, with the 'manifold labyrinth of steps' and the 'key' which is the destiny contained in it, that each destiny can have a coherence, that is, it can be cosmic and, therefore, can make sense.

BORGES. I don't know if it's cosmic, but it's certainly predetermined. But that doesn't mean that there's something or someone who predetermines it. It means that the sum of effects and causes is perhaps infinite, and that we're determined by that branching out of effects and causes. That's why I don't believe in free will. So, that moment would be the last, and it would have been determined by each step that Laprida had made since the beginning of his life.

FERRARI. The other possible deduction, Borges, is that we South Americans—since the poem talks about that—have arrived in some way at our own destiny, a South American destiny.

BORGES. And, a sad destiny, eh? A destiny of dictators. We seem to be predestined in some way—no other continent has produced people who have wanted to be called 'The Supreme One from Entre Ríos' like Ramírez, or 'The Supreme One' like López in Paraguay, or 'The Great Citizen' like I don't know who in Venezuela, or 'The Premier Worker' which needs no explanation. It's very strange, this hasn't happened in the United States . . . perhaps there's been the odd dictator—I think that Lincoln was a dictator but he didn't decorate himself with those titles. 'The Restorer of Laws' is even stranger. Nobody knows which laws it's talking about, and nobody has tried to find out either—the title on its own is enough. It's an example of what Huidobro called 'Creationism', no? A literature that doesn't have anything to do with reality. 'Restorer of Laws'—what laws? Nobody bothers about that. They all seem to have wanted an *epiteto ornens*.

FERRARI. However, it seems that we're all capable at times of maturing. Among the possibilities that our destiny had in store for us, as you said a little while ago, there is this new hope that we are experiencing now.

BORGES. One would hope so. In any case, we must be faithful to that hope, although perhaps it takes some effort. What other hope do we have? Let's believe in democracy, why not?

64

New Dialogue on Poetry

●

OSVALDO FERRARI. According to an ancient Eastern tradition, Borges, Adam talked verse in paradise . . .

JORGE LUIS BORGES. I didn't know that. I know that he spoke in Hebrew, of course. Coleridge's father was a vicar in an English town. And his parishioners enjoyed the fact that he interspersed his sermons with long digressions directly in the language of the Holy Ghost, which was Hebrew, of course. When he died, another vicar replaced him, who didn't know Hebrew and who wasn't in the habit of using it, and the parishioners felt cheated. Although they couldn't understand a word, it didn't matter—they liked to hear the vicar speak in the language of the Holy Ghost, in Hebrew. There's a passage in Sir Thomas Browne where he says that it would be interesting to leave two children in a forest—let's say, Romulus and Remus. They wouldn't imitate anybody because they would be alone, and so the primitive, Edenic or paradisiacal pronunciation of Hebrew could be recovered, for that is the language those children would speak. It seems that such an experiment was indeed carried out, but the children didn't speak—they just emitted incomprehensible sounds. Someone had assumed that simply by abandoning two children the primitive language of humanity would be recovered . . .

FERRARI. The original language . . .

BORGES. Hebrew, yes. I didn't know that Adam spoke in verse. I do remember having read in some book on the Kabbalah—one of the few books I've read on the Kabbalah—about the belief that Adam (of course, Adam had come directly from the hand of God) was the best historian, the best metaphysician, the best mathematician, since he'd been born perfect and had been taught by the divinity and by the angels. There's also a belief that he was extremely tall, and that later on he began to decline. There's a lovely phrase by León Bloy, which says that when Adam is cast out of paradise he is no longer like fire but like a dying ember. And there's a belief that the Kabbalah is a very ancient tradition, since it was taught by the angels to Adam. Adam taught it to Cain and Abel, they taught it to their children, and that tradition carried on until the middle of the Middle Ages. Now we appreciate an idea if it's new. Before, however, that wasn't the case. To be accepted, to be respected, an idea had to be very ancient, and what tradition could be more ancient than Adam as the first Kabbalist?

FERRARI. As the first one to be taught by the spirit.

BORGES. Yes, of course, in his case the angels were also Kabbalists. Well, the angels were also extremely close to God.

FERRARI. In any case, we know that literature begins with poetry.

BORGES. So the legend about Adam would support that.

FERRARI. Of course.

BORGES. I think that very little is said about Hebrew verse, apart from the parallelism, no? Because the Psalms don't employ a fixed number of syllables, and there's no rhyme or alliteration either, I think. But of course, they have a rhythm which Whitman, rather belatedly, tried to imitate.

FERRARI. Which he recovered.

BORGES. I don't know if he recovered it. In any case, he started from the Psalms of David, in the Bishops' version of the English Bible.

FERRARI. Borges' work also begins with poetry, because it begins with *Fervour of Buenos Aires.*

BORGES. Well, yes, but one would have to say poetry in inverted commas, because I don't think that's poetry. It's a more or less refined prose. When I wrote it, I remember thinking less about Whitman, who I invoked as a precursor, than about Quevedo's prose, which I was reading so much at that time. In any case, I think that book is full of Latinisms, in the style of Quevedo, which I later tried to tone down.

FERRARI. However, the invocation of Whitman persisted, because you used free verse at that time.

BORGES. In that case, yes, but I don't know if my free verse was like Whitman's or if it was like the rhythmical prose of Quevedo, or of Saavedra Fajardo, who I also read a lot at that time.

FERRARI. You have some ideas on poetry that interest me, Borges. For example, you've said that any poetry that's rooted in reality has to be good.

BORGES. And . . . one would have to say in truth, or in absolute imagination, no? Which is the opposite. . . . Well, no, but imagination has to be true as well, in the sense that the poet must believe what he imagines. I think that the worst thing is to think of poetry as wordplay, although that could also lead to rhythmical effects. I think that's a mistake, no?

FERRARI. Yes, but I think you're particularly interested in the emotional truth, let's say.

BORGES. Emotional truth, that is, I invent a story, I know that the story is untrue—it's a fantasy, or a detective story which is just another fantastic genre—but as I write I must believe in it. And this coincides with what Coleridge said, that poetic faith is the momentary suspension of disbelief.

FERRARI. That's wonderful.

BORGES. For example a person in a theatre is watching *Macbeth*. He knows that he's watching actors, men in costume who are repeating verse from the seventeenth century, but he forgets all that and believes that he's following the terrible destiny of Macbeth, driven to murder by the witches, by his own ambition and by his wife, Lady Macbeth. Or when we look at a painting, we look at a landscape and we don't think that it's an image painted on canvas. We see it, well, as if the painting were a window that looked out onto that landscape.

FERRARI. Certainly. Now, you've also said that word music, when applied to poetry, is either an error or a metaphor, that language has its own intonation.

BORGES. Yes, for example, I think I have a certain ear for what Shaw called word music, and I don't have any ear, or an extremely limited one, for instrumental or sung music.

FERRARI. They are two different things.

BORGES. Yes, they're two different things. I've talked to musicians who have no ear for verbal music, who can't tell if a paragraph in prose or a stanza of verse is well cadenced.

FERRARI. Another idea of yours about poetry is that it can do without metaphor.

BORGES. I think that, yes, apart from . . . when Emerson said that language is fossil poetry. In that sense, every abstraction would start off as a concrete word and be a metaphor. But in order to understand an abstract discussion, we have to forget the physical root, the etymology, of each word—we have to forget that they are metaphors.

FERRARI. Yes, because the etymology of metaphor . . .

BORGES. Is carrying over.

FERRARI. Carrying over . . .

BORGES. Yes, metaphor is a metaphor—the word 'metaphor' is also a metaphor.

FERRARI. Everything has a symbolic meaning, but one of the ideas that I find most interesting occurs in one way in Rilke, and in you in another though similar way. Rilke said that beauty is no more than the beginning of horror, and you've related poetry to horror, possibly reminding us of the Celtic poets—the idea that man isn't completely worthy of poetry. You've recalled that, in biblical terms, man could not look on God, because as soon as he saw Him, he would die. And you've concluded that something similar happens with poetry.

BORGES. I have a story based on that ancient idea. It's about a Celtic poet who's commissioned by the king to write a poem about the palace. And the poet performs that poem three times over three years. The first two times he turns up with a manuscript, but the last time is different—he comes without a manuscript and says only one word to the king. That word is certainly not the word 'palace' but it's a word that expresses the palace in a more perfect way. And then, once the poet has pronounced that word, the palace disappears. Because the palace has no reason to carry on existing, since it has been expressed by a single word.

FERRARI. Poetry and magic.

BORGES. Yes, that's it, and in another possible ending, I think, the king gives the poet a dagger, because the poet has achieved perfection— he's come upon that word, and he has no reason to carry on living. And also because the fact of having come upon a word that can provide a substitute for reality is like a form of blasphemy, no? What right does man have to come upon a word that can replace one of the things in the universe?

FERRARI. What you've said reminds me that, thinking in religious terms, the names of ancient cities were considered a secret.

BORGES. Yes, De Quincey recalls the example of Rome, and gives the name of a Roman who was condemned to death and executed for having revealed the secret. And then De Quincey adds that the secret name has been so well preserved that it has not come down to us.

FERRARI. Of course.

BORGES. There's a belief that if someone possesses Rome's secret name, they possess Rome, because to know the name of something is to dominate it. Something that we've talked about elsewhere is relevant here—the 'I Am that I Am' as a . . . well, as a euphemism used by God to not say his true name to Moses. That's what Martin Buber thought.

FERRARI. You mean the secret name of God.

BORGES. Yes, there was a secret name, but God, in order not to reveal that name which would have put him in Moses' power, says to him, 'I Am that I Am,' and thus evades a direct answer. It amounts to a subterfuge by God.

FERRARI. I want to ask if you have felt a relation between horror and the poet, or poetry, or beauty, the terms which we have mentioned.

BORGES. Between horror and beauty yes. I felt that before, when I thought we were unworthy of beauty. On the other hand, now I think that beauty is exceedingly common, so why not welcome and accept it?

FERRARI. The other issue that seems important to me, and that we mentioned when we were talking about Plato and Aristotle, is that the poet may still be capable of using reason and intuition at the same time, or . . .

BORGES. Or myth.

FERRARI. Yes, perhaps in contemporary society it's the poet who still manages to use both things.

BORGES. Who is capable of using both things, yes, but the poet always leans more to one or the other, no? I have had the accusation thrown at me that I'm an intellectual poet.

FERRARI. It's a false accusation.

BORGES. Yes, but it's strange. It seems that Browning was accused at first of being too decorative a poet, and then, in the end, they said that he was so intellectual that he'd become incomprehensible.

65

The Moon Landing

●

OSVALDO FERRARI. There's a contemporary event, Borges, that seems to have made a particular impression on you, and which doesn't receive much attention, in spite of having happened relatively recently—I'm talking about the moon landing.

JORGE LUIS BORGES. Yes, I wrote a poem about this subject. But for political, that is, circumstantial and ephemeral reasons, people tend to diminish the importance of an achievement which, for me, is the great achievement of our century. Absurdly, the discovery of the moon has been compared to the discovery of America. You wouldn't credit it, and yet it's fairly common. Of course, because of the word 'discovery'—since people are used to the 'discovery of America', they apply it to the 'discovery of the moon' or to the discovery of, I don't know, an afterlife, for example, no? Well, I think that once the boat had been invented, once, let's say, oars, masts, sails, rudders, had been invented, the discovery of America was inevitable. I would go as far as to say that 'the discovery' is an error—it would be more accurate to talk about the discoveries of America, as there were so many. We can begin with mythical discoveries, for example, of Atlantis which we find in the pages of Plato and Seneca, or the voyages of Saint Brendan where he came upon islands with silver greyhounds chasing deer of gold. We can leave those myths aside, which are perhaps a distorted reflection of real events, and we can turn instead to the tenth century, and there we have a reliable date with the adventure of that noble who was also a Viking, and who also, like so many people at that time from those parts, was a murderer—it seems that Eric, Eric the Red, owed a debt, as we say now, for a number of deaths in Norway. He went to the island of Iceland, there he brought more debts upon himself for further deaths and then had to flee to the West. Let's suppose that distances then were much greater than they are now, since space is measured in time. Well, he arrived with his boats at an island they called Greenland—I think it's 'greneland' in Icelandic. Now, there are two explanations: one refers to the green colour of the ice, which seems improbable, and the other, that Eric gave it the name Greenland to attract settlers. Eric the Red is a lovely name for a hero, and for a hero from the North, no?

FERRARI. For a bloody hero.

BORGES. For a bloody hero, yes. Eric the Red was a pagan, but I don't know if he worshipped Odin, who gives his name to the English Wednesday, or Thor, who gives his name to Thursday, as one was identified with Mercury—'miércoles'—and the other with Jove—'jueves'. The fact is that he came to Greenland, that he brought settlers with him, that he made two expeditions . . . and then his son, Leif Ericson, discovers the continent, he comes to Labrador and beyond what is now the border with Canada, he enters what is now the United States. Then we have more discoveries, well, by Christopher Columbus, by Amerigo Vespucci, who gives the continent its name. And later, one loses count of the number of Portuguese, Dutch, English, Spanish navigators, from all parts, who keep on discovering our continent. They were looking for the Indies, and they stumbled on this continent which is so important now, and in which we are talking.

FERRARI. They thought, as well, that it was a part of the Indies.

BORGES. Yes, they thought it was a part of the Indies, which is why they used the word 'indian' which is used to describe the indigenous peoples here. That is, it was all fated, it had to happen, and the proof is that it happened, well, historically from the tenth century. In any case, it would have happened, given the fact that there was travel by sea. On the other hand, the discovery of the moon is completely different. It's an enterprise that is not only physical—I don't want to deny the courage of Armstrong and the others—but also intellectual, scientific, it was something planned, something executed, not a gift of fate. It's something—I think it happened in 1969, if I'm not wrong—which honours humanity, not only because men from different countries participated in it but also because a landing on the moon is no mean achievement. And strangely, two novelists who wrote books on this subject, Jules Verne and H. G. Wells—well, neither believed it was possible. I remember, when Wells published his first novel, Verne was scandalized. He said: 'He's making it up.' Because Verne was a rational Frenchman to whom the dreams and the eccentricities of Wells seemed excessive. They both thought that it was impossible, although in one of Wells' books—I don't remember which one—he talks about the moon, and he says that the moon will be man's first trophy in the conquest of space. A few days after that feat had been accomplished, I wrote a poem in which I said that there was no happier man in the world than I. The cultural attaché at the Soviet embassy came to visit me, and, standing aside from the, well, territorial or geographical prejudices which are in fashion now, he said to me: 'This has been the happiest night of my life.' He forgot that it had been organized in the United States, and he simply thought: We've landed on the moon, humanity has landed on the moon. But now the world has proved oddly ungrateful to the United States. For example, Europe has been saved twice by the United States from, well, absurd cruelties—the First and the Second World Wars. And contemporary literature is inconceivable without Edgar Allan Poe, Walt Whitman and Herman Melville, not to mention Henry James. But I don't know why those things aren't acknowledged. Perhaps because of the power of the United States. Well, Berkeley, the philosopher, said that the fourth and greatest empire in history would be America. And he suggested preparing the settlers of the Bermudas, and the Redskins, for their future imperial destiny (*laughs*). Then we have that great achievement, we've seen it, it has made us extremely happy, but now we tend, ungenerously, to forget it. But, I'm monopolizing this dialogue (*laughs*).

FERRARI (*laughs*). It's just that it's very interesting. It began several years earlier . . . the beginning of that feat occurred in 1957, when the first artificial satellite—well, there it was the Soviet Union—was launched. And 12 years later . . .

BORGES. That is, those two rival countries were, in fact, collaborating.

FERRARI. Collaborating in the space race.

BORGES. Yes, they did it out of rivalry, but the fact is that we owe to their rivalry the achievement of that feat.

FERRARI. By man.

BORGES. Yes, that human feat which for me is the greatest achievement of this century. Of course, it was made possible by computers, etcetera, which were also invented in this century, eh? That is, in this century, of course, we all feel that we're in decline, but we think about ethical or economic causes, especially in this country. Well, perhaps the literature of the nineteenth century was more vibrant. Now they've invented a number of ridiculous sciences, for example, dynamic psychology, sociolinguistics. In the end, they're passing fads, no? (*Both laugh.*) Let's hope that they're quickly forgotten. However, scientifically one can't deny everything that's been done.

FERRARI. Of course, you're right, because as we've said, it's only 28 years ago that man embarked on the adventure, let's say, of leaving Earth. Yet, one doesn't talk about it . . .

BORGES. No, one doesn't talk about it because one talks about elections, one talks about the saddest subject of all, which is politics. I say, not for the first time, that I'm the enemy of the State and of States, and of nationalism which is one of the blemishes of our time. The fact that each person insists on the privilege of having been born in one or another point or corner of the planet, no? And that we're so far from the ancient dream of the Stoics, that time when people were defined by their city—Thales of Miletus, Zeno of Elea, Heraclitus of Ephesus, etcetera, who would say that they were citizens of the world. It would have been a scandalous paradox for the Greeks.

FERRARI. To come back to the Greeks. Perhaps the moon landing could be seen as the ultimate consequence of what Denis de Rougemont called 'man's Western quest'.

BORGES. That's right.

FERRARI. Which covers the adventures that we see in *The Iliad* or *The Odyssey*, and which, of course, includes Christopher Columbus' adventure.

BORGES. Well, there's a habit of talking ill of empires, but empires are the beginning of a cosmopolis, let's say.

FERRARI. Of cosmopolitanism, you say?

BORGES. Yes, I think that empires, in that sense, have done good. For example, spreading certain languages. Now I think that the immediate future belongs to Spanish and English. Unfortunately, French is in decline, and Russian and Chinese are too difficult. But, in the end, that can all lead us towards the unity we desire, which, of course, would do away with the possibility of war, which is another of today's threats.

FERRARI. Now, as part of that Western spirit, as part of that Western curiosity which has permitted discoveries over time, and now that you've mentioned empire, one should remember that Columbus made his discovery in the name of 'Christianity', and that Columbus was called 'Colomba Christi Ferens', that is, 'dove Christ-bearer'.

BORGES. Ah, how lovely, I didn't know that—of course, dove, yes.

FERRARI. Yes, Christopher also alludes to Christ . . .

BORGES. Yes, because I remember, there's an engraving—I don't know who by but it's famous—in which Saint Christopher is carrying baby Jesus, crossing a river.

FERRARI. So, can the 'Christianity' which led to Columbus' discovery be seen as a version of empire, would you say, at that time?

BORGES. Why not? Islam has now taken a political form. But, in the end, it's the way this happens—that is, in the long run . . . in the long run, all things are good.

FERRARI. At that time, the discovery was made as part of a journey into the unknown. On the other hand, these attempts by the United States and the Soviet Union to leave Earth—well, perhaps they also lead into the unknown.

BORGES. As for the moon, well, the moon of Virgil and the moon of Shakespeare were already famous before the discovery, no?

FERRARI. Of course.

BORGES. Yes, and they've been with us for so long. There's something so intimate about the moon. . . . There's a line in Virgil which talks about 'amica silentia lunae', which refers to the brief periods of darkness which allow the Greeks to get down from the wooden horse and invade Troy. But Wilde, who doubtless knew about this, prefers to talk about 'The friendly silences of the Moon'. And, in a line of my own, I've said: 'The silent friendliness of the moon / (I quote Virgil badly) accompanies you.'

FERRARI. Anyhow, even in this case, we still need the presence of the unknown.

BORGES. I think that it's completely necessary but we'll never be without it, since, assuming that the external world exists—and I think that it does, that we can know it by means of our intuition and the five physical senses. . . . Voltaire thought that it was possible to imagine a hundred senses, and that one more would change our whole vision of the world. Anyway, science has already changed it, because what for us is a solid object, for science is, well, a system of atoms, of neutrons and electrons. We ourselves are made of those atomic, nuclear systems.

FERRARI. Of course. However, the feat of landing on the moon would have astonished men from previous centuries and made them think about the unknown.

BORGES. And they would have celebrated it.

FERRARI. Wells himself, who belongs to the previous century and to our own, thought that it was impossible, as you recalled.

BORGES. Yes, but, unlike Jules Verne, Wells boasted about the impossibility of his imaginings. That is, he was certain that there wouldn't be a machine that travelled not only through space but also through time, with greater speed than us. He was certain that an invisible man was impossible, and he was also certain that man wouldn't land on the moon—he boasted about that. But now it seems as if reality has decided to refute him, and to tell him that what he thought was imaginary, was simply prophetic.

66

Russian Writers

●

OSVALDO FERRARI. Even though we perhaps haven't betrayed the Stoic ideal in the variety of subjects that we've discussed, Borges, and even though we've behaved like citizens of the world, we haven't yet dealt with the Slavonic writers—we haven't mentioned Tolstoy, for example.

JORGE LUIS BORGES. That's true. For a long time, after reading *Crime and Punishment*, I thought that Dostoyevsky was the greatest novelist. Then I read *The Possessed*, which is called *The Devils* in Russian, and then I wanted to read *The Brothers Karamazov*. But that defeated me. And though I still admired Dostoyevsky, I felt that I didn't want to read any more of him. *The House of the Dead* disappointed me too. On the other hand, I have read and reread a single book by Tolstoy, *War and Peace*, and I still think it's admirable. But I think that's the general view, that Tolstoy is superior.

FERRARI. To Dostoyevsky?

BORGES. Yes, to Dostoyevsky, no?

FERRARI. It's quite possible.

BORGES. I think that's the general opinion, in any case, among the Russians. I also read that famous Russian writer whose name I can't recall, although I'd like to—the author of *Lolita* . . .

FERRARI. Nabokov.

BORGES. Yes, Nabokov said that when he was compiling an anthology of Russian prose, he found that he couldn't include a single page by Dostoyevsky. And although that seems like an act of censorship, in fact it isn't, since I don't know if it's appropriate for a novel to have pages that can be anthologized. And I remember what Momigliano said about D'Annunzio, about his least pardonable sin, or his greatest fault, let's say, or his greatest defect, which was only having written pages that can be anthologized. Of course, a page is a unit, but a novel can't be reduced to any one of its pages, even less to one of its clauses or sentences—a novel must be read as a whole. In any case, one remembers it as a whole. So what Nabokov says may not be a criticism of Dostoyevsky, after all. Perhaps a great novelist can do without pages that can be anthologized.

FERRARI. Or all his pages could be anthologized.

BORGES. Or some of them.

FERRARI. Of course.

BORGES. Although, well, it seems that whenever one talks about novels, one inevitably thinks about *Don Quixote*. In *Don Quixote*, most of the pages can't be anthologized—they seem to have been written without any particular attention to style. But the final chapter and the first chapters, which are certainly unforgettable, are anthology pieces, and to exclude them would be an arbitrary decision on the part of the anthologist. Of course, I used to see literature in terms of what could be anthologized. I would write a sentence—generally, my sentences were long . . . well, I wanted them to be eloquent, unforgettable, four or five lines long, then I would reread it, and I would gradually edit it, but when I edited it for perverse reasons, it turned out wrong. Then I'd move on to the second sentence, and then to the third. And in the end, the whole article would be unreadable because it was made up of isolated blocks. By contrast, now I write fluently, or I try to be fluent, and then I edit what I've written.

FERRARI. Perhaps you wanted to write poetry rather than prose at that time.

BORGES. I think so. With poetry, there's an assumption that each line must be good. Although perhaps there are admirable poems without admirable lines, and awful poems, well, made up of only memorable lines. But we seem to be straying from the subject, I have this digressive habit. . . . I read the stories, as we've all read those stories by men from the Steppe. Now, the Russian language seems lovely to me—each time that I've heard Russian spoken, I've regretted not knowing it. I tried to study Russian, around 1918, towards the end of the First World War, when I was a communist. But, of course, communism then meant the fellowship of all men, the rejection of borders. Now I think it represents a new czarism.

FERRARI. A new czarism, you say?

BORGES. I think so. They made two films about Ivan the Terrible, I think. In one of them he was an abhorrent person but in the other fairly admirable. That's only natural. This Soviet government identifies with previous governments, that is, if a government is nationalist, it identifies with the country's history. But, to come back to Dostoyevsky: When I think of Dostoyevsky, I think first about *Crime and Punishment*. And I read somewhere, although I don't know if this is true, that the title was going to be *Guilt and Atonement*, and that the book, as we know it, was to have been the first part—the history of the murder, the killing of the moneylender and of the other woman. Then the section in which the police pursue him, and those unforgettable dialogues, of course, between the inspector and the murderer. And then the final section . . . I think in the last sentence it says that to recount Raskolnikov's experiences in Siberia would be to recount the transformation of a soul. That is, it would be to recount the punishment that one doesn't find in the first part, or the atonement, which amounts to the same thing. There's a terrible saying in Hegel, or which seems terrible, that punishment is the right of the criminal. That seems a cruel thing to say, but maybe it isn't. If punishment redeems, a criminal has the right to be punished. That saying has been regarded as cynical but perhaps it isn't.

FERRARI. Legal punishment.

BORGES. Yes. What do you think?

FERRARI. Well . . .

BORGES. At first sight it seems terrible: 'Punishment is the right of the criminal'—the criminal has a right to prison. Well, yes, if prison improves him—why shouldn't he have a right to that improvement, like a sick person having the right to a hospital or an operation?

FERRARI. I would contrast it with the case of the criminal who is killed without being given the opportunity to be punished in a civilized way, by legal means. Then I would say that, yes . . .

BORGES. In that case, yes, it's a crime.

FERRARI. Of course, because he has a right to punishment by the law, and not to a summary execution—he has a right to be punished in a civilized way.

BORGES. Well, I'd prefer the death penalty, because prison seems terrible to me. Xul Solar told me that he wouldn't mind being in prison for a year, as long as he was alone. But to have to live with criminals—that must be terrible, no?

FERRARI (*laughs*). It's quite possible.

BORGES. On the other hand . . . in some way, for a large part of my life, I've been in solitary confinement, no?

FERRARI. We all are.

BORGES. Yes, perhaps one is always alone . . . But in a way I feel very grateful for company, as long as it isn't excessive, as long as it isn't a matter of, well, a prison, or a cocktail party, or perhaps a meeting of the Academy (*both laugh*). As long as there aren't too many, I do like company, yes, to be with two people is extremely pleasant. On the other hand, to be with 20 people seems terrible, no?

FERRARI. Of course.

BORGES. That's the problem with heaven . . . no, but perhaps there's a meagre population in heaven, no? Since many are called but few are chosen. Here I remember that terrible phrase of Kierkegaard who says that if he came to the final judgement, and there were only one person sent to hell, and he were that damned person, he would sing *de profundis* praise of the Lord and his justice. Unless we think of that remark as a way of bribing God (*laughs*), that he wanted to be on good terms with God, but I think not.

FERRARI. A way of gaining entry to heaven.

BORGES. Yes, but better not to think that it's an act of bribery, or that God would accept that bribe, no?

FERRARI. Perhaps Nabokov is right when he says that Dostoyevsky is for him a better dramatist than a novelist.

BORGES. That's right, one remembers the conversations.

FERRARI. Yes, and the tone, and the arguments. The tragic element as well.

BORGES. Yes, but I don't think that one should condemn the melodramatic element. I think Eliot said that, from time to time, the possibilities of melodrama have to be explored. Now, of course, Dostoyevsky is melodramatic. And the Russian novel has undoubtedly exercised a great influence throughout the world. I think I've read somewhere that Dostoyevsky was a reader of Dickens, and it seems there was a time, according to Forster, a friend and biographer of Dickens, when Dickens said that he couldn't look anywhere . . . he couldn't think about a plot that didn't involve a murder.

FERRARI. Rather like Dostoyevsky.

BORGES. Yes, and one can see that because I think that the murders of his characters, Dickens' murders, are among the best, no? One can see that he felt them deeply. I remember, there's almost no novel by Dickens without a murder, apart from *The Pickwick Papers*. And his murders are, well, highly convincing and quite different from one another.

FERRARI. Perhaps even more so than in some crime novels.

BORGES. Yes, perhaps even more so, yes. Well, that's because in the crime novel the murder is a pretext for the investigation. One could write a good crime novel without a crime. For example, in one of the best detective stories, 'The Purloined Letter' by Poe, the important thing is that the letter was hidden in an obvious place, and that the letter was invisible for that reason, no?

FERRARI. There the important thing is the puzzle, let's say.

BORGES. The important thing is the puzzle, yes. Of course, a good pretext for the puzzle is the crime, since there's something that has to be investigated and discovered.

FERRARI. Now, coming back to Tolstoy. In Tolstoy, as in Dostoyevsky, we can see a fundamentally religious element. According to Nabokov, the artist in Tolstoy battled with the preacher.

BORGES. Yes, and at times the preacher won.

FERRARI. Yes . . .

BORGES. In Tolstoy's case, if I'm not wrong, he was an ascetic who renounced material goods. I read an article on Tolstoy and

Dostoyevsky, which said that Dostoyevsky experienced poverty while Tolstoy sought it so that he could experience it.

FERRARI. That's right.

BORGES. But the strange thing is that it was being used as an argument against Tolstoy. It seems to me that the act of renouncing something, and of being an ascetic, is more interesting than the fact of being poor which isn't especially praiseworthy.

FERRARI. Perhaps Tolstoy wanted to distance himself from writing, which is why he took it much further. He wanted to get closer to men by distancing himself from writing, which was probably a mistake but a very personal mistake.

BORGES. And a laudable mistake. Well, when I was young I wanted to be Lugones, and later I realized that Lugones was Lugones in a much more convincing way than I could ever be. Now I'm resigned . . . to being Borges, that is, to being all the writers I have read. And, among them, inevitably, Lugones, no?

FERRARI. So that instead of being a multitude of human beings, one is a multitude of writers.

BORGES. I think that's the case with every writer. We inherit language, and language is a tradition, language is a way of perceiving the world, and each language has its possibilities and its impossibilities, and what an author can do is extremely limited within language. Well, the most obvious example would be Joyce who has strived for the most cryptic, most complex style in the world, but his style presupposes the whole history of English literature that preceded it.

67

Spinoza

●

OSVALDO FERRARI. There's a philosophical figure, Borges, to whom
you have dedicated two poems, and who you also cite frequently in
your essays—the controversial Baruch Spinoza.

JORGE LUIS BORGES. Spinoza, yes. As a matter of fact I had to talk
about him only recently. I told you that in the United States I saw a
book titled *On God* made up of texts by Spinoza but without all that
awkward geometrical apparatus of definitions, of axioms, of corollaries. All that material had been suppressed, and the texts combined
with Spinoza's letters to his friends. And the result is a readable book,
a book that doesn't require specialist training, which can be read with
pleasure. And there isn't a single word in it, a single sentence that's
not written by Spinoza. Only that framework has been removed—
which is so awkward for the reader—of the axioms, the definitions,
the corollaries. That's all been eliminated. And the result is an easy,

174

in any case, a pleasurable read. Something that doesn't happen with Spinoza's *Ethics* which constantly directs the reader to propositions, to axioms or to earlier definitions.

FERRARI. And which is constructed almost geometrically.

BORGES. Well, that's what Spinoza himself said: 'More geometrico.' Now, he took that idea from Descartes, who was his precursor. The starting point was Descartes. Of course, because he believed, and his whole century believed, that rational thought possessed the efficacy of geometry, of that apparatus. Later on the world realized that wasn't the case. Reason accepts geometry, but it doesn't accept it because it has been explained in a geometrical way.

FERRARI. Of course. Yet there's a difference in Descartes—Descartes is a dualist or pluralist, while Spinoza is a monist, let's say. You'll remember 'God or Nature' . . .

BORGES. Yes, *Deus sive Natura*, of course. Because I think that Descartes's rigour—one talks so much about Cartesian rigour—is an apparent or fictitious rigour. Because if someone starts with rigour, and ends up in the Vatican, in Catholic dogma—well, that seems rather problematic to me. And yet Descartes does just that, and in such a way that he maintains a fiction of rigour. This conversation . . . I had it so many years ago with Carlos Mastronardi. He was talking to me about Cartesian rigour, and I told him that Descartes's rigour was a fiction, it was merely superficial, no? There was no such rigour. And one sees it in the fact that he starts with rigorous thought and ends up with something as extraordinary as the Catholic faith. It hardly seems possible. So his rigour is false. On the other hand, with

Spinoza, perhaps if one accepts those postulates, one has to reach that conclusion. And that conclusion, well, seems more plausible, because it doesn't ask us to accept a mythology. And one can accept, let's say, the equivalence of God and nature. And that's already a form of pantheism which is a very old faith—it's the basis for Shinto in Japan, for example. Like that line that we've recalled from Virgil: *Omnia sunt plena Jovis* (All things are full of Jupiter). It amounts to pantheism. Oddly, 'pantheism' is a word that Spinoza wouldn't have recognized because it was invented in England after his death to explain his philosophy.

FERRARI. That's interesting.

BORGES. Because, of course, they said that he was an atheist, and his atheism was discussed. Then, to defend him, someone said: 'No, it isn't atheism—it isn't the idea that there's no God but the idea that everything is divine.' That word was coined after Spinoza's death. He never heard it, although he would have recognized it straight away. Of course, one thinks that these words have always been with us, but each word, naturally, is a particular invention. We've talked elsewhere about 'optimism', a word invented by Voltaire to criticize Leibniz. And 'pessimism' which, naturally, arose as its opposite. Once the word 'optimism' was invented, the word 'pessimism' inevitably followed. So too once 'atheism' was invented, the word 'pantheism' inevitably followed.

FERRARI. That's right.

BORGES. But all those words were first uttered at a particular time, and a not-so-distant time.

FERRARI. Of course. Now, I think that in Spinoza you see an ethical as well as a philosophical thinker. For example, Spinoza's attitude towards freedom in the face of power. You will recall that he was excommunicated from the Jewish faith.

BORGES. Yes, the Jews claim him now but he was anathematized by the synagogue. He refused to accept Christianity. Now he's seen as a Jew—naturally, now that he's famous, they've revoked that excommunication. Nevertheless, there's the anathema, no? Which is terrible, because there it says that he is cursed, and that he must be cursed when he is standing, when he is lying down, when he is going out, when he is coming in. The sentence that they pronounced was terrible. He was left halfway between the church and the synagogue, he was isolated in that faith . . .

FERRARI. In rationalism, perhaps.

BORGES. Yes, in rationalism, but he was isolated. Bertrand Russell says that Spinoza's philosophy isn't always convincing, perhaps, but it can't be denied that, of all the philosophers, Spinoza is the most lovable.

FERRARI. How strange.

BORGES. In his *History of Western Philosophy*, he says that the most lovable philosopher is certainly Spinoza, although one might prefer other philosophical ideas. But he has persisted as a man. That is, if I say Spinoza, well, it's as evocative as if I say, I don't know, Robinson Crusoe, or if I say Alexander of Macedon. He has persisted as a figure, as a lovable and loved figure, a figure loved by everybody.

FERRARI. But Spinoza's rationalism, unlike yours, Borges, doesn't accept miracles as a possibility. For him everything obeyed invariable laws.

BORGES. Yes, he believed that everything was predestined. Perhaps he's right. But we know so little that perhaps miracles aren't impossible.

FERRARI. Of course, but he didn't see it that way.

BORGES. Yes, perhaps we're guilty of pride when we say that everything is predestined . . . perhaps chinks of freedom remain. In any case—and we've said this a number of times—free will is a necessary illusion. We constantly need it if we're talking about our past, or about that other past which is called 'cosmic process' or universal history, we can think that everything has been predestined, but as for what I'm going to say at precisely this moment, as for the way that I'm going to place my hand on this table, we have to think that it's free. If not, we'd be very, very unhappy.

FERRARI. Where you agree with Spinoza, Borges, is in his preference for thought over everything else, for the intellectual life, or the intellectual way, let's say.

BORGES. Yes, and intellectual love, as he says. Well, I try to be intellectual, but I don't know if I succeed, perhaps I often fail. And I don't know if in order to be a writer . . . the two things are important, no? Intelligence is important, but without emotion intelligence can't do anything, and without an emotional impulse there's no reason to produce an aesthetic work. Emotion is necessary—things can't be achieved with rhetoric alone, that is, if pure rhetoric exists, I think not. Without an emotional impulse there's no justification for the creation of a work of art.

FERRARI. Precisely. And in your case I see a balance between Aristotelian rationalism and Platonic intuition and emotion.

BORGES. Well, if only I could achieve that.

FERRARI. It seems a fairly typical characteristic of yours to me. Spinoza, for example, is exclusively rationalist and so doesn't accept myth, among other things.

BORGES. No. I have a sonnet about him in which I say that 'Free of metaphor and myth / He polishes a hard lens: the infinite / Map of the One who is all His stars.' Perhaps its success is in the word 'map', which suggests something vast, no?

FERRARI. That's right, but so that our listeners and readers can appreciate the complete meaning of your poem, I would like to read it.

BORGES. . . . I don't think it's necessary for you to read it, because I'm going to recite it from memory.

FERRARI. Ah, but of course.

BORGES. You will remember that Spinoza polished lenses. At the same time, he polished that crystalline labyrinth of his philosophy, no?

FERRARI. Yes.

BORGES. So in the poem, I compare those things—that dual labour of his hands polishing the lenses while his mind worked on his philosophical system. The sonnet goes like this:

'Spinoza'

The translucent hands of the Jew
Polish lenses in the half-light

And the fading evening is fear, cold.
(The afternoons are all the same.)

The hands and expanse of the hyacinth,
which pales within the Ghetto walls,
Scarcely exist for this quiet man
Who is dreaming a bright labyrinth.

Fame does not trouble him, that reflection
Of dreams in the dream of another mirror,
Nor maidens' timid love.

Free of metaphor and myth
He polishes a hard lens: the infinite
Map of the One who is all His stars.

That's the sonnet. And then I wrote another one, which I don't remember except for a line, which goes: 'Someone creates God in the half-light' or 'A man engenders God among the shadows' or something like that.

FERRARI. And it's Spinoza.

BORGES. And it's Spinoza, yes, 'A man engenders God,' a man is creating the divinity with human words, in a book that is Spinoza's *Ethics*.

FERRARI. But that poem demonstrates that you've clearly been deeply influenced by Spinoza.

BORGES. Well, I thought about writing a book on Spinoza, and then I realized that I couldn't explain what I didn't myself understand. So that book has become a book on Swedenborg . . . yes, I'm thinking about writing it some time. A secretary from the Swedenborg Society in the United States is going to pay me a visit—he's going to come and see me. And I hope to speak very little and to listen a lot to what he has to tell me, since he knows much more about the subject than I do.

FERRARI. The latest news on Swedenborg (*laughs*).

BORGES (*laughs*). The latest news, yes, about that man who died in London, and who talked with angels daily. Yes, I wrote a sonnet about him as well, but don't worry, I don't remember it.

New Dialogue on Alonso Quijano

●

OSVALDO FERRARI. In a discussion that took place in a North American university, Borges, you said that you regarded Cervantes' great character, Alonso Quijano, who transforms himself through his imagination into Don Quixote, as your best friend.

JORGE LUIS BORGES. . . . Yes, and strangely that figure is presented to us in the first chapter of the novel, no?

FERRARI. That's right.

BORGES. You'll remember that we leave our daily lives and enter the life of Alonso Quijano: 'In a region of la Mancha, whose name I do not care to recall, not long ago there lived a gentleman, one of those who keeps a lance on a rack, an ancient shield, a skinny nag and a greyhound for racing.' And so, in a few lines, we have entered that world.

FERRARI. We enter a dream world.

BORGES. Yes. What caught my attention, even as a child, is that we're told that he goes mad but we're not shown the stages of his madness. I thought that one could write a story . . . although it would be rather presumptuous, no? A story which showed the stages of his madness, which showed how, for Alonso Quijano, daily life, that dusty region of La Mancha, gradually became unreal and the world of the *matière de Bretagne* became more real. But it doesn't matter, we accept it—in that chapter, we've already entered his world. And perhaps . . . perhaps the most important thing is that a writer present us with likeable people, and perhaps that's not so difficult, because the reader tends to identify with the first character to appear. That is, if we read *Crime and Punishment*, we identify with Raskolnikov from the outset, since he's the first character we come across. And that helps the reader to become his friend, given that when one reads about him, one is him, because to read a book means to become the various characters of the book in turn. Well, I mean, in the case of a novel, if that novel is worth anything.

FERRARI. And, in a certain way, it means to be the author.

BORGES. Yes, in a certain way, it means to be the author as well, all of that—a series of metamorphoses, of changes, that aren't painful but are pleasant. But that idea of Unamuno's, that Don Quixote is an exemplary character, seems mistaken to me, because he certainly isn't. Rather, he's a bad-tempered, erratic man. But he's harmless (*laughs*) . . . I wrote something once about what would happen if Don Quixote killed a man. But my anxiety was ridiculous, because one realizes from the outset that he isn't capable of killing anybody, that he's a likeable character. And the writer doesn't expose him at any moment to that danger. And then I thought about the possible consequences of that impossible act by Don Quixote, I thought about what might happen, and I don't know what possibilities I suggested. But the fact is that we regard Alonso Quijano as a friend.

FERRARI. That's right.

BORGES. But not Sancho. I regard him as rather impertinent. Even as a child I was conscious that they talked too much. I imagine, more plausibly, that there must have been long periods when they rode together in silence. But as the reader expected colourful dialogue, Cervantes couldn't let them be quiet. When I read *Martín Fierro*, I thought the same thing, I thought that it was very strange that Cruz told Fierro his whole story straight away. I thought that it would have been more plausible if he'd told it to him gradually, little by little.

FERRARI. So that, for you, the most important thing about Cervantes' book is . . .

BORGES. Is the protagonist.

FERRARI. The creation of the man Alonso Quijano.

BORGES. Yes, Alonso Quijano who gets confused with Don Quixote. The author deliberately confuses them at times. In the first part in particular, one feels that he's not Don Quixote, that he's Alonso Quijano. Besides, he's treated as an outsider wherever he goes in Spain. The second part is different, because by then the whole of Spain has read the first part and is expecting him and encouraging his madness. And then, at the end, Sancho proposes that they move on to the pastoral genre, do you remember? And Alonso Quijano rejects that. He's convinced by this point that he's Alonso Quijano, and that he can't go back to become a wandering knight, or a shepherd.

FERRARI. Yes, and in 'A Soldier of Urbina', you will remember, and in 'Alonso Quijano Dreams', in both poems . . .

BORGES. I don't remember the second poem but I do the first. I even know it by heart, because sometimes they ask me for a sonnet, then I haver between 'Everness', 'Allusion to a Shade of Eighteen Ninety-something', about the knife-fighter Juan Muraña, from Palermo, and that poem, 'A Soldier of Urbina', which doesn't mention Cervantes directly but the reader gathers that it's about him.

FERRARI. In the two poems I've mentioned, you relate the epic dreams of Don Quixote to the epic reality that Cervantes had the fortune to experience in his life.

BORGES. Yes. What is strange is that it seems that neither Cervantes nor any other writer of his time was aware of the importance of the discovery of America.

FERRARI. In spite of it being a contemporary event.

BORGES. They are more interested in the most trifling, most disastrous battles of Flanders than in the discovery of a continent. The same thing seems to have happened in England—they sent Cabot out to travel to China because they didn't realize that America was there, blocking the way.

FERRARI. But Cervantes asked to go to America.

BORGES. Yes, and Groussac says that they could have given him some post in Nueva Granada, for example, and that perhaps we owe the writing of *Don Quixote* to the fact that they denied him that post. That is, what appeared like misfortune to Cervantes was a good thing for him and for the rest of humanity.

FERRARI. We were saying, then, that Cervantes had experienced what you call 'the epic flavour' in his life.

BORGES. Yes, he liked to refer to the battle of Lepanto, he mentions it a number of times.

FERRARI. And as you say in your poem, 'To erase or lessen the cruelty / of the real, he sought to dream.'

BORGES. 'And the Roland and Breton cycles / gave him a magic past.' Yes, the *matière de France* and the *matière de Bretagne*, to which we must add the *matière de Rome la grande*, which includes the adventures of Alexander of Macedon, who reaches the wall of paradise and also the bottom of the sea. That's all in the *matière de Rome*.

FERRARI. From Italy he also read Ariosto, and many other authors.

BORGES. Of course, and when Cervantes talks about 'lively scrutiny', he talks about the 'Christian poet Ludovico Ariosto'. And one could write an essay on Ariosto and Cervantes, that is, the two appreciated the particular qualities shared by those three *matières*—from Brittany, France and Rome. At the same time, they realized that it was all a little bit ridiculous, a little extravagant.

FERRARI. The chivalric quality, let's say.

BORGES. Yes, that quality. Even in the first canto of *Orlando Furioso*, when Charlemagne is mentioned, it becomes a little ridiculous. At the same time it was wonderful for Ariosto who realized, well, that it was all unreal. Perhaps he liked it for that very reason. And in Cervantes it's even more pronounced.

FERRARI. The contrast with reality is wonderful.

BORGES. Yes, the contrast, but I think that they were both similar in that way, no? In having a feel for the world of chivalry, yet knowing that it was all unreal . . . rather derisory in any case. In Cervantes' case, completely derisory.

FERRARI. So the development of his novel lies in the contrast between reality and dream.

BORGES. Yes, and that dream is the dream of the *matière de France* and *de Bretagne* more than anything, more than Rome, since Alexander or Caesar are barely mentioned.

FERRARI. I'm particularly interested in your identification with the character, almost more than with the author, I would say, with Alonso Quijano rather than with Cervantes.

BORGES. But I think that's happened to everyone, no?

FERRARI. One would have to see . . . it's possible.

BORGES. I think that Unamuno wrote that Don Quixote is now more real than Cervantes. Well, it's true that we imagine Alonso Quijano directly while we imagine Cervantes through biographies, or people's accounts . . .

FERRARI. Or we speculate about him . . .

BORGES. Or we speculate about him, yes. On the other hand, with Alonso Quijano, and with the Don Quixote who he tries to become, we have a direct relation. The exposition is clear, there can be no other.

FERRARI. Agreed, but the fact that Alonso Quijano's dream was the dream of a library is similar to you, I think, similar, that is, to your own inclination.

BORGES. Ah, of course, yes. I think I wrote in a sonnet that, unlike Alonso Quijano, I'd never left my library. Although I've travelled all over the world, I don't know if I've ever left those first books I read.

FERRARI. Yes, you remain constant to that first library.

BORGES. And, besides, being short-sighted, my first memories are not, let's say, of the Palermo neighbourhood, nor even of my parents' animated faces, but of books, illustrations, maps, well, of the spines of books—why not—of the bindings. Those are my first memories, they're really more memories of books than of people.

FERRARI. So your father's library was of vital importance in your life, as you've said.

BORGES. I think so, and I don't think I've ever left it, which is fortunate for me but less fortunate for my readers, the fact that it has led me to write more books. In this house, I try to be in my father's library, since in this house I don't have any books of my own.

FERRARI. Certainly, but we've already talked about contrasts. Don Quixote's story, strangely, takes place in Spain, the country where realism has most weight.

BORGES. That's right. They boast about it, because they regard the picaresque novel in that way, no? Although, in fact, it's a fairly puritan form of the novel. In the picaresque novel, sex is excluded, for example.

FERRARI. Yes, but Cervantes himself broached that subject.

BORGES. You mean in 'Rinconete and Cortadillo'?

FERRARI. Yes, precisely, and in the *Exemplary Novels.*

BORGES. Of course. All in all, the picaresque novel must have been a revelation for Europe, since it had such a great influence on the English novel, on the *Simplicissimus* of Grimmelshausen in Germany and, later, on the *Gil Blas* of Lesage.

Celtic Culture

●

OSVALDO FERRARI. In one of your writings, Borges, you explain that just as authentic German culture reaches its final flowering in Iceland, so Celtic culture took refuge in Ireland. . . . You say that in the archives and libraries of Ireland, one could find evidence of the linguistic and literary culture of the Celts.

JORGE LUIS BORGES. Yes. It was lost in the other countries. In Wales also, the Mabinogion are from Wales, they're stories, some of them very beautiful, which Lady Guest translated. Her translation was read by Renan who used it to attack the Germans in the Franco-Prussian War. And there's that lovely story which we have talked about before, about the two young kings who play chess on the peak, the high peak of a mountain, while below the armies fight, below is the ebb and flow of men in combat. And then a moment comes, and at that moment, which is clearly decisive, one of the kings says, 'Checkmate' and makes a move. And a man arrives on horseback with the news that the other king's army has been defeated. So one realizes that the game of chess is a magical procedure, because the armies are directed by the moves of each player, and when one of the players says, 'Checkmate,' the army of the other is defeated. I've used a similar idea in a poem about chess. The pieces think they enjoy free will but they don't—the hand of the player moves them. The player thinks he enjoys free will but he doesn't—he is directed by a god who, for literary reasons, is controlled by other gods. And so, among the chess pieces, an infinite series is formed, a chain of infinite links. I wrote two sonnets on this subject, both titled 'Chess'. But since we're talking about Irish culture—I don't know if we've talked about this before, it's a very strange subject. I was made a member of the Academia Argentina de las Letras. And when I talked there I referred to this strange subject (since we were talking about academies)—that nowhere had the academies been as important as in Ireland, when Ireland was made up of small kingdoms. At that time, the study of poetry included the study of all the other disciplines, for example, genealogy, astrology, botany, mathematics, ethics—that was all studied by poets. And there were various categories. And only people who'd passed an exam were allowed to write poetry. Once they'd passed from the first year to the second, they were allowed to use certain metres and certain subjects—but that was all. Only in the end, when they reached the level of high poet, could they use all the metres, all the names of the fabulous genealogies, all the rhetorical figures. And so an extraordinarily complex poetry was created (which was maintained by the State). But a time came, according to legend, when one of the kings of Ireland ordered two poets—who had completed their

12 years of study, and were now high poets of Ireland—to produce a eulogy for him. The poets recited their poems. And each poet probably understood the other's poem, but no one else did. So the king dissolved the school of poets—he put an end to the academies, just like that. Besides, those poets were more expensive than the kings—they had the right to more slaves, to more cows, to more money . . . they ended up as, let's say, a serious expense for the State (*both laugh*).

FERRARI. They would also have had a right to more leisure.

BORGES. To more leisure . . . well, who knows. If they invented and had to practise an extremely complicated system of poetry, which is similar to the Scandinavian system, the Anglo-Saxon system in which certain metaphors appear . . . we've talked so many times about that—'the path of the swan' for the sea, the 'meeting of swords' for battle, etcetera. It was similar to that but much more complex. So that a high poet, after 12 years, knew everything. Of course, what we call 'everything' is limited compared to the sum of possible things, but, in the end, he knew everything that could be known in Ireland at that particular time.

FERRARI. It seems to me that, like Renan, you identify an extremely peculiar characteristic of that ancient Celtic culture—that after being converted to Christianity, they still retain the memory of the pagan myths and the ancient legends.

BORGES. But I think that also happened in other places. You see, I've just finished writing a poem about Góngora. And the subject is that Góngora, who of course was Catholic, uses the Latin gods, who were really the Greek gods but with different names. That is, he doesn't talk about war but Mars or, as the Greeks would say, Ares. He doesn't talk about the sea but Neptune or, as the Greeks would say, Poseidon. These mythologies have carried on feeding men's imaginations irrespective of their theological beliefs. I think that now, in Ireland, two languages are taught—English, and Erse which is the Celtic form and which was more or less unknown before, especially by people in the countryside. It was a language which was of interest to the erudite, to philologists. Which is what happens with Guaraní here, no?

FERRARI. Another remarkable aspect of the ancestry of Celtic culture is that their first men of letters were their priests, the druids.

BORGES. The druids, yes, I think that Caesar notes that there were druids in all the Celtic lands, for example, in Belgium, in France, in Spain, but that the school of druids was in England which was a Celtic country in those days. And that they went there to complete their studies—of what I don't know, perhaps magic. Now, Caesar attributes a belief in the transmigration of souls to the Celts. He sees the influence of Pythagoras there. But that seems unlikely, it seems that what he heard was that men can change into animals, which is, well, our idea of the *tigre capiango*, of the werewolf. And that he confused it with the idea of transmigration. In the case of transmigration, the soul of a man passes into another body, that is, if a man is particularly ferocious, then he will pass into the body of a tiger, because for the tiger being ferocious isn't a problem, no? So that each soul finds its appropriate home.

FERRARI. Regarding Celtic poetry, you tell us that in spite of its complexity, of its extreme rigour, it can at times be fantastical.

BORGES. Yes, I particularly remember what was written in Wales. There's a poem, which Robert Graves collected, in his book *The White Goddess*, and the title is lovely—it's called 'The Battle of the Trees'. I don't know exactly what it refers to. I think that a verse has been preserved, and that verse talks about transmigration. I read it in a quotation in Arnold, and I remember this fragment which I hastily reconstruct: 'I have been a glimmering fish / I have been a bridge that crosses seventy rivers / I have been the surf on the water / I have been a word in a book / I have been a book in the beginning . . . '

FERRARI. That's lovely.

BORGES. A splendid enumeration, eh? It moves from one thing to another, and in a surprising way, no? I remember that ending: 'I have been a word in a book / I have been a book in the beginning.' Of course, it all relies on the play on 'in', which is quite particular. A word 'in a book' as in space. On the other hand, a book 'in the beginning' as in time. But it doesn't matter—it works very well. Then it says, 'I have been a sword in the hand / I have been a hand in the battle,' and it continues with an extremely lengthy enumeration—there are about 20 or 30 terms, and all of them are surprising. At the same time, each one prepares the reader for the next.

FERRARI. Also in Ireland, you tell us that the theme of navigation, of sea voyages in particular, recurs in its literature.

BORGES. Well, that also happens in Germanic poetry and in Portuguese poetry. I once wrote a book, or what claimed to be a book, on Portuguese literature which seems to have a special genre dedicated to shipwrecks and voyages. Books about voyages, of course, but unfortunate ones since they include shipwrecks.

FERRARI. But the voyages, in the Irish imagination, were always directed towards the West . . .

BORGES. Yes, towards the Isle of Saint Brendan. And other fantastical isles. There's one that says that 'silver greyhounds chase deer of gold', I remember. Then there's another circled by an eternal flame, and yet others with fantastical beings, especially that Isle of Saint Brendan which was later linked to the discovery of America, no? The Irish imagination has populated the North Atlantic with an archipelago of imaginary, marvellous isles.

FERRARI. As well as having a particular way of imagining nature, the Irish have a special love for nature and landscape.

BORGES. Yes, a sense of the beauty of trees. For example. I think that the word 'druid' has been traced to the 'amadryads', that is, there's the idea that the druid was linked with trees.

FERRARI. That love of nature is particular to England, as well as Ireland . . .

BORGES. Yes, landscape was almost unknown in literature before the Romantic movement in other European countries. There's almost no landscape. Not, I think, in painting either. Now, according to Ruskin, the first painter who really sees the rocks, the clouds, the mountains, the sea, is Turner. Until then, as a general rule, landscape was used as a background, and that background was conventional. The important thing was human character. Japanese painting is different. In Japanese painting, the landscape was always thought about—if that word 'always' is valid—or it was perceived. Which is something that a lot of people don't do. For example, you read *Don Quixote*, and, apart from some green meadow clearly taken from Italian literature, from the conventions of Italian literature, there are no landscapes. That's why Doré's illustrations are so lovely—but they don't have anything to do with Cervantes' text. You see the nobleman with his squire and they're surrounded by vast landscapes, but those landscapes don't feature in the book. I wondered, when I read the first page of the *Glory of Don Ramiro* many years ago, by Rodríguez Larreta, if that first page wasn't a mistake. Because I think that there, or in any case in the first pages, he talks about the landscape of Toledo. Now, I don't know if the Toledans, in the sixteenth or seventeenth century, were able to see that landscape, I don't think so—I think that the landscape was invisible. As it is in popular landscape poetry. There, as a general rule, the interest lies in the characters and their passions.

Quevedo

•

OSVALDO FERRARI. There's a classic writer you admire, Borges, who we haven't talked about yet, a Spaniard who was neither sentimental nor plaintive, you've said, and who we don't remember for the creation of a literary type so much as for the quality of his writing.

JORGE LUIS BORGES. Cansinos Assens?

FERRARI. No, no, I'm talking about Quevedo.

BORGES. Quevedo.

FERRARI. Yes, the most noble Spanish stylist, according to Lugones, I seem to remember . . .

BORGES. Well, I've distanced myself from Quevedo over the years, in the same way that I've distanced myself from Lugones. I think that one always sees the effort in Quevedo and Lugones—they never seem to flow. I was compiling an anthology of sonnets, and I have never found a sonnet, well, I have never found sonnets by Quevedo or Lugones without some blemish, without some line where the author falls into the sin of vanity. Because the baroque is open to criticism on ethical grounds, I think, the baroque is open to criticism because it's guilty of vanity. But, in Quevedo's case . . . however, there's a sonnet, the one that goes:

> Retired to the peace of these deserts,
> With a few, learned books gathered together,
> I live in conversation with the deceased
> And I listen with my eyes to the dead.

That's lovely, but I don't know if the fourth line can be justified.

FERRARI. You find his *conceptista* style too involved.

BORGES. Yes, it seems to me that the fourth line has been written rather for the sake of an idea. . . . There's the Spanish saying that goes 'To talk out of your elbows.' Here we have the idea of listening with your eyes. And yet it's right, because when one is reading a text one tends to read it aloud, so one is listening with one's eyes. Although perhaps that contraposition of listening and eyes is rather harsh, no? Then it goes:

> If not always wise, always awake,
> They either adapt or advance my theme,
> And in silent musical counterpoint
> They speak waking to life's dream.

That's lovely and it's right too. At the end he says:

> In irrevocable flight the hour slips away;
> But in the best reckoning,
> that hour improves us in reading and study.

It's a calm ending which isn't like Quevedo, no? The fact that the final line is so gentle.

FERRARI. Yes. Now, you used to consider Quevedo as a writer's writer, perhaps because you found that he suited the sensibility of writers.

BORGES. Yes, and because he also writes rather as a professional writer, no? But I don't know if that's a good thing. They also said that about Spenser, who was 'the poet's poet', that was said about Edmund Spenser. Then people talked about the writer's writer, that they give pleasure to one's sensibility, to one's emotions, to whatever. But in Quevedo's case, one feels that pleasure is primarily literary, that is, one feels more than anything the value that he gave to words. Now, I don't know if that's a virtue, perhaps it's better for the reader to forget about words. In Quevedo and in Lugones, who are so similar, one always remembers their words.

FERRARI. That's why you said that Quevedo's greatness is verbal.

BORGES. Did I say that? Well, yes, of course.

FERRARI. Turning to the defence that Quevedo makes of logical reasoning against, let's say, superstition, the refutation of myths that one finds in his attack on those lines by Empedocles . . .

BORGES. I don't remember them. How do they go?

FERRARI. Where he said that he had been a fish, that he had been . . .

BORGES. Ah, yes, hang on . . . 'I have been a fish that rises from the sea.' I think Empedocles said that, yes. Of course, Quevedo's refutation is a sort of joke, no?

FERRARI. Well, he uses it to refute the theory of the transmigration of souls in particular, which he regarded as pure superstition and which he attacked from the point of view of logic.

BORGES. Yes, but I don't know if myth can be refuted by logic.

FERRARI. Ah, of course.

BORGES. And, besides, the idea of having lived in many forms might be right, that is, although one hasn't lived in many forms, one might feel that one has done so without leaving one's own life. Because if I think about my past life, well, there are years and dates and actions that are so distant from me that they could have been lived in other, not human, forms.

FERRARI. In your own life, you say?

BORGES. In my own life, I think so. . . . In India, for example, everybody accepts the idea of reincarnation, but they accept it because it doesn't contradict experience. If one remembers something that one did a long time ago, well, one remembers something that was done by someone else and one accepts that. The imagination seems to be amenable to the myth, which is perhaps right or wrong, of reincarnation.

FERRARI. So Plato converges with India.

BORGES. Yes, I think so.

FERRARI. Because once we have memory, then we have been that other or that earlier thing.

BORGES. Yes, because, in the end, at an emotional level, it's perhaps easier to accept the idea that one has lived in another body, in another form, than in a human body and form, than the idea of accepting archetypes. Archetypes seem inconceivable, and the imagination seems somehow reluctant to accept them. On the other hand, the idea of having been 'a mute fish that rises from the sea' as Empedocles of Agrigentum said is an idea that one accepts easily, at least in theory (*laughs*) or as a possibility.

FERRARI (*laughs*). Things are always possible in theory. Returning to Quevedo, you say that in *Marco Bruto*, for example, Spanish and the Latin of the Silver Age meet. I wanted to talk to you about that Silver Age which is linked to Seneca, Tacitus and Lucanus.

BORGES. In my poem 'Another Poem of Gifts', I talk about Lucanus and Seneca who, before the Spanish language had emerged, wrote the whole of Spanish literature, and I talk specifically about that, about that 'silver Latinity' which Quevedo later imitates. Well, Quevedo translated some of Seneca's epistles. I've read two of the epistles to Lucilius in Quevedo's work, in his translation. Admirably translated, of course, since they were the model that had been suggested, in any case, by *Marco Bruto*.

FERRARI. Now, with regard to Quevedo's poetry, although you say that you find occasional blemishes in his sonnets, I think that you also find distinction.

BORGES. Yes, but it's hard to find a sonnet by Quevedo or Lugones in which there isn't some blemish. And some blemish which isn't, let's say, inadvertent, but sought, and unfortunately, encountered. It seems that what for us is a blemish would for them have been beautiful. It's so difficult to judge these things. For example, I remember those lines by Góngora that go:

> Oh, great river, great Andalusian king,
> of noble though not golden sands!

Well, from the point of view of logic, or for me, the idea, the admission that the sands are not golden—it doesn't seem effective. Perhaps Góngora liked the idea—the idea of affirming but doing so grudgingly, no? Because if not, why write that? Or did the rhyme force him to? No, I don't think so, I think that he liked the idea of 'of noble though not golden sands'. The opposition pleased him in some way. So we can't judge him, since it's something so personal that we don't know whether we should censure it or praise it.

FERRARI. Well, it's similar to what you say about Quevedo's best pieces. Apart from the ideas, or the concepts, that inform them, they have a literary existence. The literary existence of a text can be independent of other aspects in certain cases, no?

BORGES. Well, one might think that a poem doesn't correspond to an emotion, or to a particular subject but that it's another object in the world—a verbal object. And I have a poem about just that, called 'The Other Tiger'—I don't know if you remember it—in which I set out to describe a tiger. Once I've done it, I realize that my tiger isn't the tiger but simply a verbal object, a construction, an edifice made of words, and then I talk about the other tiger. But as I'm talking about it, the other tiger becomes as artificial as the first one, and so, in the end, I'm left alone in the evening, in the great evening of the National Library, searching for that other tiger, the one that isn't in the poem . . . I think that poem is, perhaps, one of my best. It incorporates a chain of infinite links, and each one of those links is a tiger,

202

and each one of those tigers is purely verbal, and none of them is the tiger I'm looking for.

FERRARI. That reminds me of another of your poems, 'The Panther'. The other aspect of Quevedo I wanted to talk to you about was his sceptical vision of relations with women. I don't know if you recall that aspect of his work.

BORGES. Yes . . .

FERRARI. He talks presciently.

BORGES. Well, I can't agree with Quevedo on that . . . For me, there's something so pleasing in a woman, in any woman, something which of course can't be defined . . . there's pleasure in simply being with a woman. It doesn't have anything to do with love, or with sensuality— it's the presence, rather, of something gently distinctive, distinctive enough to be perceptible yet not so much as to separate us. This occurs in every example of friendship, I think, but, in the end, I would say that there's something about friendship with a woman, or simply about the presence of a woman, that's not there in the presence of a man.

FERRARI. Besides, you say that women think intuitively, unlike men who think dialectically. And that women's thinking complements the thinking of men, because it involves intuition.

BORGES. Now I'm coming to the conclusion that no one thinks, not in one way or another (*both laugh*). But that's a form of scepticism. Now, of course, if women think intuitively, that involves a single mental leap. Then it's easier to be right. On the other hand, with logical thought, it's like a chain with various links, and error might be lying in wait in each one of those links.

FERRARI. That's right.

BORGES. It's easier for error to occur in a long process than in a single act of feeling, as is the case with intuition. With a logical process, however, yes, it's easier for errors to creep in.

FERRARI. Of course, and you will remember that in the East, for example, in Zen Buddhism, intuition is considered the highest form of intelligence.

BORGES. Of course, because it's a direct act, because it's a single act. The other form of thought is an operation, and operations are always prone to error.

The Mystic Swedenborg

●

OSVALDO FERRARI. There's a mystic who's also a theosophist, Borges, who you seem to know very well, since you refer to him frequently. He's the visionary Emerson described as the archetypal mystic.

JORGE LUIS BORGES. Swedenborg, yes. . . . Well, one could summarize his teaching. . . . According to Jesus Christ, man's salvation is ethical, and there are those provocative sayings, such as 'The last shall be first' and 'Of the pure in heart is the kingdom of Heaven' and even 'Let the children come to me.' On the other hand, in the eighteenth century, we have the great Swedish mystic Swedenborg, and his teaching is different. He based all his teaching on long personal dialogues he conducted with the angels, in London, dialogues that went on for many years. He was a notable man of science, he'd distinguished himself in metallurgy, anatomy and astronomy too. But then he left all that behind after Christ first appeared to him in London. From then on, he devoted his life to visiting the various regions of heaven and hell which is also the name of perhaps his most popular book, *De Caelo et inferno*. But there are others. . . . There's one on the Last Judgement which, according to him, has already occurred. Those two books are written in a dry Latin. Of course, Swedenborg isn't a poet, but they're written with the precision of a traveller, as if he were describing regions of Asia or Africa . . .

FERRARI. As if rather than visions they were concrete landscapes.

BORGES. Yes, because those visions are meticulous. But that could be a subject for another conversation. Perhaps the most important thing is that he believes that man's salvation must be intellectual as well as ethical. And there's a sort of parable of his that refers to an ascetic. That ascetic sets out to achieve salvation. He renounces everything, he lives in the desert, dies and then reaches heaven. But when he reaches heaven he's lost, according to Swedenborg, because everything that exists on earth, let's say, everything that involves forms and colours, all those things exist in heaven but in a much more intense and complex way. And, besides, there's even a hint of a fourth dimension, since he says that the angels can talk to one another but that they're always in God's presence. It's very strange, no?

FERRARI. Yes, it's very strange.

BORGES. So that poor man (the ascetic) is in heaven. But the angels' conversation is an intellectual conversation, of course, it's theological and extremely complicated, and this poor man can't follow a word of it. So they wonder what to do with him. Of course, to send him to hell would be absurd, since he would be extremely unhappy, and he wouldn't be able to live with the demons either. . . . Ah, I'd like to add here that, according to Swedenborg, nobody is judged and sent to heaven or hell but throughout our lives we continually prepare ourselves for one of those eventual destinies.

FERRARI. With each act.

BORGES. Yes. When you die, you reside in an intermediate region, and then strangers come up to you. If you feel attracted to some of them, you go off with them. If you feel repulsion towards the others, you leave them alone. They can be angels or demons. And the people who have prepared themselves for heaven are attracted to the angels and find the demons repulsive. On the other hand, the people who have debased their lives, the people who have stained themselves with sin, they feel more comfortable with the demons and find a relative happiness in hell. I return to the case of the ascetic. During his life, the ascetic has renounced all pleasures, all appetites. But heaven isn't like that, a place of penitence. On the contrary, it's the life of earth, only much fuller. To send him to hell because he can't follow the intellectual conversations would clearly be unfair. In the end, the solution they find is for the ascetic to project a sort of illusory desert around himself. And they leave him there, alone.

FERRARI. In a wasteland.

BORGES. In a wasteland, that is, he repeats the life that he led on earth but with a crucial difference, since on earth he did it in hope of heaven. By contrast, now he is in that illusory wasteland but without any hope, since it can't be changed. It's terrible. There's another parable—I don't know if they are parables or real-life events for Swedenborg—which is the story of a damned person who somehow manages to ascend to heaven. He's in heaven, and there's a splendid light, but that light burns him. There are heavenly fragrances but to him they smell fetid. That is, he's already disposed for hell, he feels wretched in heaven. Swedenborg is not only an ethical but also an intellectual thinker.

FERRARI. He appreciated the intellect, and he argued for its importance as well.

BORGES. Of course, he argued for its importance, and his books are the books of an extremely intelligent man, but they're written without any great appeal apart from their content. He describes the various regions of heaven, the various regions of hell. . . . Now, he travelled through it, he sees hell as a series of swamps, then there are huts, the ruins of burnt villages, also taverns and brothels. And sounds that seem horrible to him but that are heavenly music for the damned. And as for the devil, I think that some Lutheran theologian shares his view that the Devil is more of a professional title, that he's the Boss. But as they live in a world of envy and rivalry, the world of politicians, let's say, none of them lasts for long, because the other devils are always conspiring in favour of someone else who succeeds him and against whom they conspire in turn. So that the Devil isn't a single individual but various individuals who hate one another. And they lead a terrible life, but that life, of course, is more tolerable for them than, well, than an insufferable paradise.

FERRARI. I see . . .

BORGES. And yet, the Lord presides over both realms, heaven and hell. And the universe is made of a sort of equilibrium between those two regions—that shadowy, criminal, sinful zone, and the serene, conservative, philosophical heaven. Well, all that comes from several books. I have several biographies of Swedenborg. . . . He went to England because he wanted to meet Newton, but he never got to meet him. And later on he witnessed, well, the first visitation of Jesus Christ to London. And his servants heard him. He was walking, they heard his steps, no? The clear sky—he was walking in the air and talking to the angels. Talking with the angels in the streets of London too. I wrote a sonnet about it.

FERRARI. Yes, I would like to read it.

BORGES. Well, we should have a conversation about Blake at another time, because Blake adds to the, let's say, ethical and intellectual salvation a third form of salvation which he says is essential for all men—aesthetic salvation. So that Blake is a rebellious follower of Swedenborg, since he criticizes Swedenborg, but he's also inconceivable without Swedenborg. Now Blake was a great poet, something which Swedenborg wasn't and wouldn't have wanted to be either. So we have Swedenborg's vast work, all written in Latin, apart from the odd report on mining which was written in Swedish, and those years of his life. . . . I don't know if he was lonely in London . . . since if he was talking to the angels he can't have been that lonely.

FERRARI. But I have seen many of Swedenborg's books in your library, and from different periods of his life, I think.

BORGES. Yes, I read the first one in Buenos Aires, I think, and later on I learnt that there are four volumes in the Everyman's Library, among them a short treatise on the Last Judgement. Besides, I wrote a prologue for an edition of Swedenborg, which was published here and which is also included in that book of mine called *Prologues*. Now, if you want to read that sonnet . . .

FERRARI. Yes, I'm going to read it, but first I want to ask you, since you habitually describe yourself as agnostic, about the source of your faith, of your belief in a mystic like Swedenborg.

BORGES. No, no, no, I don't know if that's right. I know that he was sincere, and that he was a man, well, a famous mathematician, astronomer, metallurgist, that he travelled throughout Europe.

FERRARI. A varied man.

BORGES. Yes, and he abandoned all those scientific disciplines because he thought he'd been chosen to spread the faith. Now, it seems that he never insisted on it in conversation—he did that in his writings but he didn't talk about those things in conversation. He led a rather sober life, apart from when someone came over to London from Sweden. Then they would both celebrate that visit . . . I suppose, in the taverns or perhaps with women, I don't know, that has been insinuated. Now Swedenborg has many followers, particularly in the United States. De Quincey talks about having a conversation with an English gentleman in Manchester, who was a follower of Swedenborg, and the father of Henry and William James was also a follower of Swedenborg.

FERRARI. They were followers, then, of Swedenborg's doctrine of the New Jerusalem.

BORGES. Yes. And there's a church which is extremely beautiful . . . because one always thinks of churches as dark places but this one is like a kind of conservatory, made of glass, that is, it's a place for the worship of clarity . . . which is consistent with Swedenborg's doctrine.

FERRARI. I will read your poem to Emanuel Swedenborg:

> Taller than the others, this distant man
> Walked among men,
> Occasionally calling the angels
> By their secret names. He would see
> What earthly eyes do not see:
> The bright geometry, the crystal
> Labyrinth of God and the sordid
> Whirling of infernal pleasures.
> He knew that Glory and Hell
> Are in your soul, and in its myths;
> He knew, like the Greek, that the days
> Of time are mirrors of Eternity.
> In dry Latin he went about recording
> Last things without why or when.

BORGES. Well, I have put into verse what I've just told you.

72

Painting

●

OSVALDO FERRARI. You told me recently, Borges, that, according to Ruskin, the first painter in his time to truly see nature was Turner.

JORGE LUIS BORGES. Yes. Ruskin also has a book misleadingly, or mistakenly, titled *Modern Painters*, which is raised, let's say, to the greater glory of Turner.

FERRARI. In particular.

BORGES. Yes, its principal theme is that nature—of course, he's talking about the West, no?—had been used as background. Painters would mostly paint the faces, sometimes their apprentices would paint the hands, and then landscape was a sort of afterthought. Now, according to Ruskin—but I can't judge his analysis—Turner was the first to really see the clouds, to see the crags, to see the trees, to see the mist and certain effects of light. According to Ruskin, that was all Turner's personal discovery. He would examine Turner's paintings extremely carefully, with a magnifying glass, according to Xul Solar who was also an admirer of Turner. And Chesterton has said that the hero of Turner's paintings is 'the English weather', not the succession, or chronology of weather but, well, the different behaviours or habits of weather, particularly sunsets, mists and light. All of that more than form. I understand my personal opinion is worthless, but I repeat what Xul Solar told me—that Turner is unsuccessful with the human figure but a great observer of landscapes. And I remember that in one of the volumes of Ruskin's book there's a reproduction of a bridge, of a particular bridge, and then there's the same bridge drawn extremely carefully and extremely finely by Ruskin himself. But, if I remember rightly, Turner seems to have removed two arches—he's simplified the whole, or he's enhanced other things. And Ruskin approves of that, and explains that Turner was right aesthetically, although he gave a misleading image of the bridge.

FERRARI. Turner's skies are notorious.

BORGES. The skies, yes, the sunsets.

FERRARI. Oscar Wilde said that they were musical skies.

BORGES. Yes. I also remember another of Wilde's sayings, that nature imitates art.

FERRARI. Ah, of course.

BORGES. And that sometimes it imitates it badly. They say that he was in a lady's house, the lady took him out onto the balcony to look at the sunset, so he went out with all the others, and what was it? According to Wilde, a second-rate Turner (*laughs*).

FERRARI. That real sunset?

BORGES. Yes, an imitation by nature, no? That is, nature isn't always a good follower.

FERRARI. Precisely in the period they were discussing . . .

BORGES. Yes, there'd always been the idea that art imitates nature, but Wilde said the opposite, that nature imitates art . . . which is possible to the extent that art can teach us to see in a certain way.

FERRARI. Of course.

BORGES. I mean, if one has looked at lots of paintings, one is bound to look at nature in a different way.

FERRARI. One becomes better at observing.

BORGES. Of course, and as we're talking about nature—I've written a prologue for the work of the visionary engraver and poet William Blake. And he, the least contemporary of men. . . . Well, in an age of neoclassical mythology, he invented his own mythology with divinities who don't always have attractive-sounding names, like Golgonooza or Urizen. He says that, for him, nature's spectacle is always diminished in some way. He called nature—which was so revered by Wordsworth—'the vegetable universe'. And he says another thing—I don't know if it's for or against nature—that sunrise for many people is simply a disc, similar to a pound coin, which rises brightly. But for him it's different: When I see the sunrise, he says, I seem to see the Lord, and I hear thousands and thousands of angels who are praising him. That is, he saw everything mystically.

FERRARI. A beatific vision.

BORGES. Yes, a beatific vision, exactly.

FERRARI. That was Blake's vision. Now, even though you declare that you don't have an ear for music, apart from milongas and the blues . . .

BORGES. Well, I don't know to what extent they're music, although I would say that . . . I think that the spirituals are music, yes, really, Gershwin is music, no?

FERRARI. Of course, which you also like a lot.

BORGES. I like him a lot, but Gershwin doesn't always write that type of music. Stravinsky also liked jazz a lot. What strikes me when I listen to jazz is that I hear sounds that I don't hear in any other music. Sounds that seem to be coming from the bottom of a river, no? As if they were being produced by different elements, yes, and that incorporation of new sounds creates a resonance.

FERRARI. That's right, that's what jazz has done. I was saying that, on the other hand, you have an eye for painting.

BORGES. No . . .

FERRARI. It's demonstrated, for example, in that poem of yours, 'The Unending Gift' which you dedicate to the painter Jorge Larco.

BORGES. Yes, but I don't know if it was about painting. It was about the fact that when a painting has come into being, it is something limited. And when it doesn't yet exist, it can still renew itself, branch out, proliferate infinitely in the imagination. And, besides, well, I remember that Shaw in *The Doctor's Dilemma* mentions three painters . . . Titian, Rembrandt and Velázquez. When the painter is dying, he says that beyond the confusion of his life (he's talking about morality, no?)

he's been faithful . . . and then he talks about God, how he has blessed his hands, since he believes in the mystery of light and the mystery of the shadows, and he believes in Titian, Velázquez and Rembrandt.

FERRARI. And he would hope for the heaven of those painters.

BORGES. I suppose so. I remember a long, extremely eloquent, deliberately rhetorical passage by Shaw that Estela Canto knows by heart. She knows so much of Shaw by heart. That rhetorical side of Shaw hasn't been noticed by many people, and he accentuated it, he brought back to the theatre what had been forgotten—long rhetorical speeches. And they were effective as well, because 'rhetorical' isn't necessarily a slight. Well, I had the fortune of knowing a great Argentine painter, Xul Solar, and he was always talking to me about Blake, and about the Swiss painter Paul Klee who he thought was superior to Picasso at a time when to talk ill of Picasso was considered heretical, no? Perhaps that time has not yet passed, I don't know (*laughs*).

FERRARI. And you have described Xul Solar as a genius.

BORGES. Xul Solar, yes, of course, perhaps. . . . I've known many talented men, this country abounds in them as perhaps does the whole world. But not geniuses, apart from Xul Solar—I'm not sure. As for Macedonio Fernández, he was—orally. But in writing . . . people who've looked for that in his writing have felt let down or confused.

FERRARI. He expressed his genius in conversation, as you've said.

BORGES. Yes, I think so. Now, they're going to publish a book by Xul Solar—I'm going to write the prologue—with some of his writing but, strangely, his writings in everyday, current Spanish, not in his Panlengua which was based on astrology, and nor in Creole, which was Spanish enriched with other languages.

FERRARI. Which Xul Solar had invented.

BORGES. Yes, because he invented those two languages . . . well, he also invented the Panjuego. Now, as he explained the game to me—I never got to understand it—each turn of the Panjuego is a poem, a picture, a piece of music, or a horoscope. Well, if only we could be sure of that. There's a similar idea in Herman Hesse's *The Glass Bead Game*, except there one realizes throughout that it's about music and not really about a Panjuego which is what Xul wanted, a universal game.

FERRARI. As for your relationship with painting, Borges, we mustn't forget that you're the brother of a painter.

BORGES. Of a great painter, I think, eh? Although I don't know if the word 'great' adds anything to the word 'painter'. Brother of a painter, let's say. Now, as she explores subjects like angels, gardens, angels who are musicians in gardens . . .

FERRARI. Like the painting of the Annunciation, for example, which has the city of Adrogué in the background, which is in your house.

BORGES. Yes, which she wanted to destroy.

FERRARI. How dreadful.

BORGES. No, it's because she thinks that she was still very clumsy, that she couldn't paint when she made it. Well, what I know is that she sketches the plan of each painting and then she paints it. That is, the people who've described it as a naive painting are completely wrong. But art critics, of course, their profession is to get things wrong, I'd say . . . or all critics.

FERRARI. Like literary critics?

BORGES. Like literary critics, yes (*laughs*), who are specialists in error, no? In cautious error.

FERRARI (*laughs*). Then we have one of your neighbours.

BORGES. Doctor Figari?

FERRARI. Pedro Figari, who lived round the corner, on Marcelo T. de Alvear.

BORGES. And he died here, round the corner on this block. Ricardo Güiraldes introduced me to him. He was a lawyer, he must easily have been 60 years old when I think he suddenly discovered that he could paint, but not draw—he couldn't draw, he drew directly with the brush. And I think that he took those subjects of black people and gauchos from the book *Rosas and His Age* by Ramos Mejía. And Pablo Rojas Paz called him 'Figari, painter of memory' which seems right to me because that's what he paints. They aren't realist paintings because they include gauchos in 'calzoncillo cribado'. Well, and those pants were never worn in Uruguay. But, so what? He wasn't looking for accuracy, and all his paintings are really paintings produced by memory or, rather, paintings of the imagination.

FERRARI. To such an extent that when Jules Supervieille praised the light in Figari's paintings, Figari replied, 'It is the light of memory.' That confirms what you've said about him being a painter of memory.

BORGES. Ah, yes! I didn't know that, and I didn't realize either that Figari could be so pithy. He explained each picture from the point of view of the anecdote it contained. For example: 'This man is very worried, what is troubling him? These black people, how happy they are, they're playing the drum, borocotó, borocotó, borocotó, chas-chas!' He was always repeating that onomatopoeia: borocotó, boro-cotó, borocotó, chas-chas! (*both laugh*). He would explain every painting in a jovial way, without referring to colours or form but to the subject, to what he called the painting's anecdote.

73

Voltaire

●

OSVALDO FERRARI. We recently talked, Borges, about Victor Hugo's book on Shakespeare and about Hugo's vision of the classics. And I've just come across Hugo writing about Voltaire, where he starts off saying that, to a large extent, Voltaire is the result of his father, who condemned literature, and of his godfather, a literary enthusiast who encouraged Voltaire.

JORGE LUIS BORGES. I don't know if that's fair. Voltaire is, after all, one of the great literary figures.

FERRARI. Of course, but Hugo adds that perhaps those two competing impulses warped Voltaire's imagination.

BORGES. Yet, we have Voltaire's stories. Some of those stories were perhaps suggested by Swift, others by *The Thousand and One Nights*, others by Captain Gulliver's adventures, but he produced something completely distinctive. He also had the idea of taking the East, and a fantastical East . . . of course he did it in an ironic way, completely different from the style of *The Thousand and One Nights*. No, without doubt, Hugo admired Voltaire.

FERRARI. Of course.

BORGES. Because I think that to not admire Voltaire is one of the many forms of stupidity.

FERRARI. Although Hugo regrets the way that Voltaire's work is scattered across different genres.

BORGES. Well, yes, Voltaire's drama in particular. I think that it was Lytton Strachey who said that, in his work, drama reached unprecedented heights even though he didn't have a sense of the ridiculous.

FERRARI. Which is what has been most commonly associated with him, of course.

BORGES. Of course, yes. His dramatic works completely lacked that. Although perhaps the dramatic tradition was so strong that the absurd was a part of the genre.

FERRARI. Hugo lists the successes and failures of the different plays that Voltaire produced in his lifetime.

BORGES. Yes, but now we would think that they have all failed, no?

FERRARI. In what way?

BORGES. In the sense that, when we think about Voltaire, the last thing we think about is his dramatic work. We don't think about his poetry either, about *La Henriade*.

FERRARI. But *La Henriade* reveals Voltaire's taste for the epic.

BORGES. Yes, but it didn't turn out very well for him. Someone once observed that there wasn't enough in the work to nourish the horses that appear in it (*both laugh*). However, without meaning to, and perhaps without knowing he was doing it, Voltaire wrote an epic and that is his book on Charles XII of Sweden, who Voltaire described as the most extraordinary man in the world. I think that, from the historical point of view, the book is deeply flawed since Voltaire's knowledge was limited. Despite that, it's an epic.

FERRARI. He wrote that essay on epic poetry where he says, for example, that an epic poem must be based on reason but embellished by imagination.

BORGES. Well, that basis in reason is something that we don't know . . .

FERRARI. It's typical of his time.

BORGES. Yes, it's typical of his time. Of course, to defend reason, even as a human ambition . . . although I don't know if we have ever been reasonable, I would say not. In any case, the cult of reason is a good thing, it's beyond question. Even though we don't achieve it or, rather, even though we don't always achieve it, since life would extremely seldom be, well, completely irrational. For example, Wells' *Outline of History*. Of course, he wanted men to forget their passions, boundaries, nations, he wanted history to be seen as a common human enterprise. And of course he had to rewrite what he encountered, which is, precisely, the history of war and of conquest . . .

FERRARI. The history of what really happened.

BORGES. Yes, the history of what really happened, which is a military history, sadly. In any case, that's what comes down to us. But philosophy and art also come down to us, which are different. Perhaps one day a universal history can be written whose great figures aren't the violent likes of Alexander or Charles XII, or Tamburlaine or Napoleon or whoever. For the moment, when we think about the past, we're forced to think about that, which is also dramatic. It has an aesthetic value. One would imagine that Wells' *Outline of History* would be different from the others, yet it differs very little. We've also talked about the other excellent universal history, by Chesterton, I think it's called *Everlasting Man*, I found out about it through Francisco Luis Bernárdez. Now, that's a very strange book—there's not a single date in it, there are very few proper names, and it's all told in such an affecting way . . . I remember reading the chapter about the Punic Wars. When I came to the end of it, I was crying.

FERRARI. As always, the epic moves you.

BORGES. Yes, exactly.

FERRARI. Now, Hugo makes links in the eighteenth century, of course, between Voltaire, Rousseau and Mirabeau.

BORGES. I don't know, I feel so distant from Rousseau now. Although I've done everything I could as a good Genevan, I've even read *Émile*, one of the most boring books ever written.

FERRARI (*laughs*). But you didn't get as far as *The Social Contract*.

BORGES. No, not *The Social Contract*. But I read the *Confessions* which reveals an extremely unpleasant character. When he wrote that book,

Rousseau seems to have realized its pathetic possibilities and so attributed a series of offences to himself that he didn't actually commit. The one, for example, about having abandoned his children and about not being their real father.

FERRARI. Hugo also maintains that in the middle of that French society, which was breaking apart, before the Revolution . . .

BORGES. Of course. For the Revolution to occur that must have already happened, no? But one could say that about anything, eh? That when something happened, it had already happened some time before but in a more private way. That is, events simply confirm something that's already occurred.

FERRARI. Yes, the preceding events are invisible but they're revealed later on.

BORGES. Yes, I think so. And certainly that could be used, let's say, as an argument in favour of Rosas, and the other Rosas that we've suffered, that if they came to power it's because there was something . . . well, 'something rotten in the state of Denmark'.

FERRARI. Aside from what they did to achieve power.

BORGES. Yes, of course, yes. One might also think this would be a form of consolation—that when something happens to you, something bad, it simply means that you've received a letter informing you about it.

FERRARI. In which you're informed about something that was already going on.

BORGES. Yes, so events would be symptoms of already latent illnesses.

FERRARI. That's right, it's like being ill.

BORGES. Yes, that is, if they decapitate me, it means that they've already chopped my head off (*both laugh*).

FERRARI. In the man's heart, they have already chopped it off, of course.

BORGES. And what goes on in the heart and the mind is more important than what happens in mere external events, in mere reality.

FERRARI. You're right, because it's what happens in consciousness.

BORGES. Of course. We're certain of consciousness but not of the reality of reality. We have immediate evidence of consciousness. On the other hand, reality is more or less. . . . When I say that I was born in Buenos Aires in 1899, it's a mere act of faith, because I don't remember being born in Buenos Aires in 1899. Nobody can remember their birth, no? Although now, according to the psychoanalysts, we can even remember our experiences prior to birth . . . which is an act of faith that, personally, I don't share. How strange to base 'a science' on something as hypothetical as that. Of course, we say a science in inverted commas, like psychoanalysis, which is based in part on that, on an assumed relation between children and their parents, for example.

FERRARI. The past in particular is reassessed.

BORGES. Yes, and a past that is also fairly speculative, or of a speculative nature. González Lanuza began writing an autobiography, and he said, 'I'm sorry to hurt or to distress the psychoanalysts but I have really loved my mother and my father' (*both laugh*). 'I would rather,' he said, 'not hurt their feelings, but the truth forces me to say that I was a happy child, and that I have loved them both equally.'

FERRARI. Coming back to Voltaire. Hugo explains that in the middle of that French society that was breaking up, Voltaire appeared 'like a serpent in a swamp, ready to transmit his venom and influence what was to come'.

BORGES. It's so hard to associate Voltaire with the word 'venom'. . . . Apart from the alliteration . . . but aside from that no, eh?

FERRARI. I assure you that Hugo associates them quite readily. He attributes . . .

BORGES. Well, yes, but as Hugo liked antitheses, he might possibly have thought that 'Voltaire' and 'serpent' were an antithesis, as when he talks about the star and the spider, light and shade. Perhaps it was for that reason.

FERRARI. A literary antithesis, shall we say?

BORGES. Yes. But there was already something snake-like in Voltaire, no? Or he was perceived that way. He was perceived as diabolic.

74

The Nineteenth Century

●

OSVALDO FERRARI. A little while ago, Borges, one of your comments suggested an identification, or a greater affinity, with the last century than with the present one.

JORGE LUIS BORGES. It's true, I was born in the penultimate year of the last century, in '99, I'm a relic from that century. At the same time, if I think that the nineteenth century produced the twentieth, well, I've provided the strongest possible argument against that century. But the nineteenth century was produced by the eighteenth which was perhaps better. As for the seventeenth century, I don't know, I have mixed feelings.

FERRARI. One can easily see that the majority of your favourite authors are from the nineteenth century.

BORGES. Well, they were born in the nineteenth century.

FERRARI. Born then, yes.

BORGES. Of course, the division into centuries is arbitrary. We can't think without generalizing, which is also a generalization, no?

FERRARI. That's right.

BORGES. Thinking is impossible without generalization, it seems, since in order to think we need abstract words. Well, here there are two possibilities—either abstract words are simplifications of other words, or the Platonic archetypes do exist. We have to choose between two things, that is, either the word 'white' is a way of referring to the colour of rice, or the colour of snow, or the colour of the moon, or the colour of teeth. Or one has to suppose, like the idealists, that there are archetypes. Or, rather, that snow, rice, the moon, teeth, participate in an archetype which is whiteness. But it seems more plausible to suppose that we seek a rather, well, vague word to help us think, which brings us close to nominalism, which assumes that individual objects exist and that similarities have been found that help to suggest abstract words.

FERRARI. Or, in the other case, to suggest Platonism, let's say.

BORGES. Yes, which assumes that every object is a knot where the archetypes converge . . .

FERRARI. And that there are archetypal words.

BORGES. Yes, that the word 'whiteness', for example, works for snow just as it works for rice, and for the moon.

FERRARI. The extension of white, of course.

BORGES. Yes, we can choose between the two ideas. Now, according to Coleridge, every man is born Aristotelian or Platonic, that is, he's born an idealist or a nominalist. One can't conceive of a third type of man. So we're Aristotelian or Platonic and, according to Coleridge, we can't be anything else. But, generally we're a bit of both.

FERRARI. Or in the East we are Confucian or followers of Lao Tzu.

BORGES. Of course. Now, I was reading in *The First Thousand Years*—a history of Japanese literature by a Japanese author—that Zen Buddhism came to Japan, and that Buddhism and Confucianism are the same thing. Or, according to the fairly inevitable metaphor that he uses, they are two sides of the same coin, that is, there's no inherent need for conflict between them, although historically there has been and it has frequently been bloody.

FERRARI. Yet one would associate Buddhism more with Lao Tzu than with Confucius.

BORGES. Yes, but since the conflict had been established between Confucius and Zen Buddhism, what they were looking for was reconciliation. Because, officially, Taoism didn't count, or it was, as you say, identified with Buddhism. As a matter of fact, Confucius' world seems rather mystical. And I think that at some point Confucius said that one has to respect supernatural beings, but it's best to keep them at arm's length (*both laugh*). Which was a polite way of rejecting them, no?

FERRARI. More or less like Plato with the poets.

BORGES. More or less, yes. Of course, we believe in the Trinity, but it's better for the Trinity to keep its distance, no? For it not to interfere too much (*laughs*). In the meantime, let's respect it out of, well, courtesy . . . or as a perhaps necessary precaution.

FERRARI. I was saying before that you often refer to the vision of nineteenth-century writers, like Chesterton or Shaw . . .

BORGES. Ah yes, and the truth is that literature seems so fertile. Now, there's another hypothesis that I've heard, and it's that the nineteenth century really ended in 1914.

FERRARI. Ah, that's quite probable, of course.

BORGES. Because in 1914 the war came, and then distrust among nations, well, passports . . .

FERRARI. Well, it was the century of the ideology of progress, of positivism, and of nationalist and socialist ideas. . . . Many things were born in that century and their influence continues into our own.

BORGES. I would say that politicians, in general, are backward readers, no? (*Laughs.*) A French writer once said that ideas are born gently but gain in ferocity as they age. It's true, because one starts with the idea, for example, that the State should manage everything, which is better than allowing a private company to manage things, better than everything being 'left to chaos or to individual circumstance'. But that leads to Nazism or Communism, of course. Each idea starts life as a beautiful possibility, and then, well, as it grows old, it's used by tyrants, for oppression. But in the beginning . . .

FERRARI. All ideas are innocent . . .

BORGES. Yes, we can even say that they're poetic, and that later they become prosaic and terrible, yes, inexorable.

FERRARI. Now, at the beginning of the last century the movement appears that you consider, I think, the most important in the history of literature—Romanticism.

BORGES. Yes, although Romanticism arose in the eighteenth century, so it must have arisen with Macpherson's *Ossian*, and with Bishop Percy's English and Scottish ballads.

FERRARI. That is, in Scotland and England.

BORGES. Yes, in Scotland rather, since Bishop Percy was from Northumbria, that is, he was on the border with Scotland. And then it spread across the world. In any case, we have the official date of the Romantic movement in England, which is 1798, the year of the publication of Coleridge and Wordsworth's *Lyrical Ballads*, and in France, 1830, the year of the production of *Hernani*. I don't know what the official date is in Germany, if there is an official date, for official dates are clearly, well, conventions. And, of course, I don't know if there was really a Romantic movement in Spain, apart from Bécquer who was a sort of pale reflection of Heine. I don't think that there was a Romantic movement.

FERRARI. Well, possibly Espronceda . . .

BORGES. Yes, but he seems rather rhetorical and he is rather oratorical. The Spanish Romantic poets are rather oratorical. In any case, they come late to the feast. One would have to look more closely at Italy. And here, here we would have . . .

FERRARI. Echevarría.

BORGES. Echevarría, I don't know exactly what the date would be, it must be after 1830.

FERRARI. Of course, in Rosas' time.

BORGES. Of course, and the poem of his that's remembered, which was so criticized by Lugones, the one where he talks about the pampa and says that it stretches out mysteriously, vaguely, like a huge, green ocean. Now, that comparison, I think that it's false—the plain is always compared to the sea. Personally, I see it in a different way, because there's a mystery to the sea, there's a continual change in the sea that isn't there with the plain, as far as I can see.

FERRARI. The sea is a plain in movement.

BORGES. And yet, the desert, which is a sort of plain, has, at least for the imagination, a completely different association. Besides, there's something in the word 'desert' that's not there in the word 'plain'. Well, I have no right to talk about these things—I was always short-sighted, and now I'm blind. But I get the impression that the plain is the same all over the world. When I was in Oklahoma, for example, I thought that I was in the Buenos Aires region. And quite possibly, if I went to the Steppe, or if I went to Australia, or if I went to what is called the Veldt, in South Africa, I would feel the same. On the other hand, they say that every hill is different, we could almost say that every hill is an individual.

FERRARI. While the plain is anonymous.

BORGES. The plain is anonymous and spread out, and if you've seen one you've seen them all. But not with mountains—mountains are different.

FERRARI. Towards the second half of the last century, we have another of your favourite poets, but now one of the symbolists . . . I'm talking about Verlaine.

BORGES. Ah, of course. But I think that I've said that if I had to choose one poet, I'd choose Verlaine, although I sometimes hesitate between Verlaine and Virgil. And some people have told me that Virgil is simply a faint echo of Homer. Voltaire said, 'If Homer made Virgil, then Virgil is the best thing he ever made.'

FERRARI. And as we suggested at another time, if Virgil later made Dante, then he's also one of his best works.

BORGES. Yes, of course.

FERRARI. We should also recall it was in the nineteenth century that Nietzsche made the declaration that 'God is dead.'

BORGES. . . . And yet, it doesn't look like that, eh? It looks as if he hasn't died. In any case, he lives on as a hope. . . . Shaw said, 'God is in the making,' and that making of God would be, well, the universe, including the minerals, the plants, the animals, men. Our conversation here too would be an example of God's making.

FERRARI. Well . . .

BORGES. As for the idea that 'God is dead'—it's an extension of the idea of the 'twilight of the gods', of the moment when the gods die, and the demons, of course. But there's no mention of humanity there—it's strange—in that song of the witch's, or the prophet's, prediction. No, with a sort of haughty disdain they talk about the gods and the demons in that Scandinavian 'twilight of the gods'.

FERRARI. Humans don't count for anything.

BORGES. No. The songs of the 'Poetic Edda' talk about the gods, and that they will return after their 'twilight'.

FERRARI. So that you think that mythology must have influenced Nietzsche?

BORGES. Certainly I think that, and the proof is there in the title of his book, *Twilight of the Idols*.

FERRARI. Mythology and philosophy.

BORGES. I suppose that there must have been a constant interchange, eh? Myth . . .

FERRARI. And reason.

BORGES. . . . And reason, yes. I was thinking about myth. I think that the difference between myth and fable or whatever type of fiction, is that—I've thought about the classical authors in particular—the classics are books that are read in a certain way. Whereas myth is a type of fiction, dream, fable, which is read as if it were susceptible to numerous interpretations and as if it had a necessary meaning.

FERRARI. Of course, yes.

BORGES. Because if not, I don't know what the difference would be between a myth and a fairy story. The proof that they're different is that one listens to a fairy story as something entertaining while with myth, well, the word 'myth' is already a fairly reverent word.

FERRARI. One listens to it as an expression of fate, in the way that fate appears in Greek mythology.

BORGES. Yes, fate appears there.

75

Virgil

●

OSVALDO FERRARI. One of your constant favourites among the classical authors, and within the epic genre, Borges, seems to be Virgil's *The Aeneid*, ahead of even *The Iliad*. Perhaps the subtlety with which *The Aeneid* is written is also another aspect . . .

JORGE LUIS BORGES. Clearly. Besides, I know *The Odyssey* through various versions, through versions in English . . . I think that in English there are 30-something versions of *The Odyssey*. There are fewer of *The Iliad*, since, well, England and the sea are a single entity. On the other hand, more versions of *The Iliad* have been made in German, because Germany and the land, like England and the sea, go together, no? So I've read many versions of the *The Odyssey*, I have the old version by Chapman, who was a contemporary and rival of Shakespeare and I think that, well, they were rivals in love, and that Shakespeare mentions him indirectly in some of his poems. But, well, I seem to have got distracted, as I'm talking about *The Odyssey* rather than *The Aeneid*. Perhaps the best English version of *The Odyssey* is by

Lawrence of Arabia. He published it and signed it 'T. B. Shaw', which is the pseudonym he adopted when he resigned his military post as colonel and joined the Air Force. In the case of *The Aeneid* which, of course, would have been impossible without *The Iliad* and *The Odyssey*, we have, as you said at the beginning, two virtues that are hardly ever encountered, or that are only encountered in *The Aeneid*—it's a matter, more than anything, of epic inspiration, because, clearly, the epic of Aeneas, well, is seen as the founding epic of the Roman empire, and it's well known that it was written in the time of Augustus. And then, there is the care with which each line is written. It's very strange, it's almost like the work of a *précieux* poet, as if a poet who felt each line, the special quality of each line, had used that meticulous art (*in tenui labor*) for a vast epic. And we must bear in mind that in the Middle Ages, and perhaps up until the Romantic movement, the great poem was *The Aeneid*, since they respected Homer but that was no more than an act of faith. For example, he appears in *el nobile castello*, when those great shades of the classical poets, there are five of them, approach Dante and welcome him as the sixth of their group. One of the five shades approaches with a sword in his hand and he is Homer. How strange that a poet should work towards future poets, who he can't predict, and who he perhaps wouldn't understand or wouldn't like. Because one would have to know if Homer, or the Greeks who we call Homer, would have approved of *The Aeneid*— possibly not. And what would Virgil have thought of *The Divine Comedy*? He wouldn't have understood a lot of it, he'd have understood only the parts that refer to pagan mythology, for example, the minotaur and the centaurs that appear in the *Inferno*. Well, and he appears too, but he's changed into another character, because there's no reason for the historical Virgil to be similar to that great figure, to that Virgil who is the most important figure in *The Divine Comedy*. And one might even think that the most important part of that work, although it's all important, is the friendship between Virgil and Dante, because Dante knows that he will be saved but that his companion is damned, excluded from the sight of God, and so he leads a mournful life with the other four great shades.

FERRARI. Like Aeneas earlier in *The Aeneid*.

BORGES. That's right.

FERRARI. In the sixth book.

BORGES. Yes, in the sixth book, which must have served as an inspiration for Dante, because that idea of the journey to . . . well, the whole idea of *The Divine Comedy* is in some way an extension, a wonderful extension of the sixth book of *The Aeneid*. But, how strange, when I think about *The Aeneid* now, I remember fewer incidents than phrases, but that's the same with every poet . . . and, I think that now we could call Virgil baroque.

FERRARI. Each of his lines has been carefully worked.

BORGES. Yes, each line. For example, he produced that wonderful expression *Troya fuit*, which is generally translated very badly into Spanish as 'Aquí fue Troya', which loses all of the expression's power. On the other hand, 'Troya fue' is tinged with sadness . . . 'Troya fue' is like saying: Once one could have said 'Troy is' but now we can only say 'Troy was'. That 'was' is wonderful. Of course, it's a literary device, but all literature is made up of devices. I remember now that Chesterton notes that the whole world, every country, has wanted to be a descendant of the Trojans rather than the Achaeans.

FERRARI. It's odd.

BORGES. And that brings us to the suspicion that the real hero of *The Iliad*—for us, and perhaps for Homer too—is Hector.

FERRARI. The Trojan.

BORGES. The Trojan, yes, and the title is proof, *The Iliad*, that is, it refers to Ilion.

FERRARI. To Ilion, that is, to Troy.

BORGES. Of course, because it could have been called the *Achillea*, like *The Odyssey*, but no, it's called *The Iliad*. Both have a tragic destiny, since Achilles knows that he will never enter Troy, and Hector knows that he's defending a city that's condemned to fire and extermination. Both are tragic figures, both struggling, well, Hector for a lost cause and Achilles for what will be a vengeful cause but at a time when he's already dead, a cause whose triumph he will never see.

FERRARI. One appreciates the Greek sense of fate there.

BORGES. Yes, and then, the vastness of the sea, because in the action of *The Iliad* we have the battles and also some scenes between the gods . . .

FERRARI. Yes, but it's very interesting to see the way that each character in *The Iliad* submits to the fate of the gods, to the Greek sense of fate, we could say.

BORGES. Yes, well, the gods are also subject to it.

FERRARI. In their turn.

BORGES. I think the word that symbolizes fate, in Greek, is equivalent to 'wyrd' in Old English. That's why the three witches at the beginning of *Macbeth* are also the weird sisters, that is, the fatal sisters or, rather, the Fates. Those sisters are also the Fates and Macbeth is an instrument of the Fates and of his wife's ambition. How it affects him, well, when she says that he has too much of 'the milk of human kindness'. That is, one feels that essentially he isn't cruel, that he's driven by the prophecy, by his faith in the prophecy which Banquo for his part doesn't share, because the witches appear, they make their prophecies, they disappear, and Banquo says, 'The earth has bubbles, as the water has, and these are of them.' So that he sees in the witches the chance phenomena of the earth, bubbles.

FERRARI. Paganism persists, in some way, even if it's attenuated.

BORGES. Fate also appears in Scandinavian mythology, as 'nornn, yes, the Norns. As for Scandinavian mythology, *The Aeneid* seems to have exercised such a fascination in the north and on the Saxons that Virgil's rather weighty epic inspired *Beowulf* (I think that two passages from *The Aeneid* have been detected in it). You'll also know the Scandinavian god Thor. Well, I've read in some Scandinavian book that Thor was Hector's brother.

FERRARI. Hector once again, the Trojan.

BORGES. The Trojan. That is, the Scandinavians, stranded up there in their north, wanted—well, contradicting Hitler the future ethnologist—

to be Trojans. The sound of the names Thor and Hector is similar also.

FERRARI. It's an example of the North's need to feel connected to the South, as you said on another occasion.

BORGES. Yes. On the other hand, the prestige of Rome, always the prestige of Rome. And all of the South, well, of course, the barbarians are bound to feel the prestige of . . .

FERRARI. Of the ancient culture.

BORGES. Of that culture, yes. A classic case would be the Tartars—the Tartars or Mongolians conquered China, and then, within two or three generations, they've become Chinese gentlemen studying the *Book of Changes* and the *Analects* of Confucius, yes (*laughs*).

FERRARI. Coming back to the South, it surprises me that Virgil acknowledged that he was a follower of Lucretius, given that he was such an idealist, or so fantastical, in contrast to the materialism of Lucretius who followed on, naturally, from Epicurus.

BORGES. Yes, one doesn't seem to sense any similarity between them, but Lucretius must have had an influence on Virgil. Now, naturally, Dante doesn't mention Lucretius. And then, the five poets welcome him and greet him as an equal because they know that he will write *The Divine Comedy*. Let's see, who were they? Virgil, Homer, Horace, Ovid and Lucan. But Lucretius is excluded. Well, naturally, Lucretius was an atheist so he has to be excluded, no? Although he begins with an invocation to Venus, and Venus would be an equivalent there of Schopenhauer's will, or the creative evolution of Bergson, or the life force of Shaw, a type of force like this, or as Glanvill said, 'God is a will,' a will manifested in the stones, the plants, the animals, in ourselves, in each one of us. Yes, there's certainly religious feeling in Lucretius but in a rather pantheistic sense, I think.

FERRARI. Well, even though he denies religion, denies the gods and the influence of the gods on men.

BORGES. Yes, but he feels that for him there's something sacred, let's say, in the universe, in life.

FERRARI. He doesn't say it but he feels it, that's right.

BORGES. That's why Hugo, who clearly wasn't a Christian, in his book on Shakespeare, makes a list of great poets, or men of genius, and he begins with Homer and continues with Lucretius, and I think that he excludes Virgil and Dante, yes, and throughout there's a sort of parallel between Aeschylus and Shakespeare, which one understands later when he says: 'How can those two great figures resemble each other?' 'By being different,' he replies.

FERRARI. And who do you feel closer to, Borges, Lucretius or Virgil?

BORGES. . . . It's difficult to answer that, I think that, let's say, intellectually Lucretius, but in literary or poetic terms—Virgil.

FERRARI. Perfect.

BORGES. I've read Lucretius in Monroe's English version which is regarded as the best. But with Virgil . . . in the end, I have barely heard Virgil's voice from a distance in the seven years that I've worked at the study of Latin and the love of Latin.

76

On Friendship

●

OSVALDO FERRARI. Beyond our own borders, I think that you see the creative possibilities of friendship. One of the most famous examples is the spiritual friendship between Plato and Socrates.

JORGE LUIS BORGES. That would be the classic example, no?

FERRARI. Of course.

BORGES. But there have been so many since.

FERRARI. Well, Jaspers maintains that Plato's philosophy is based on his lifelong personal association with Socrates, that the most important aspect of his philosophy is not nature or the universe, or man, or any proposition, but the way that those things emerge from his friendship.

BORGES. That's certainly possible. Now, I've said, and doubtless I've said it more than once, that the Platonic dialogues relate to, or emerge from, Plato's nostalgia for Socrates. That is, Socrates dies but Plato plays at him still being alive, still discussing various subjects. It's similar to the idea of *magister dixit*. We have an example in Pythagoras. Pythagoras doesn't write anything down so that his thought can branch out among his followers. And Plato, in spite of the physical death of Socrates, carries on playing at, or imagining, Socrates being alive, Socrates applying his theory of the archetypes to all things. And so Plato develops the primitive idea, the idea of archetypes of the good, imagining archetypes of the bad, archetypes of all things. In the end, one arrives at an archetypal world which includes as many archetypes as individual entities and which would need another world of archetypes in its turn, and so on into infinity.

FERRARI. But this would imply, among other things, that the great feeling of friendship was at the beginnings of Western philosophy.

BORGES. Yes, friendship and thinking that death is an accident, and that a particular line of thought can be carried on in the minds of followers beyond the physical death of their teacher. Pythagoras would be the classic case, no?

FERRARI. Of course, that's a part of his philosophy which maintains that the spirit exists before birth and carries on existing beyond the death of the body.

BORGES. And beyond the individual, of course.

FERRARI. Naturally.

BORGES. Because I think that, for example, Aristotle never talks about Pythagoras on his own. He talks, rather, of 'the Pythagoreans'. So he isn't sure whether Pythagoras thought in a particular way, but his group carries on thinking for him after his physical death.

FERRARI. It was a form of spiritual community, let's say.

BORGES. Yes, that is, coming back to what one assumes is our subject, which is friendship, then it carries on with people who knew him personally. Pythagoras carries on thinking through many minds, who are the Pythagoreans and who must have come to think things that he hadn't thought.

FERRARI. But always in the spirit of the teacher.

BORGES. Yes, for example, I think that the idea of cyclical time doesn't occur in Pythagoras. Yet the Pythagoreans professed it, as did the Stoics.

FERRARI. As they did too, yes. Now, turning to your life, Borges, we have to talk about your friendship with Macedonio Fernández.

BORGES. Yes, it has been a tutelary friendship. . . . But, how strange, that physical death seems to suit that type of friendship, no? Since, well, that famous line of Mallarmé's, 'Tel qu'en Lui même en fin l'éternité le change' (Such as into Himself at last eternity changes him), which refers to Poe. That is, when someone dies, one has the image of that person, which isn't altered by their contemporary circumstance, and that image can be manipulated as one wishes. So that we could say that the image of a friend is perhaps stronger after their death. One can also shape it, no?

FERRARI. Improve it?

BORGES. And perhaps improve it, because I don't know what Xul Solar would have made, for example, of this or that event. But the Platonic Xul Solar would have thought the same as we do about this, no?

FERRARI. Of course.

BORGES. And the Platonic Macedonio as well, although perhaps not as an individual. Of course, while a person is alive they are changing and they are ungraspable. On the other hand, when they're dead, they have the stillness of a photograph, of a fixed image.

FERRARI. Jaspers also says that perhaps every young person aspires to find their Socrates.

BORGES. Ah, that's a lovely idea.

FERRARI. . . . And I'm thinking that when you talk about the tutelary friendship of Macedonio, it suggests that you found something similar in him.

BORGES. Well, many of us found that in Macedonio, all of his followers, or his interlocutors who were his followers, of course, since we felt that he was our teacher. He didn't like the idea of being a teacher.

FERRARI. Which proves his status as a teacher.

BORGES. Yes, I think so. On the other hand, in Doctor Johnson's case, or in the contemporary case of Gómez de la Serna, or of Rafael Cansinos Assens, they felt like they were teachers of a group. José Ingenieros too.

FERRARI. That is, with Macedonio, one didn't suspect any didactic intention.

BORGES. No, with Macedonio it was curiosity and doubt more than anything . . .

FERRARI. He shared that.

BORGES. Yes, he shared that. But, in fact, he was the teacher, and people didn't come to hear us but to hear Macedonio Fernández.

FERRARI. So that it didn't matter whether he wrote or not, because he had followers.

BORGES. Yes, but he didn't see them as followers. And, besides, as he had the habit of attributing his opinions to an interlocutor, he would say, for example, 'It's dangerous to talk about music without knowing what Santiago Dabove has said about this subject' (*laughs*). And lots of people have flirted with that danger, no? Of talking about music without knowing the opinion of Santiago Dabove, who wrote a book of stories, *Death and Its Suit.*

FERRARI. And later on, many of your friendships have been linked to work, that is, you've worked in collaboration with many of your friends, as in the case of Bioy Casares, and your friend Silvina Ocampo.

BORGES. And I've found that women make excellent friends—they have an admirable capacity for friendship.

FERRARI. Of course.

BORGES. Something which a lot of people deny, I don't know why . . . well, of course, I think that women are more sensible and more sensitive than men . . . more sensitive, I'm not sure, but certainly more sensible, in general, no? The proof is there in the fact that women aren't prone to fanaticism, whereas men, especially in this country, are easily roused to fanaticism and to, well, indefensible causes. They have to be fanatical to expound them, otherwise they wouldn't make sense to anybody.

FERRARI. It's also been said that women are less harmful in friendship than in love. What do you think?

BORGES. Love is a vulnerable relationship, no? It requires constant confirmation, and if that confirmation is lacking there is doubt, and if a few days go by, and one hasn't heard anything from her, one is in despair. On the other hand, one can go a year without hearing from a friend and it doesn't matter. Friendship, well, friendship doesn't require one to confide in someone, unlike love. And love is a state of suspicion—it's fairly uncomfortable, eh? One can see or not see, one can know or not know what the other person is doing. Now, perhaps there are people who experience friendship in a jealous way, but not me. There are many people who experience friendship as one experiences love, they even want to be the other person's only friend.

FERRARI. That's a mistake, it's possessive friendship, let's say.

BORGES. Yes, and love tends to be possessive.

FERRARI. Of course.

BORGES. Otherwise, it's regarded as a betrayal. But not with friendship, quite the opposite.

FERRARI. Now, in the prologues that you've written for the works of writers like Alfonso Reyes or Pedro Henríquez Ureña, or even other writers you didn't know personally, like Almafuerte or Ascasubi, there's a type of emotion that one has to relate to the feeling of friendship.

BORGES. Yes, you're right. In the case of Henríquez Ureña and Alfonso Reyes, we *were* friends. Well, before I used to criticize people, but not now. I haven't written a single antagonistic, or vaguely hostile, line in a long time. I don't see the point of it. Besides, well, for example, Schopenhauer thought that Fichte was a charlatan. Now similarities have been discovered in both their doctrines—they coexist in the history of philosophy. De Quincey had a very low opinion of Alexander Pope. And now one can admire them both impartially, no? So, in the long run, tradition wins out, and tradition is primarily made up of revolutions. The Romantic movement for example, is opposed to the great century, the century of Louis XIV. Well, now we look at Hugo, and we're forced to think of Racine or Boileau. And we don't think about how they were enemies.

FERRARI. A triumph of tradition.

BORGES. Yes, which also creates a form of unity from those heterogeneous elements. And what is now heterogeneous for us might become a whole in very little time, since everything ends up as tradition. The history of literature is the history of a series of antagonistic groups.

77

Chesterton

•

OSVALDO FERRARI. There is one of your favourite authors, Borges, who's not known well enough in Argentina, although you think that his Catholicism perhaps brings him close to many Argentines—I'm talking, of course, about your beloved Chesterton.

JORGE LUIS BORGES. Yes, of course. Well, his Catholicism has harmed his reputation in England. And then perhaps that word coined by Shaw—ChesterBelloc—they were seen as a kind of monster. The association of his name with Hilaire Belloc has also harmed his reputation. I think that Belloc had a bad influence on Chesterton. Belloc was a very intelligent man but easily drawn to fanaticism while Chesterton had a very generous mind. He was tolerant, but Belloc pushed him towards fanaticism and caused him to be read for his opinions. That's what has always harmed writers. For example . . . well, there are so many examples. Here we have Lugones, who has been judged for his political opinions, in particular, the opinions of his later years. One forgets that before that he was an anarchist, a socialist, a supporter of the Allies in the First World War and then, later on, he published *The Hour of the Sword*. And Kipling is viewed as part of the British Empire. Whitman is viewed favourably, of course, because he represents democracy. Political opinions are the least important part of a writer's work, they're superficial. In Chesterton's case, we have a man of genius, and . . . to reduce that to his Catholicism is an injustice. I remember that Shaw said the Catholic Church, the Vatican, was a small ship which would capsize when Chesterton, who was an enormous man, got on it (*both laugh*).

FERRARI. Yet . . .

BORGES. Well, that's simply a joke, but the truth is that it has been forgotten that Chesterton . . . for example, he's written detective stories, as we all know. But as Xul Solar once pointed out to me, those detective stories aren't merely detective stories, which would be no disgrace for the genre was invented by Edgar Allan Poe and then developed by Dickens, and . . . by Chesterton. But those stories are also many other things, since each of Chesterton's stories ends up in some way as a picture, then like a theatrical piece, then like a parable. There are also his landscapes. The characters are like actors who appear on the stage—they're always extremely vivid, visually vivid. And then there's the solution which is always ingenious. And, strangely, no one talks about the criminals—Father Brown, the detective in Chesterton's stories, never accuses anybody throughout his whole career. One doesn't know terribly well what happens to them, since the important thing is the enigma, and the ingenious solution of that enigma. And, besides, each of Chesterton's detective stories suggests a magical explanation. I think that if the detective genre dies, and it's possible that it will die, since it seems that death is the fate of all literary genres—well, those stories will still be read for their poetry and, perhaps, for their magical suggestion. There's a story called 'The Invisible Man' in which the solution appears towards the end—the man is invisible because he's so visible, he's a postman who wears a striking uniform but since he comes and goes every day, he's seen as part of the house's routine. But the person who has been murdered makes clockwork dolls which work as servants, and the story implies that the man has been devoured by those iron dolls—a supernatural solution. Perhaps those stories owe some of their power less to the logical explanation than to the false magical explanation offered by Chesterton, which merges with the atmosphere of each house. For example, the story will be different depending on whether it occurs in the Highlands, in a garden suburb close to London, or in an office. Now it has been forgotten that Chesterton was so many other things, that he was, for example, an admirable poet. 'The Ballad of the White Horse', which refers to the wars between the Saxons and the Scandinavians, was published, I think, in 1912, and it's an admirable poem, full of metaphors that would have delighted Hugo. For example, one that I've doubtless cited before, the one where the Viking gazes covetously at Europe, as if Europe were a fruit that he was going to taste. And he thinks about how wonderful marble and gold are, and he says, 'To what can I compare marble and gold?' Well, Chesterton sought impossible comparisons—but that's why they're so effective—so he says, 'Marble like solid moonlight' or 'Gold like a frozen fire.' They're impossible, but precisely because they're a rational impossibility, they are, well . . .

FERRARI. A possibility for poetry.

BORGES. A possibility for poetry, a possibility for the reader's imagination which accepts those impossible images and doesn't think that they're impossible . . . the idea of a 'frozen fire' is so delightful, and especially in English, which has the alliteration on the *f*. 'Gold like a frozen fire,' no? He thinks to what can he compare marble and gold, which are such ancient things, and he comes across those impossible metaphors—that's how he finds what is perhaps the only way of exalting those things, and they have so much power precisely because they are ancient.

FERRARI. He does the same thing in the poem 'Lepanto'.

BORGES. . . . Yes, I don't remember any metaphor from it but I remember phrases like 'Don John of Austria is shouting to the ships'—to the ships, not to the crew.

FERRARI. That's lovely.

BORGES. Yes, and then, when he describes the monstrous paradise of Allah, he says that God Allah is walking among the trees, and adds that he 'is taller than the trees', so that everything becomes monstrous, because one doesn't imagine paradise like that, no? It must be a pagan paradise, that is, an evil paradise according to Chesterton, I suppose. That God is walking among the trees is something we read about in the first chapter of Genesis. But that he's taller than the trees—there's something terrible, something monstrous in that. And Chesterton constantly gets that type of thing right, even in the most unexpected places. For example, one comes across splendid phrases in his book on Blake, in his book on painters, in his history of England too, which may essentially be false but it doesn't matter, because everything is said in such a beautiful way that one wishes that things had been like that.

FERRARI. His book on Saint Thomas Aquinas is also wonderful.

BORGES. That's right, because it seems impossible. I think that Claudel was fairly alarmed at the idea of Chesterton doing a book on Saint Thomas Aquinas. And yet, when he did it . . . well, Claudel was one of Chesterton's first readers, and he considered translating *The Innocence of Father Brown*, which was admirably put into Spanish by Alfonso Reyes. Claudel considered translating it . . . no, what he was going to translate was *The Man Who Was Thursday*, yes, he translated that book into French.

FERRARI. Well, *The Man Who Was Thursday* fully reveals Chesterton to us as a writer.

BORGES. Yes, and it's strange, because it's an increasingly fantastical book, that is, the first chapter is slightly unreal, but by the end, when Sunday (the leader of the society of anarchists) flees on an elephant, it has become wholly fantastical.

FERRARI. Of course.

BORGES. But it happens gradually. From the imaginative it arrives at the impossible, and it does so in such a way that the reader believes in the ending as he or she has believed in the first chapters. What Coleridge said, that poetic faith is the willing suspension of disbelief. And if the work in question is strong, there's no difficulty in suspending it because it imposes itself. Yes, I've thought about Argentine history . . . I've thought that one can question all the facts that history records, apart from one—the murder of the black man by Martín Fierro. It's impossible to think that didn't happen—it was written so effectively, no?

FERRARI. Ah, for precisely that reason?

BORGES. Yes, I think so. I can question any fact, but that fight with the black man . . . and at the end: 'Finally with one thrust / he lifted him on his knife / and like a bag of bones / he threw him against a fence.' Well, that has to be true.

FERRARI. It's so vivid.

BORGES. Yes, it's so vivid. One can question everything else but not the death of the black man.

FERRARI. Talking of literary effectiveness, I think that Chesterton has been really effective in his detective stories because he developed a special narrative technique . . .

BORGES. Yes, because there was the convention that the stories were recounted by a not particularly intelligent friend of the extremely intelligent detective, which is the technique of the first detective story, 'The Murders in the Rue Morgue', by Poe. Which Conan Doyle takes up and modifies, so that the detective isn't an ingenious automaton with the narrator anonymous—the two are friends who love each other, Sherlock Holmes and Doctor Watson (clearly, a simpleton who is always marvelling at his companion). And in Conan Doyle's case, the fact that they're detective stories is perhaps the least important part of it—perhaps the important thing is the friendship between that odd couple, no? It could be placed in the venerable tradition of Don

Quixote and Sancho, Doctor Johnson and Boswell, except that Boswell did it deliberately, he was intentionally Sancho to Doctor Johnson's Don Quixote. He ridiculed himself because he wanted to create that couple who live on in the imaginations of men. In Chesterton's case, we have so many things . . . we have the book on Saint Francis of Assisi, the book on Saint Thomas Aquinas. He said that in Saint Francis' case, an outline, a sketch was enough, but, in the case of Saint Thomas Aquinas, one had to think more of a plan, the plan of a great building. And that in some way defines them both. We also have Chesterton's books of criticism—there's a book on Browning, and another on Dickens in the famous collection of the Everyman's Library. All of Dickens' work was published there, and Chesterton did the prologues, and they paid him a few pounds sterling for them.

FERRARI. As for Chesterton's poetry, you've considered it a weakness that he sometimes constructs his poems in the form of parables, that there's evidence of an intentional construction, that is, there's something rather contrived about his poems.

BORGES. That is, Chesterton was also an intellectual poet.

FERRARI. That seems right to me.

BORGES. Yes, but that could be used against Chesterton. After having read and admired a poem, and having felt and been moved by that poem, one realizes that the author already had the poem's line of reasoning in his mind before he wrote it. And I don't know if it's a good thing that one poem should be so similar to another . . . and, to a game of chess, for example, or that the poem should be a sort of narrative.

And that usually happens with Chesterton, yes, one realizes that from the beginning he is working towards an end, and one is aware of that perhaps too often.

FERRARI. He didn't have the patience to wait for the revelation, let's say (*laughs*).

BORGES. No (*laughs*).

78

The Book of Heaven and Hell

•

OSVALDO FERRARI. One of the first conclusions that is suggested to me, Borges, by the book you compiled with Bioy Casares, the *Book of Heaven and Hell* is that, like the authors included in the book, you reject the idea of a heaven and a hell.

JORGE LUIS BORGES. Yes, because I don't think I'm worthy of reward or punishment. Now, one of Shaw's characters, Major Barbara, says, 'I have got rid of the bribe of heaven.' Then, if heaven is a bribe, hell is clearly a threat, no? And both seem unworthy of the divinity since, ethically, bribery is an extremely lowly activity . . . and punishment also.

FERRARI. The concept of punishment and reward.

BORGES. Or threat—the idea of a threatening god seems ridiculous. It's already ridiculous for a man to threaten someone, but for a divinity. . . . Of course, the idea of reward is also bad, because if one does good deeds, one appreciates that, having done good deeds, having an easy conscience, is already its own reward—one doesn't need additional rewards, and immortal or eternal rewards even less so. But. . . . Everything is so implausible. . . . My father would say to me, 'This world is so strange that anything is possible, even the Trinity.' A sort of *reductio ad absurdum*. Now, I recently had a terrible nightmare, so terrible that I don't dare tell it to you because, if I tell it to you, I will have to remember it, and I think that my duty is to forget nightmares. Yet, there's a special horror in nightmares that isn't there when we're awake, not even at the most dreadful moments. I've come to fear that our nightmares are like glimpses of the hell that might be waiting for us. And perhaps each of us is creating his hell in some way, by means of his nightmares, and his heaven through his happy dreams. In the end, that's merely a fanciful hypothesis—if only it could offer some literary possibility. I don't think so, I'm not thinking about writing a story about it either, but that would be its only value. I suppose that, for each person, the pleasurable and the terrible correspond to different images. And for each of us there is something that's especially terrible. For example, for María Kodama, snakes are especially terrible—she sees a snake and she feels horror. For me, of course, I don't think that they're particularly beautiful but I don't feel disgust or a particular fear. Yet other people do. Coleridge said that when we're awake, our emotions are created by images. For example, if a lion comes in here, we're afraid of the lion, and if a sphinx settles on our chest we find it difficult to breathe. On the other hand, in a nightmare, one starts with the emotion, or the sensation, and then looks for a symbol for it. If I'm asleep and feel something pressing down on my chest, which could be the sheet or the bedspread, then I dream that a sphinx has sat on top of me. That sphinx isn't the cause of the feeling of something pressing down—it's the feeling of something pressing down that suggests the sphinx to me. It has also been said that, when one is in love, the image of the woman is a pretext for the prior emotion, no? There's an illustrious literary example—the tragedy of *Romeo and Juliet*. Romeo goes to a ball to find a woman with whom he's in love, let's say—he's predisposed for love. And then he sees Juliet, and on seeing her he's dazzled, and he says, 'Juliet teaches the torches to burn bright.' And he falls in love with her because he was predisposed for love . . . well, he's presented with a symbol which isn't the woman he was looking for but Juliet, and he falls in love with her. Now, that could be applied to so many things.

FERRARI. Of course, now this idea about nightmares, this idea that one can spend time in hell while still on earth.

BORGES. Rimbaud's idea.

FERRARI. Rimbaud's idea, but I think we can see it clearly in your story 'The South'.

BORGES. Ah, that's possible, yes.

FERRARI. In what happens to your character, Dahlmann, before his train journey.

BORGES. Ah, yes, of course. In that case, one would have to assume that the second part of the story is a hallucination, which is what I think. But, in the end, my opinion isn't worth more than any other reader's, no? When I wrote that story, I'd been reading Henry James, and I thought: I'm going to apply his practice of writing deliberately ambiguous stories. Then I wrote that story with surroundings that are completely alien to Henry James, since the setting is the Buenos Aires region, and it's a setting with gauchos which he would never have heard of in his life. But I thought: I'm going to apply that method. Now, I was reading a book about Melville, and there's a story of his that has never been explained. It's said that he wrote a deliberately inexplicable story as an appropriate symbol for the world, which is also inexplicable.

FERRARI. How remarkable.

BORGES. I don't know if that's plausible, it seems strange that someone should write an inexplicable story, but to him it seemed that since the world we live in was inexplicable, at least for us, the best symbol would be . . . that story is called 'Benito Cereno', now I remember, and it occurs on the Chilean coast, on some ships that are close to the Chilean coast. And the protagonist is Spanish, he's called Benito Cereno. I don't know if that surname exists or if Melville invented it thinking that it sounded Spanish. And the story is a fitting symbol of the inexplicable universe we live in.

FERRARI. Yes, coming back to the book you compiled with Bioy Casares. Among the first texts is an extremely short one that illustrates very well the idea that devotion to God shouldn't have to come from imagining heaven or hell but from God himself.

BORGES. Is it by a Persian mystic?

FERRARI. It's by Attar.

BORGES. Ah, of course, the author of the *Conference of the Birds*, he's the famous Persian Sufi poet, that is, one of the Muslim mystics. As for the word 'Sufi', it has two etymological roots: one which has something to do with wool, because Sufis dress in wool, and another which is much better in any case, which our imagination accepts more readily, which is the idea of 'sophia' or wisdom. So that the Persian word is a corruption of the Greek word, 'sophia'. What's the text?

FERRARI. It's fairly short, it says: 'Lord, if I worship you for fear of Hell, may I burn in Hell. And if I worship you for hope of Heaven, exclude me from Heaven. But if I worship you for yourself, do not deny me your imperishable beauty.'

BORGES. Well, it would be like a version, but a much more lovely one of that famous sonnet

> It is not the heaven that you have promised me,
> my God, that moves me to love You,
> nor does the hell that is so fearful move me
> to cease sinning against You

which Saint Theresa wrote, although it's not by her, no?

FERRARI. It's anonymous.

BORGES. Yes, but then it comes to a sad conclusion, which is the idea that she feels that she loves God simply, well, out of pity for Christ's human suffering, because she says:

> You move me, Lord; it moves me to see you
> nailed on a cross and despised.

It seems extremely sad to feel pity for God at that moment. In his eternity, that episode of the cross and of being a man must have been negligible—it must have been an instant in his eternity. But the idea is a bit like that, no? That is, the idea of rejecting what Shaw called the bribe of heaven and the threat of hell.

FERRARI. Later it says:

> Finally, your love moves me, and in such a way
> that even if there were no heaven I would love you,
> and though there were no hell I would fear you.

BORGES. Yes, it's like another version . . . but I think that the Persian poet put it better.

FERRARI. Yes, it's much more beautiful, yet they both cast light on the same idea.

BORGES. Yes, the idea is the same.

FERRARI. And then we have your own poem, 'Of Heaven and Hell'.

BORGES. Well, yes, I imagine hell or heaven as the image of a face.

FERRARI. Yes.

BORGES. And that face, which is perhaps our own, or perhaps the face of the beloved, as I say, can be terrible or it can be beautiful, according to our mood. But heaven and hell are reduced to a single image.

FERRARI. In the last stanza you say:

> In the clear glass of a dream I have glimpsed
> the promised heaven and hell:
> when Judgement Day sounds in the last
> trumpets and the millenarian planet
> is destroyed and your ephemeral pyramids,
> Oh time, suddenly cease to be . . .

BORGES. Well, that recalls Shakespeare, because Shakespeare talks about time and its pyramids.

FERRARI. It ends:

> The colours and lines of the past will trace
> in the gloom a sleeping, still, faithful, changeless
> face (perhaps the face of the loved one, perhaps your own)
> and the direct contemplation of that face,
> unceasing, whole, beyond corruption
> will, for the damned, be Hell,
> and for the chosen, Heaven.

BORGES. Ah, there I say it, but perhaps too explicitly, no?

FERRARI. Yes, I think one detects Swedenborg's presence.

BORGES. Yes, perhaps it would be a good idea to rewrite that poem and make it a bit more enigmatic. It seems too reasoned.

FERRARI. I don't see it like that—I really like it as it is.

BORGES. Some friends have told me that the poem fails because I've worked too hard on it, or because I was working under a false assumption.

FERRARI. Without wanting to flatter you, I don't see such a failure—I think it's very effective.

BORGES. I don't know, I wrote it so long ago that I'm resigned to it. I'd completely forgotten it, I didn't think that you were going to remind me of it. It was so long ago that nobody talks to me about it any more, and I don't remember it, it's like a revelation that has come this morning.

79

Lucretius

●

OSVALDO FERRARI. When we were discussing the classical Latin authors, Borges, you told me that you couldn't conceive of Lucretius and his *De rerum natura* without the existence of the Greek philosophers.

JORGE LUIS BORGES. Yes, that's obvious. Now, of course Lucretius has been . . . deliberately forgotten, because the fact of his having sung the praises of atheism, of his wanting to free men from the terror of the afterlife, well, that can't earn the approval of believers. However, a notable exception would be Victor Hugo who, in his book *William Shakespeare*, makes a list, a sort of annotated, extremely eloquent, catalogue of great poets. And Virgil is excluded from it, while Lucretius is not. And strangely, that idea of the infinity of the world, that idea of the infinitely vast, of the infinitely small, the idea of infinite space and of infinite worlds which gave Pascal a sense of vertigo, rather excited Lucretius. He greeted all that with enthusiasm. I remember reading Spengler's *The Decline of the West*, he talks about Apollonian culture, the culture of the cavern and Faustian culture, and indicates that it is typical of Faustian culture to be, well, enthusiastic about an infinite world, with infinite possibilities. And all that was already there in Lucretius, long before the author of *Faust* came along, or before that spirit was thought about. But it seems to me that the Germans, when they write . . . every German writer feels obliged to claim that everything he's written was actually there in Goethe's work. So, it's natural to call that form of contemporary culture 'faustian'. Well, now, in that book, Hugo includes Lucretius and quotes a line . . . I don't know if I'm scanning it right: 'Then Venus, in the forests / joined the lovers' bodies.' And one sees how both images intertwine and enhance each other, no?

FERRARI. That's right.

BORGES. Because the forest suggests the idea of trees joining together, and then, the lovers' bodies too. The word 'forests' is already an intermingled word, let's say, no?

FERRARI. Yes. In any case, the result is perfect.

BORGES. The result is perfect, yes. Now, I don't know how the legend came about that Lucretius died mad. There's a poem by Tennyson about that, but perhaps it all arose from the idea that someone who criticized the gods, or criticized religion, had to be punished. That's why that legend came about.

FERRARI. Which is hostile to Lucretius.

BORGES. Yes. He wrote that great poem in which he defends the system of Epicurus. He talks about atoms and, as FitzGerald said, he manages to make poetry from the hardest atoms. And it's true, because it's a philosophical poem, it's an exposition of the philosophical system of materialism according to which the world is made up of an oblique motion of atoms. And Lucretius makes a great poem out of that. And he begins with a hymn to Venus who, of course, represents love. She isn't, let's say, simply, a deity. Rather, one understands that this Venus doesn't obey any mythology other than, well, the fact of love, of the will to continue.

FERRARI. Of union.

BORGES. Yes, of multiplying, all that, yes.

FERRARI. Now, Lucretius expounds a particular materialism.

BORGES. He believes in, let's say, an enthusiastic materialism, in the sense that to become enthusiastic means to be filled with God. Lucretius' materialism is a materialism full of God. It could also be the idea of pantheism. There's a line in Virgil where he refers to pantheism even though the word didn't exist then: *Omnia sunt plena Jovis*, 'All things are full of Jupiter'. It's the same idea. And then, when Lucretius talks about the fear of death—I recall that he believes in the death of the body and the soul also—he says that mortals can think: 'I am going to die and the world will carry on.' And now I come back to Hugo, who laments precisely that in a poem where he says, 'I will go alone, in the middle of the feast.' Now, Lucretius says that's true, that there will be an infinite time after death, that one won't be there in person but that, in the end, why regret that infinite time after death, which won't be ours? Since we don't regret the infinite time that came before our death, which we haven't shared either. And then, he says, 'And where were you during the Trojan War?'

(*Laughs.*) So, if not having been in the Trojan War doesn't bother you, why does it bother you not to be around for later wars, or other circumstances, no?

FERRARI. He believed in the eternity of matter, that's the strange thing.

BORGES. In the eternity of matter, yes.

FERRARI. Unlike the idealism of Virgil, Lucretius' materialism was, although it seems inconceivable, a materialism that involved faith, we could say.

BORGES. A materialism that involved faith, yes, but these things aren't uncommon. . . . My word, we seem to be condemned to talk about Argentine writers. Why condemned? It's only natural that we should talk about Argentine writers (*both laugh*). The example of Almafuerte, for example, who was a mystic without God.

FERRARI. Ah, you're right.

BORGES. Or the example of Carlyle, in England, also an atheist mystic, a mystic without God, or, in any case, without a personal god. Of course, one can be mystical and not believe in the divinity, or believe, let's say, in a general divinity of the spirit, a divinity that's imminent in each man. But not in another god, or another Lord, as in, another person.

FERRARI. So Lucretius proposed living life in the best way possible, and not harbouring hopes about what happens after death, like a good follower of Epicurus.

BORGES. Yes, well, it's what I've tried to do, but I'm sure that I've always acted ethically. In any case, I think so. . . . I could go further and say that to hope for reward or to fear punishment is immoral. If you do good deeds because they will be rewarded, or for fear of being punished, I'm not sure how good your good deeds really are, I'm not sure how ethical they are. I would say that they aren't, that if we fear punishment or wish for reward we're no longer ethical people.

FERRARI. Of course, because then it's a conditional eternity, a conditional immortality . . .

BORGES. Well, talking of conditional eternity, I'm going to come back to Goethe. Goethe believed in the immortality of the soul but not of all souls. He believed that there are certain souls—among which he perhaps included his own—that were worthy of surviving beyond physical death. But not others. That is, according to the life one leads, one can deserve to be, well, immortal, or in any case, to pursue another life after death. If not . . . one is left to fall. Now, how strange that falling from life should be the ideal proposed by Buddha's teachings, since nirvana is to fall from the wheel.

FERRARI. The karmic wheel of incarnations.

BORGES. Yes, and the greatest thing to which man can aspire, according to the 'Smaller Vehicle', according to the original Buddhism, is to fall from the wheel and not be reincarnated.

FERRARI. Of course.

BORGES. And it seems as if Buddhism doesn't require intellectual acceptance. No, it requires something which seems much more difficult, and it's that at the moment one dies, one shouldn't want to carry on . . . that one really should have resolved not to continue.

FERRARI. It implies that determination.

BORGES. Yes, that is, to accept death, well, with open arms, and perhaps with joy also. To accept death.

FERRARI. That helps one to achieve nirvana.

BORGES. Precisely. It seems that the least important part of Buddhism is to accept the doctrine intellectually—what is important is to accept it, let's say, intimately, essentially. Without that acceptance, the other sort is useless. You can think that you're one of Buddha's followers, you can accept all his teachings, but if you don't assimilate them fully, you're condemned to reincarnation. So it has to be a full, a total acceptance. The other sort of acceptance isn't that important.

FERRARI. It's more a matter of spiritual than intellectual acceptance.

BORGES. Yes, spiritual especially.

FERRARI. There's an idealism with which Lucretius clashes, and it is precisely the idealism of Plato . . .

BORGES. Ah, of course. Plato's idealism assumes that there are universal forms.

FERRARI. Yes, and he refutes Plato point by point. And he feels compelled to maintain, for example, that the senses can't be wrong, that the senses are infallible.

BORGES. Yes, which is fallible, of course. Well, according to contemporary science, what we perceive, what our senses perceive, doesn't have anything to do with reality. For example, we see this table, but this table is really a space, there are systems of atoms that are spinning. That is, they don't have anything to do with the visible table, nor with the table you can touch. Reality is something completely distinct from what our senses present to us.

FERRARI (*laughs*). Reality is invisible.

BORGES. It's invisible, it's inaudible (*laughs*), inedible, impalpable . . .

FERRARI. Now, Lucretius went on to say that the sun, the moon and other stars were the same size that we see from the earth. And that's a clear failure of his belief in the infallibility of the senses. He believed that if the senses were mistaken then reason was mistaken.

BORGES. Well, why not? That he was a great poet is beyond question, that he was a bad physicist is less important, no?

FERRARI (*laughs*). Of course.

BORGES. Now, of course for us, although we have some knowledge of astronomy, the sun carries on rising and setting. And we know that's not the case, we know that it's the earth that spins round but for our senses it's the sun that spins. We can talk about the sun rising, about it appearing, about it setting, about it declining, about daybreak. And all that is faithful to our imagination. And what I think Lucretius refutes, somewhere, is the idea of a cyclical history—there's a reference to that, well, to circular time.

FERRARI. To the circular time of the Stoics.

BORGES. Yes, of course. He assumes that the universe carries on but that it's not subject to anybody's will, no? That everything, well, arises from the random clash of atoms.

FERRARI. That's why we were saying that he believed that matter was eternal, that through the permanent forms of atoms it takes progressively different forms.

BORGES. And up until recently people believed that. I think that now there's a belief in entropy. That is, it's assumed that the universe is losing its energy, and that a moment will come when it becomes still, no? So that would be the opposite, or something different from his belief.

FERRARI. How strange, Borges, that the classical Latin writers have brought us to entropy.

BORGES. Indeed.

On France

●

OSVALDO FERRARI. Generally, when we talk about France, Borges, you recall an eminently literary nation, the nation of formal literary tradition, or the nation that epitomizes literature, let's say.

JORGE LUIS BORGES. Yes, and the nation of literary schools. That means that the French, the French writers, want to know exactly what they're doing. That's how a writer steals a march on literary historians—the writer has already classified himself and writes according to that classification. On the other hand, England is a country of individuals. They're individualists, and they're not interested in the history of literature. They don't want to define themselves either, but it seems that they express themselves . . . spontaneously, no? In France . . . they're intelligent, lucid people, they're interested in order, and, more than anything, they believe in the history of literature. They believe in the importance of schools. That's why France is the country of literary manifestos, of groups, of polemics. And all that is relatively rare in other countries. I'll take the example of England because, as Novalis said, 'Each English person is an island.' Each English person is an individual, and not so concerned about the position he or she might occupy in a literary history. That is, a book like Thibaudet's, which discusses French literature, and discusses it well, discusses it in terms of generations. It's a sensible discussion, but in other countries it wouldn't seem sensible. Now, that doesn't mean that France lacks imagination, or invention. It means, rather, that, in general, the writer wants to know what he's doing, that the writer is interested in the theory of his work. But other countries seem to be more interested in the execution of the work or the work's imagination, if you will. That would be another argument in favour of France.

FERRARI. Of course.

BORGES. In favour of reason, of the clarity of the French mind. But that doesn't mean that France is short of, well, rather inexplicable figures: I— don't know how far a writer like Rabelais, or a writer like Rimbaud, who was a symbolist, or a writer like Léon Bloy fit into a tradition. But they would have liked the idea of a literary-historical tradition. I don't believe in literary schools any more. Flaubert stopped believing in them too, because he said, 'Quand un vers est bon, il perd son style', 'When a line is good, it loses its style.' And I think he also said that a good line by Boileau, who represents classical tradition, the tradition of the century of Louis XIV, is as valuable as a good line by Hugo, who is Romantic. But I'd go further: I would say that when a line is good, yes, its school is irrelevant and it doesn't matter who has written it, nor does it matter when it was written. That is, literary historians can't easily appreciate good lines or good passages. And I try to write, let's say, atemporally, although I know I can't really do that, since a writer has no reason to try and be modern as he's inevitably modern. Up until now, nobody, as far as I know, has lived in the past or in the future—each person lives in the present, in his present. And that present is very hard to define precisely because it's so close to us, it's invisible, and so various that it's inexplicable. I don't think that we can understand our present history but, perhaps, well, the twenty-first century—if we accept that rather arbitrary division into centuries—will be able to understand what is happening now. But not us—we have to live and suffer things. And of all that, of course, the present is the most vivid.

FERRARI. Of course, but France is a special case. I recall that when we talked about James Joyce, we said that in *Ulysses*, and in *Finnegans Wake* especially, Joyce attempted to create something like a final judgement on literature . . .

BORGES. And more than anything on the novel, no? Yes, I think that Joyce must have thought that *Ulysses*, and later *Finnegans Wake*, were definitive books. When his book closes, he brings all previous literature to a close in some way. He must have felt that, even though literature carried on after him . . .

FERRARI. But I think there were a lot of French writers and poets who thought like Joyce.

BORGES. The idea of a definitive book?

FERRARI. Yes. Though some of them were 'revolutionary' within a particular style or school, ultimately, as you say, the historical tradition of the academy, of the French schools, ended up incorporating them.

BORGES. Well, but that's precisely how tradition works . . .

FERRARI. In terms of that dialectic?

BORGES. Yes, in terms of that dialectic, or the fact that once something has happened it belongs to history. It amused me that in Italy there's now a futurist museum. Futurism has led to the destruction of museums, the destruction of libraries, like Qin Shi Huang in China. Yet, now, futurism is a museum piece. I don't know if that would have pleased or saddened the founders of futurism—perhaps it would have saddened them. But, of course, as that present wanted to be the future, and all times, including the future, will eventually be past, everything will end up as a historical subject, everything will end up as a museum piece. And what I say to criticize history will also be a historical fact, and will be studied in terms of this period, of these circumstances . . . and doubtless in terms of social, economic and psychological circumstances. It seems that, for now, we're condemned to history. Now, if we could manage to forget history, everything would be different. But I don't know if that would make a difference, since language is a historical phenomenon, that is, we can forget Latin, but what we're speaking, Ferrari, is in some way a dialect of Latin.

FERRARI. Of course . . .

BORGES. So that history reaches us. But some times have less of a historical awareness than others. Now we have developed a strong historical sense, a geographical and political sense as well. But all that can disappear. I hope that it does disappear, or at least abates.

FERRARI. That's why Murena talked about the writer's art of becoming anachronistic, or of countering time.

BORGES. I didn't know that but it's good that idea.

FERRARI. I think so.

BORGES. Well, Bioy Casares and I brought out a secret magazine—there were 200 copies, I think—which was called *Destiempo*, precisely because we didn't want to be contemporary.

FERRARI. It's the same idea.

BORGES. Yes, but by calling it 'untimely' we were already . . . doubtless that title belongs to a particular period. In the same way that futurism now is confused with something as old-fashioned as 'L'art nouveau' and which now seems to us, well, completely obsolete, no? Or like something very old, since it seems that the recent past, that the immediate past, is viewed as more archaic or primitive. One feels that difference particularly sharply.

FERRARI. I think, on the other hand, that you've maintained that literary life is even more conscious in France than in other countries.

BORGES. Yes, and that's why there are schools, and writers write in terms of those schools and that period. And now the idea of a compact between the author and his period is very common, though I don't think that it's necessary. That is, however independent I think I am, however anarchistic, I'm writing in 1985, and I'm using a language that belongs to 1985. So we can't escape our period either.

FERRARI. It's inescapable.

BORGES. It's inescapable, in such a way that there's no point in trying to escape it, no? We're inevitably, incurably modern—we can't be anything else.

FERRARI. France, then, is like the ancient Celtic Ireland we were talking about before, another example of a rigorously organized literary life.

BORGES. Yes, and of extremely conscious people who want to know what they're doing. Even when they're excessive, they know what they're doing. Something more innocent is possible than what happens in France. Perhaps people can be excessive without realizing it, or without aiming to be. On the other hand, while the other countries have chosen a writer to represent them, France's literary life is so rich that there have always been at least two contemporary traditions— they haven't been able to confine themselves to one.

FERRARI. When I think about the nineteenth century in France, I think that your favourite authors would be . . . let me guess: Verlaine for poetry and Flaubert for the novel.

BORGES. Yes, above all, Verlaine for poetry, because . . . perhaps Flaubert was too conscious in his work, no? I don't think he was so inventive. . . . But I don't know what other French novelist we could consider. . . . Now, in Verlaine's case, what interest can the symbolist school have for us? Perhaps it doesn't interest us at all, but Verlaine does. Verlaine himself mocked the symbolists, and he said, 'I don't understand German.' The word 'symbolism' seemed too abstract to him.

FERRARI. And in Flaubert's case, I think that you see the exemplary attitude of the writer to his work.

BORGES. Yes, the idea of literature . . . and, as an act of faith, as something that is exercised, well, that is practised rigorously, with a form of abnegation as well. And perhaps that produces less fortunate results than a writer who lets himself write, who takes pleasure in just writing, who plays around a little with it. And I don't think that Flaubert played with writing. Perhaps he was a priest who was too conscientious to do it well, no? Perhaps he lacked that innocence, which I think is necessary, and which one finds in spite of everything in Verlaine, eh? With Verlaine, one thinks about his fate, one thinks about certain perversions, but that doesn't matter—Verlaine like Oscar Wilde, is a child at play. And here I remember that lovely remark that we've cited more than once, by Robert Louis Stevenson, who said, 'Yes, art is a game, but one has to play it with the seriousness of a child at play.'

FERRARI. Ah, but how wonderful.

BORGES. That is, a child plays seriously, the child doesn't laugh at his game, and that's a good thing, no?

FERRARI. It's a serious game, of course.

BORGES. Yes, it's a serious game, the two ideas come together: the idea of the game, of *homo ludens*, and the idea that every game needs certain rules to exist. Literature also has its rules, although, unlike a game of chess, for example, its rules aren't entirely defined. In literature, everything is so mysterious, it's like a type of magic, I would say, one is playing with words, and those words are primarily two things, or several things: each word is what it means, then what it suggests, and then its sound. These are the three elements that make each word so complex. And then as art, as literature consists of combining those words, there has to be a sort of balance between the three elements: the meaning, the suggestion, the rhythm. Those three essential elements. Doubtless, if this conversation goes on any longer, we'll be able to find others (*both laugh*), since literature is so mysterious. Clearly, rhetoric doesn't exhaust it.

81

Mark Twain, Güiraldes and Kipling

●

OSVALDO FERRARI. You've found similarities, Borges, between three novels that come from writers and places that are completely different from one another. I'm talking about *Huckleberry Finn, Don Segundo Sombra* and *Kim*.

JORGE LUIS BORGES. Of course, they are three links, the framework, let's say. In those three books we find the idea of a society and a world seen through two different viewpoints: the fugitive black man and the boy, and that whole world of the United States before the Civil War. Now, Kipling claimed to be a fervent admirer of Mark Twain and eventually met him—Twain gave him a corn-cob pipe. . . . I don't remember the exact date of *Huckleberry Finn* but I think it's from 1880-something. And then in 1901 *Kim* was published. Kipling wrote that book in England, in the rain, feeling nostalgic about India. And there we have a much richer world than *Huckleberry Finn*, because it deals with the vast world of India, and the two characters, Kim and the lama. Kipling, who was a very reserved man, says that his novel is clearly picaresque, but I don't think so because the two characters, at the end of the book, according to the lama's vision, are saved. Güiraldes had read *Kim* in the French version which, according to Kipling himself was excellent. In his *Don Segundo Sombra*, we also have a world—the world of the Buenos Aires region, the plain that literary types call the pampa, seen through the eyes of those two characters, the old cowboy and the boy (Fabio). It's worth pointing out that they follow the same scheme. But it's hard to imagine three books more different than *Huckleberry Finn* by Mark Twain, than *Kim* by Kipling and *Don Segundo Sombra* by Güiraldes.

FERRARI. That's right.

BORGES. Emerson said that poetry is born of poetry. On the other hand, Whitman criticized 'books distilled from other books', which is a denial of tradition. Emerson's idea seems more accurate to me. Besides, why not suppose that among the many impressions that a poet receives, impressions of other people's poetry play an important, and legitimate, part?

FERRARI. Of course.

BORGES. And one sees this particularly, I think, in Lugones' books, since—as we must have said before—behind each of his books is a tutelary reading. Yet his books are personal. Those readings that I'm talking about were available to everyone, but only Lugones wrote *Strange Forces, Sentimental Calendar* and *Twilight of the Garden*. And behind other books, in the end, are other influences, although I don't think that's an argument against anybody. And, well, as I don't believe in free will, I've come to assume that each of our acts, each of our dreams or each of our daydreams is the work of all prior cosmic history, or, less grandly, of universal history. Doubtless, the words I speak now have been caused by the thousands of inextricable events that precede them. So those antecedents that I find in *Don Segundo Sombra* aren't a criticism of the book. Why not take that genesis for granted? In the same way that every man has parents, grandparents, great-grandparents, why not assume that also happens with books? Rubén Darío said it better: 'Doubtless Homer had his own Homer.' That is, there's no such thing as a truly primordial poetry.

FERRARI. I want to support your assumption, Borges, by noting that Waldo Frank agrees with you, since he saw a relation between *Don Segundo Sombra* and *Huckleberry Finn*.

BORGES. Ah, I didn't know that.

FERRARI. Yes, he notes it in the preface to the English edition of *Don Segundo Sombra*.

BORGES. Well, I don't know that edition, but I'm pleased to have agreed with Waldo Frank. Besides, it means that what I've said is plausible, because if the same thing occurs to two separate people it's likely to be right.

FERRARI. Yes . . .

BORGES. And yet, the fact that the framework is the same doesn't prevent the books from being completely different. Of course, the United States before the Civil War, before 'The War between the States', as they say in the South, which is the world of *Huckleberry Finn*, has nothing to do with that heavily populated and infinite world of India, the world of *Kim*, which in its turn has nothing to do with the elemental Buenos Aires region of *Don Segundo Sombra*.

FERRARI. Now, as for the possible inversion of the relation of authority between age and youth, I remember you saying that an older man can learn from a younger man.

BORGES. My father would say that it's children who educate their parents. In my case I don't think so—my father educated me, I didn't educate him. Perhaps he just said that as a witty remark. But perhaps it also contains some truth, no?

FERRARI. You've made a similar observation about your friendship with Bioy Casares.

BORGES. Ah, yes, of course, in the sense that Bioy has influenced me, and Bioy is younger. One always assumes that the older person influences the younger one. No doubt it's reciprocal.

FERRARI. You attribute to each of the three writers we've discussed a purpose, an intention. At the same time, you always maintain that the most important part of a book is not the purpose that the writer has proposed.

BORGES. Well, in Mark Twain's case, I don't think that he had a pedagogical purpose, no?

FERRARI. No.

BORGES. I think that he simply shows us that world. And there's a feature that's very attractive, and it's strange—that the boy helps the runaway slave. But that doesn't mean that intellectually, that mentally, he's against slavery. Quite the opposite—he feels remorse because he's helped that slave to escape, and that slave is the property of someone in the town. And I don't think that has been noted as one of Twain's ironic traits. It must have been because he thought, 'The boy would have thought that.' He can't have thought that he was acting for the noble cause of the abolition of slavery. That would have been completely absurd. In Kim's case, Kipling's idea is that a man can be saved in many ways, so the lama is saved by the contemplative life and Kim is saved by the discipline that the active life imposes on him, since Kim doesn't see himself as a spy but as a soldier. In the case of *Don Segundo Sombra*, the boy becomes progressively more gauchesque and he learns many things. Enrique Amorim wrote a novel, *The Countryman Aguilar*, which is a response to *Don Segundo Sombra*, where the protagonist becomes progressively more gauchesque and brutalized.

FERRARI. The other possibility.

BORGES. The other possibility, but I think that both are plausible, and both are artistically legitimate.

FERRARI. Of course, but in the case of *Huckleberry Finn* you say that it's a merely happy book, that is, it made me think about the joy of adventure.

BORGES. Yes.

FERRARI. And that seems right, because that delight in adventure occurs in Mark Twain's stories.

BORGES. Yes, and, besides, it's as if the narrative flowed like the Mississippi, no?

FERRARI. Ah, of course.

BORGES. Although I think that there they travel against the current, I'm not sure.

FERRARI. Twain was a pilot on the Mississippi.

BORGES. Yes, so that he must have been attracted to the river. What I don't remember is whether they travel south or north.

FERRARI. Twain seems to have had a varied personal life—as a gold prospector . . .

BORGES. That's right, a gold prospector in California, a pilot on the Mississippi.

FERRARI. A traveller.

BORGES. A traveller in his own country and abroad, because he describes travels in the Pacific in other books. And then, in the end, fate takes him to England, to Germany, he feels a great affection for Germany. I think that he died in 1910. . . . Yes, because he said that he was going to die when Halley's Comet returned. I remember that year was 1910, and that we all felt here that the comet was one of the illuminations to celebrate the centenary of independence. Everybody felt that, although, of course, we didn't say it. We all thought: Since everything is illuminated, it's only right that the sky should be too. I don't know if we got as far as expressing it, or if we realized that it was a ridiculous idea. Nevertheless, Halley's Comet was understood and welcomed in that way here.

FERRARI. In 1910.

BORGES. Yes, and it's the year that Mark Twain dies in the United States. And one of his biographers, Bernard Devoto, says, 'That burning dust of the comet has disappeared from the sky, and the greatness of our literature with it.'

FERRARI. Relating the passage of the comet to Twain's death.

BORGES. Yes, exactly.

82

'Buddha and Personality'

●

OSVALDO FERRARI. Earlier, Borges, we talked about Buddhism, and you demonstrated a thorough, extensive knowledge of that religious philosophy. Recently I discovered that you already possessed that knowledge in 1951 when you wrote 'Buddha and Personality'.

JORGE LUIS BORGES. Yes, I think that, of all the religions, Buddhism is the one that requires least mythology. That is, Hindus, for example, can worship their multiple gods and can also be Buddhists. But one can be a Buddhist and not believe in a personal divinity. And, besides, in the later forms of Buddhism, Mahayana or the Great Vehicle, and Zen Buddhism, one can deny—perhaps one should deny it for patriotic reasons—the historical reality of Buddha. Because it's understood that the important thing is the law. And when Buddha dies, according to the legend, his disciples cry, but he doesn't tell them, like Christ, 'Where two of you gather, I will be the third.' No, he tells them, 'When I am dead, think about the law I have taught.' That shows how important doctrine is for him. I had a long discussion with

Kasuya Sakai, who is a Buddhist, a Japanese Zen Buddhist who got annoyed with me because I believed in the historical reality of Buddha. He disagreed—for him, Buddha hadn't existed, but the law did, and it's the law that matters. And there's the idea that the important thing is, well, the spirit—the spirit and not the letter. I read in a book about Buddhist monasteries that there's one in which, for example, all the disciples are gathered, they're with the teacher, the fire is lit, the hearth and then, the teacher, as he's explaining the doctrine, one by one he takes images of Buddha and throws them into the fire. . . . As for the sacred writings, they are used for various ends, even dishonourable ends, to show how important the spirit is rather than the letter. I know of some Buddhist monks, and some Buddhist saints who are revered in Japan, who have never read the Sutras, Buddha's sermons, but who had reached nirvana through their own meditation, by their own means. That is, they insist above all on the spirit. Buddhism doesn't require any mythology of us—we don't have to believe in a personal god, we can if we want to, and if not, not. But we have to act ethically, that's the important thing.

FERRARI. But he denies personality. For example, he denies Buddha himself.

BORGES. Yes, he denies personality. There are various psychologies in Buddhism, and almost all of them deny the self. I have a book called *The Questions of King Milinda*, which is a sort of Buddhist catechism. Milinda was a king in a particular region of India, who should be called Menander but Menander became Milinda. He goes to a Buddhist monk and asks him questions. And so the book is a long catechism, and it begins with a denial of the self. The example that the monk gives is the carriage in which the king has arrived. He asks him how he has got there, and the king replies that he has got there in a carriage. And the monk replies that if the king has said that it must be true, and then he asks if the carriage is the axle, if it is the seat, if it is the wheels. Then, the king says no, it's all those things together. In the same way one also comes to break down, and eventually to deny the self, or personality.

FERRARI. And to believe in the void.

BORGES. Yes, and to believe in the void.

FERRARI. Now, in that text of yours, 'Buddha and Personality', you talk about . . .

BORGES. I don't remember it, I wrote it so long ago . . .

FERRARI. Well, there you compare Buddha's personality to the personality of Jesus.

BORGES. Ah, I think so. Tell me, is it in *Other Inquisitions*?

FERRARI. No, it's in the issue celebrating twenty years of *Sur*, in 1951. In that essay you said that there had been many attempts to compare the personalities of Buddha and Jesus.

BORGES. Yes, certainly.

FERRARI. But you added that in fact it's a futile exercise.

BORGES. Well, because the Gospels are written . . . of course, one looks for conviction, but one looks to be moved as well. The example of Buddha is quite different, as is the example of Socrates. They look to teach a law, or laws that can lead to a state of calm. To a certain extent, it's the opposite of something that aims to move.

FERRARI. In Buddhism, then, there's a metaphysics and an ethics.

BORGES. A metaphysics and an ethics. That happens with Confucius as well. When one reads Confucius' *Analects*, at the beginning one is a little disappointed because there are no moving passages. But that's because Confucius doesn't want to convey anything moving—he wants to convey something reasonable. So the book's style is reasonable as well. On the other hand, the style of the Gospels is, well, a splendid drama, of course.

FERRARI. In that same essay, Borges, you contrast Buddhist ethics with aspects of Western ethics, and you cite a letter by Julius Caesar and a magnificent passage from that letter which talks about his political opponents, who he frees although there's a danger they will return to oppose him once again, Caesar says, 'I do it because I only wish to be as I am, and for them to be as they are.'

BORGES. Yes, now I'm not sure if that's the historical Caesar or the Caesar in Shaw's comedy *Caesar and Cleopatra*.

FERRARI. The literary Caesar.

BORGES. Yes, well, let's say Caesar, and we're safe then, eh? I'm not sure if that features in Seutonius, I think not. It doesn't matter, Caesar is now an image that we can enhance—why not, if he's been enhanced by Shaw. . . . Perhaps Plutarch enhanced him as well.

FERRARI. Caesar's remark is magnificent, but it betrays the Western obsession with personality, which is distinct from Buddhism.

BORGES. Yes, because in Buddhism, personality is considered erroneous. To such an extent that they deny the historical personality of Buddha.

Because that would also be a form of egoism, no? I mean, in the etymological sense of the term.

FERRARI. Of course, you also indicated in that essay that the Western novel prefers 'the flavour of souls', in Proust and in other novelists. And in Buddhism the negation of that flavour of souls, of that individuality of souls.

BORGES. Yes, I think that the novel leads readers to vanity and egoism. Novels talk about a single person and the features that distinguish them from other people, which encourages the reader to try and be a specific person and to have features that distinguish them from other people. So that reading a novel indirectly promotes egoism and vanity and trying to be interesting. Which is what happens with all young people. When I was young, I was purposefully unhappy, because I wanted to be, well, Hamlet, or Byron, or Poe, or Baudelaire, or a character in a Russian novel. On the other hand, now I try to seek calm, and not think about the personality, well, of a writer called Borges, who lived, let's say, in the twentieth century (*laughs*), although he was born in the nineteenth. I try to forget those pedantic circumstances, no? I try to live calmly, forgetting that character who is my companion.

FERRARI. Yet through your knowledge of Buddhism, Borges, we see that the path of literature is different from scientific knowledge, although it can lead to wisdom.

BORGES. I don't know if I've achieved wisdom, but to believe in wisdom is already an act of faith, of course. Besides—perhaps I've said this many times—one can create something that one doesn't possess.

For example, a person can create happiness but not feel happy, they can create fear but not be frightened. And one can offer wisdom but not possess it. Everything in the world is so mysterious.

FERRARI. Not personally to reach nirvana while everybody else reaches it.

BORGES. Yes, it's as if we were a conduit through which things happen, no? As if we were a medium through which things occur. In the case of poetry that would be especially true, perhaps, since poetry uses us—we allow poetry to pass through us, in spite of ourselves, and then we cause the reader to feel it. But it isn't something we invent—aesthetic emotion is something that happens to us, and which then happens to the reader, although perhaps in a quite different way.

FERRARI. In that sense, one could think that poetry is an extremely close relation to mysticism.

BORGES. Yes, it would be hard to find much difference between them. Of course, the rhetoricians find a difference—they reduce poetry to a series of techniques.

FERRARI. Indeed.

BORGES. And perhaps we will have to resign ourselves to those techniques for poetry to visit us. But, in the end, they're mere contrivances.

FERRARI. However, the existence of many mystical poets demonstrates that the two aren't alien to each other.

BORGES. Ah no, of course, the existence of Blake or of Angelus Silesius . . .

FERRARI. Or of St John of the Cross.

BORGES. Or of St John of the Cross would suffice. Strictly speaking, logically speaking, a single example is enough.

FERRARI. Of course.

BORGES. Perhaps it's a mistake to provide more examples, because then things seem less certain. In the same way that many proofs for the existence of God are a proof that there is no God, since so many different proofs are used.

FERRARI. Well, before theology came along they didn't produce those proofs, it's theology that introduces doubt.

BORGES. Yes.

FERRARI. Very well, Borges, we will perhaps return to Buddhism a third time, because we see that your knowledge of it is not exhausted.

BORGES. I've talked little about Buddhism and a lot about other things, but perhaps it's better that way.

83

Irish Literature

●

OSVALDO FERRARI. A short while ago, Borges, we talked about the past, about Ireland's Celtic past, and we proposed then to talk again about the great riches of Irish literature over time.

JORGE LUIS BORGES. Yes, they're riches that seem to contradict any statistics—a poor island, stranded in the north-west of Europe, but which seems to have specialized in men of genius, and which has enriched English literature, since English literature is inconceivable without all those unforgettable Irish writers.

FERRARI. That's right.

BORGES. Now, strangely, it's an old tradition—I think that it's the ninth century when we have that great figure, Scotus Eriugena, which means 'Irishman born in Scotland'. They called Ireland 'Scotia', and Scotland is the name that the Irish brought over there. Reading histories of philosophy, including scholastic philosophy, which certainly has a very rich history and extremely varied thinkers, I realized that Scotus Eriugena is unique because he's a pantheist. The manuscripts attributed to the *Aereopagiticus* had come to France, but there was nobody who could read them. And then this monk from Ireland comes along . . . in Ireland, they'd preserved the knowledge of Greek. I'm not sure if it was the Saxons or the Scandinavians who invaded them. In any case, the Irish monks had to flee their monasteries . . . those monasteries were distinctive, each monk was alone in his hut, with ditches in cultivated patches of garden to hold off the barbarians. One of the monks who managed to escape was Johannes Scotus Eriugena. He was called Charles the Bald, and he translated the text of the *Aereopagiticus* from the Greek. Nobody else knew Greek or Latin. And then he wrote his philosophy, which is a pantheist philosophy. Oddly, there's a poem by Hugo, 'Ce que dit la bouche d'ombre', which corresponds exactly to the philosophy of Scotus Eriugena. And that philosophy can also be found in *Back to Methuselah* by another Irishman, although he may not have read Scotus Eriugena—George Bernard Shaw. The idea is that all things flow from the divinity, and that, at the end of history all things will return. And that allows Hugo to create a splendid passage in which he imagines every type of monster, of black dragons, whatever, and among them the devil. And they all return to the divinity. That is, the divinity becomes reconciled with all his creation, even his monsters.

FERRARI. Even with the evil creations.

BORGES. Yes. After Scotus Eriugena, much later, we have another incredible Irish writer—Jonathan Swift, to whom we owe *Gulliver's Travels*, among them that terrible voyage, the voyage to the Yahoos, men who end up like monkeys and those other people, whose name mimics the neighing of a horse and who make up a republic of rational horses. There are other names later on, among them, surprisingly, the Duke of Wellington, Arthur Wellesley, who defeats Napoleon, and who was Irish. And I've forgotten, perhaps, someone who is certainly no lesser a figure, the philosopher Berkeley. Berkeley who first develops idealism and was an important influence on Hume. Well, Hume was Scottish, and they were both an influence on Schopenhauer. There are so many illustrious Irish writers that one doesn't know where to start. Perhaps the greatest poet of the English language in our time, William Butler Yeats. There's also a writer who is unjustly neglected, George Moore, who began by writing very silly books but ended up writing wonderful books in a new type of prose, books of secrets, of secrets about unreal things, about things that he'd dreamt up but which are told as if the author were confiding in the reader. And there's another name who, in spite of the sadness or perhaps the notoriety of his fate, we think about him perhaps as an intimate friend, or like a child as well—Oscar Wilde, of course. And why not mention another Irishman, who has created two characters that are perhaps the most famous anywhere—the creator of Sherlock Holmes and Doctor Watson, Arthur Conan Doyle. Doubtless, you'll be able to add your own names.

FERRARI. Yes, but I would like to pause on the inevitable name of Shaw.

BORGES. But, of course, Shaw, who in *Back to Methuselah* repeats exactly the universal history of Scotus Eriugena—the idea that all things, all beings, flow from the divinity and return in the end to the divinity. And Scotus Eriugena thought all that up in the ninth century and he ends up giving Shaw a dramatic and extremely entertaining form for that work.

FERRARI. Now, Swift, Shaw and Wilde show us shows that Ireland has produced a particular type of genius, the humorous, the ironic, the satirical genius. And we could say critical genius as well, critical, in part, of England.

BORGES. Ah yes, yes, of course. And we haven't mentioned Goldsmith, we haven't mentioned Sheridan, well, we haven't mentioned the poets of the 'Celtic twilight'. Yeats was a part of that group at first but then, fortunately, he emerged from that twilight and wrote what were perhaps the most poetic and most precise works. And I don't know how we've managed to forget him, really it's a colossal oversight—we haven't mentioned the author of *Ulysses* and *Finnegans Wake*, who was also Irish.

FERRARI. Who we were talking about recently, James Joyce.

BORGES. Yes, we haven't mentioned Joyce. And we could also include the admirable and strange dramatist O'Neill. Since his family was Irish. When one tries to make a list of Irish geniuses, one quickly gets lost and becomes guilty of unforgivable omissions.

FERRARI. We haven't talked before about the writer you say is perhaps the greatest contemporary poet in the English language, Yeats.

BORGES. Well, what Yeats did with the English language is more admirable than what Joyce did, since Joyce's writings are rather like museum pieces, no? On the other hand, the poetry of Yeats is different, it's something that astounds us, like Hugo's poetry, for example.

It's extraordinary. I always remember that untranslatable, senseless line that works its magic all the same: 'That dolphin-torn, that gong-tormented sea.' How strange—the sea torn by dolphins and tormented by gongs. I don't know if it can be justified logically but it's clearly a magical combination. And one finds so many of these combinations, and such unforgettable lines, in Yeats. I remember the end of one of his plays where one of the characters is a swineherd who sees some splendid women slowly descending the stairs. And he asks what they are there for, and they tell him, 'For desecration and the lover's night,' that is, they are there for profanation, for the night of the lover. They are the last words. It's wonderful, no?

FERRARI. Wonderful. For my part, I've chosen a passage that you had come across before, in Shaw.

BORGES. Which one?

FERRARI. 'Hell, heaven and earth.' It's very short and I think it's exceptional. I don't know if you remember it, I'm going to read it.

BORGES. Yes, I'm listening, thank you very much.

FERRARI. 'Hell is the home of the unreal and of the seekers for happiness . . . '

BORGES. My word.

FERRARI. 'It is the only refuge from heaven, which is, as I tell you, the home of the masters of reality and from earth, which is the home of the slaves of reality.'

BORGES. It's splendid, eh? And all of theology is there.

FERRARI. And I think that it coincides with your own vision.

BORGES. Well, my vision coincides with Shaw's, more like, and more like what I say, what I've thought . . .

FERRARI. I'm talking about your conception of reality.

BORGES. I think it's dangerous to think without an awareness of Shaw, no? It's imprudent (*both laugh*). For me to think without Shaw and without Schopenhauer is impossible. I remember a remark by Macedonio Fernández, who said that, whatever he thought, Berkeley and Schopenhauer had already thought for him (*laughs*).

FERRARI. I see that Shaw has been a companion in your thinking.

BORGES. Yes, I hope that he carries on being so.

84

Góngora

●

OSVALDO FERRARI. Recently you told me, Borges, that you had been writing a poem about Góngora.

JORGE LUIS BORGES. A second poem. Before I wrote one that begins, 'Mars is war, Phoebus the sun, Neptune the sea / my eyes can no longer see / because the god erases the world.' That is, I thought that the Greek gods, who Góngora didn't believe in, well, in this case they had obscured his sight, they had eclipsed his vision of things so that instead of war he saw Mars, instead of the sun he saw Phoebus, instead of the sea, Neptune.

FERRARI. He saw mythologically.

BORGES. He saw mythologically and through a mythology that was dead for him. So, I imagined that poem, but then, on reflection, I thought that it was unfair, that another poem could be written in which Góngora responded to me and told me that to refer to the sea, to something as various, as vast, as inexhaustible as the sea, is no less mythological than to refer to Neptune. And as for war—we know that all wars are terrible, but the word 'war' is already perhaps no less mythological than 'Mars.' And as for the sun—'Phoebus', of course, is and isn't the sun. So we could conclude that all languages are as arbitrary as that precious style of *culteranismo* which refers to Phoebus rather than the sun. And even when Góngora refers to Phoebus, to Mars and to Neptune, he recognizes that there's something sacred in those things, and perhaps in all things. Since if I say Phoebus, I imply that there's something sacred about the sun. And if I say Mars, I imply something at least sacred and inexplicable about war. That is, I thought that every word, or that a complete language, can be described as mythological, since they limit the world, the world which is constantly changing, to a series of fixed words. Now, that could lead us to an idea, well, to an impossible mission, which is, if each moment is new, if what I perceive now, talking to you, isn't precisely what I've perceived at other times, then I would have to find a language that was constantly renewing itself. If not, we're limited to, let's say, the 10,000 symbols, to the 10 symbols, or whatever, of each language. Of course, I don't know how one could create this language . . . it's an impossible project.

FERRARI. With the help . . .

BORGES. Except that a language that was constantly renewing itself could be made up of compound words, well, combining adjectives, as Japanese does, or declining verbs. But that wouldn't be enough either—we would always have to use some symbols that had been used before.

FERRARI. Except that here we also draw on the help of mythology.

BORGES. Ah, yes, but one would have to create a mythology for each moment.

FERRARI. Of course.

BORGES. But we could imagine a utopia, a utopia that will never be realized, of the imagination: Why not depict a world in which language is constantly growing and changing? And there perhaps one would have to think less about the meaning of words than about their cadence—it would be a language close to music. In any case, it's an impossible literary project, but it's not impossible for there to be a school that proposes it (*laughs*), since new literary schools seem to be appearing all the time, no? Yes, and they try to do all sorts of things. Of course, that adventure would be the greatest adventure of language or of literature—a language that grew and changed in response to the passage of reality. Now, that happens over long periods of time. For example, there are words that were used when I was small that are not used now. But no, what I would suggest would be a language that was changing every instant—not every 50 years. That words change is beyond question, and particularly the atmosphere of words. And that's very important for poetry, that is, it's not just the meaning that changes, that's the least of it, but also the connotation.

FERRARI. The project you propose seems more of a possibility for poetry than for language in general.

BORGES. For poetry . . . and I would say for music (since I don't know anything about music, I see it as fertile, as endowed with infinite possibilities). That motto of the Spanish Real Academia: 'It is fixed, clean and spreads light,' well, the idea that it implies of fixing language is impossible. And yet, Doctor Johnson, in the eighteenth century, believed that the time had come when the English language could be fixed. And now we realize that the language of Doctor Johnson is admirable but antiquated. Poetry depends, above all, on connotation, on the atmosphere and rhythm of words.

FERRARI. Without doubt.

BORGES. That's why Stevenson said that one should never use a distracting word.

FERRARI. That's clear.

BORGES. Of course, that means it has to flow, because, for example, neologisms get in the way. Except in German which is accustomed to compound words. I think that we talked once about *Weltanschauung*, which Ortega y Gasset translated extremely clumsily as 'cosmovisión'. Compound words are rare in Spanish, and 'cosmovisión', in particular, is extremely conspicuous. The first part is Greek and the second Latin. On the other hand, in German, both words are Germanic. German is accustomed to compound words—someone says *Weltanschauung* and the listener doesn't realize that it's the first time they've heard the word.

FERRARI. Coming back to Góngora's poetry, Pedro Henríquez Ureña claims that he's the great example of devotion to form, yet . . .

BORGES. That's true. Yet, Gongora's best poems aren't the most precious ones, or the most 'Gongorine'. For example, I remember that: 'The hours will hardly forgive you, / those hours that are wearing down the days / those days that are gnawing at the years'. They could have been Quevedo's best lines if Góngora hadn't written them first. If someone didn't know anything about Quevedo, and one wanted to let them know what he was like, the best thing would be to recite those lines by Góngora. Because by knowing, by hearing those lines, he would have the essence of Quevedo. And Góngora later risked jokes that aren't always successful, no? I think that we've recalled that one, 'monocled gallant of Galatea' which refers to the cyclops. Now, Góngora couldn't foresee that there would be a type of glasses called a monocle—he was thinking about the Monoculos, the race of imaginary beings mentioned by Pliny, I think. So that 'monoculo' meant, strictly, a person with one eye.

FERRARI. Yes, a cyclops.

BORGES. Of course, it applies specifically to the cyclops, to Polyphemus. Then comes that sort of unfortunate pun, 'gallant of Galatea'. I've discussed with Bioy Casares 'Oh great river, great Andalusian king of noble though not golden sands!' which seemed a lapse of Góngora's to me. But Bioy told me that it was precisely that idea of one thing rather than another that he liked about Góngora.

FERRARI. You're talking about the poem 'To Córdoba'.

BORGES. Yes, exactly.

FERRARI. Henríquez Ureña adds that the greatness of Góngora's poetry resides not in its subjects, and only rarely in its feelings, but in its delicacy, the splendour of what he calls his pictorial imagination.

BORGES. Well, I don't know to what extent it's pictorial, because, in the end, what do we have: the contrast between red and white. For example, 'Shine, gold sun, adorn and colour / the luxuriant peak of the high mountain, follow with delightful gentleness / the rosy passing of the white dawn.' He liked those fairly simple contrasts between colours. But, in poetry, perhaps those colours are more obvious if one sees them . . .

FERRARI. In a painting.

BORGES. Yes, that's why I say that pictorial character refers more to language. Because in fact, if one put red and white in a painting, it would seem too simple, no?

FERRARI. Obviously, now, Remy de Gourmont, for his part, called Góngora 'that great aesthetic malefactor'.

BORGES. Ah, I think he was right.

FERRARI. And he compared him to Mallarmé.

BORGES. Well, perhaps Mallarmé's best lines are superior to Góngora's best lines.

FERRARI. You will recall, perhaps, that in his time Góngora was criticized by Lope and Quevedo but in his turn he called Lope de Vega 'Vega because he is always flat.'

BORGES. Yes, 'Rightly Vega, because he is always flat.' I remember that, and he called him 'Duck of the wishy-washy Castilian water'. That's not so pleasant, but then it isn't meant to be insulting.

FERRARI. On the other hand, he said about Quevedo that he had 'lines of a low tone, sad the colours'.

BORGES. How strange, I talked about that with Henríquez Ureña. Yes, because we were talking about how far what we feel in response to a poem from the seventeenth century was felt by the author. And he told me that what we feel is what they felt. But I think not—I think that as time goes by language changes, and one feels things in a different way. And what the author felt matters little, since texts are there to be renewed by each reader, no? Journalists are always asking me what my writing means. Yesterday I was asked, for example, what the message was of the poem 'The Golem' and the story 'The Circular Ruins'. And I told them that there's absolutely no message, that they simply occurred to me, that I had, well, amused myself with that imagining, and that I'd recounted it to the reader so that he could feel the same thing. If I say 'story', I think about something imaginary. But now it's the moral of the story that people think about. One assumes that every story has a moral, and that the author knows what it is. I think that we've already mentioned that Kipling said that an author can be allowed to imagine a story but not know what its moral is, and that the moral must be produced by the reader or by time, let's say.

FERRARI. Of course, one doesn't realize that the author, or the creator, acts without preconceptions, without plans, that he allows himself to be carried by his inspiration.

BORGES. I think that plans are dangerous, that is, it's better to write with a certain innocence. And above all, it's better for the reader to think that what they are being told, or what they are hearing is, well, something that arose of its own accord, and that it hasn't been directed. It's better for things not to seem prefabricated.

FERRARI. That they have the spontaneity of creation, of course.

BORGES. Yes, I think that Schopenhauer talked about writers who write without having thought, and he said that it was better to think first and then write. In that case, I venture, with all humility, to disagree with Schopenhauer. I think it's better for both processes, writing and thinking, to be simultaneous, that is, that as one writes, one thinks.

85

The Poets of New England

•

OSVALDO FERRARI. Some time ago, Borges, we talked about what I think is your favourite part of the United States, about New England. And we also talked about the particular things that have happened in that region which has produced excellent poets.

JORGE LUIS BORGES. Yes, there's a book by Van Wyck Brooks, *The Flowering of New England*, which refers precisely to that long period in which men of genius, and an extremely diverse genius, suddenly arise, and they're almost neighbours. Take Edgar Allan Poe, who is born in Boston, take Emily Dickinson, devoting her whole life to poetry and declaring that publication is not an essential part of the poet's fate, take Herman Melville and that splendid nightmare, *Moby Dick: or The White Whale*, and take Ralph Waldo Emerson, who corresponded with all of them, and who for me is the greatest of the intellectual poets, since, unlike other intellectual poets, he had a lot of ideas. There are others who are called intellectual but they are

simply cold, or ineffectual. Then Jonathan Edwards, who came earlier and who learnt to feel predestination as something joyful, who
said that at first the idea that everyone was already predestined to
hell or heaven seemed terrible, because one softened it by saying, no,
that there were people who were predestined to heaven, but the fact
is that the people who weren't predestined to heaven were going
to hell, so it amounts to the same thing. And then Longfellow and
Prescott, and Frost, who is the most famous poet of that region,
although he was born in California. . . . Then there's a name without
which the literature of the whole world—in any case, the literature
of the West—is inconceivable, and that's Edgar Allan Poe. He's the
father of so many things . . . even the detective genre which he creates
unwittingly in those three stories: 'The Murders in the Rue Morgue',
'The Purloined Letter' and 'The Gold-Bug'. There is the detective
genre in essence.

FERRARI. Indeed.

BORGES. He also influenced Baudelaire—Baudelaire prayed to Poe
every night.

FERRARI. Ah, I didn't know that.

BORGES. Yes, Baudelaire's translation of Poe's work is, of course, superior to Poe's text, since Baudelaire had a finer artistic sense than Poe
. . . and Poe, as a poet, is a minor poet, although he was, of course,
a man of genius.

FERRARI. Yet he was a better short-story writer.

BORGES. Yes, of course.

FERRARI. But we also find poets like Robert Lowell in that region, among the contemporaries.

BORGES. Yes, that's right, he also belongs to a family of writers.

FERRARI. Yes, among them Amy Lowell, I think.

BORGES. Yes, of course, I met him.

FERRARI. Robert Lowell?

BORGES. Yes, when he was here, in Buenos Aires. My word, I don't know if . . . perhaps it would be indiscreet to recall this . . . he was at a gathering, talking away, and some people came from the US embassy and took him off to an asylum. How sad to be there like that, talking, feeling safe, and then two people appear, silent but inescapable . . . and take him away. But let's forget that. I was with him in England and no doubt he'd forgotten that episode, and I forgot it too.

FERRARI. Of course.

BORGES. At least while we were together.

FERRARI. I see. Now, among the New England poets you seem to prefer Frost.

BORGES. Yes, I think that one has to view Frost as a follower of the English poet, Browning. In any case, I think that Frost emerges from Browning's work, from Browning's poetic habits.

FERRARI. Frost's themes are, to a large extent, rural themes.

BORGES. They're rural, yes. Well, he was a farmer.

FERRARI. Of course. I don't know if they fall within the boundaries of New England but we also find remarkable poets in the United States, like Wallace Stevens.

BORGES. I don't know where he was from precisely.

FERRARI. Me neither.

BORGES. We'll have to guess (*both laugh*).

FERRARI. And also Edgar Lee Masters and his book of epitaphs, *The Spoon River Anthology.*

BORGES. Edgar Lee Masters must be from the Middle West, of course, and I don't know about Spoon River. In any case, one thinks of that region, yes, and the references to Lincoln in that book, for example . . . a splendid epitaph. Now he wanted his anthology to be read as a novel, since there are relationships between the people who are the subjects of the epitaphs, but I don't know if the reader can follow that. For example, one of the dead people speaks, and he says that he hasn't been very happy but that he could always count on, find support in, the affection of his wife. And then when she speaks, it turns out that she couldn't stand him and that she had a lover. That is, all those epitaphs amount to a sort of chronicle of the Spoon River area, but I don't know if readers realize that. I think they read each epitaph as if it were an individual poem. In the second number of *Sur*, I translated two of Edgar Lee Masters' epitaphs from the *Spoon River Anthology.*

FERRARI. Those epitaphs are so remarkable that, if you'll allow me, I'd like to read one now that has particularly impressed me.

BORGES. But of course.

FERRARI. It's the one in which Horace Burleson speaks.

BORGES. I remember the one about that woman who Lincoln loved, who says, 'Beloved in life of Abraham Lincoln, / Wedded to him, not through union, / But through separation.' How lovely, eh? And then she says, 'Bloom for ever, O Republic, / From the dust of my bosom!'

FERRARI. Well, it has remarkable qualities.

BORGES. Which is the one that you recalled?

FERRARI. As I said, it's John Horace Burleson's epitaph, and it goes:

> I won the prize essay at school
> Here in the village,
> And published a novel before I was twenty-five.
> I went to the city for themes and to enrich my art;
> There married the banker's daughter,
> And later became president of the bank—
> Always looking forward to some leisure
> To write an epic novel of the war.
> Meanwhile friend of the great, and lover of letters,
> And host to Matthew Arnold and to Emerson.
> An after dinner speaker, writing essays
> For local clubs. At last brought here—
> My boyhood home, you know—
> Not even a little tablet in Chicago
> To keep my name alive.
> How great it is to write the single line:
> 'Roll on, thou deep and dark blue Ocean, roll!'

BORGES. And of course, that character is like a character in a novel, no?

FERRARI. Like an everyday character from the town.

BORGES. Yes, that's very good, because one can read a whole life in those lines, no?

FERRARI. Exactly.

BORGES. And the man's character.

FERRARI. That's right, it's all there.

BORGES. And the contrasts. Besides, it's written with a certain irony as well, of the poet towards his creation.

FERRARI. With great irony: 'epic novel of the war' (*laughs*).

BORGES. Yes (*laughs*).

FERRARI. Another of the names, but I don't know if he's one of your favourites, is William Carlos Williams.

BORGES. Ah, yes, of course.

FERRARI. Well, there's a whole host of poets, but, naturally, we'll always come back to Whitman.

BORGES. And in my case, Emerson.

FERRARI. Emerson, even as a poet?

BORGES. As a poet, I'd say for me as a poet more than anything. I prefer—I know that this is a personal fancy—but I prefer his poetry to his prose. His poetry seems more essential to me. Besides, it's profoundly original, but spontaneously original, not scandalously original, it's spontaneously different from everything that's called poetry. Yet one doesn't sense any rebellion. It's as if he naturally expressed himself in that cold way, in that reserved way, because reserve can also be a poetic virtue. One always assumes that it isn't, that the poet must be effusive and confessional . . . but reserve makes up a great part of the character of many people. And if a poet writes in a reserved way, he is expressing himself, he's expressing that reserve which is one of his aims or one of his characteristics.

FERRARI. Of course, and in this case, of a man, of a poet capable of thinking, as you say, capable of ideas.

BORGES. And of original, and very interesting ideas, and his poetry has something of the engraving . . . of sculpture about it, no? It seems ridiculous, but it has something in common with Seneca in its pithiness. Although, of course, what they both imagined was completely different.

FERRARI. We must also recall, I think, although he left the United States, and lived for so long in Europe . . .

BORGES. Henry James?

FERRARI. No, Ezra Pound, who also devoted an energy to the study of poetry that few have equalled, no?

BORGES. Yes, in the case of Henry James, he felt, let's say, not only the affinities but also the contrast between the American and the European—that was his subject. Now, he believed that the Europeans were, of course, more complex, more intelligent, but ethically inferior to the Americans. He discovered something ethical in the American which, I don't know . . . possibly he was thinking above all about that region, no?

FERRARI. About New England?

BORGES. Yes, at a time when Protestantism was still strong. Now, I think that it isn't, eh? Of course, that country has changed so much. Well, the world has changed so much . . .

86

On Metaphor

●

OSVALDO FERRARI. I'm interested in the way that your ideas about literary metaphor differ from other writers, Borges.

JORGE LUIS BORGES. Yes, I began, let's say, by proclaiming the cult of metaphor that Leopoldo Lugones had taught us. How strange, all of that generation that was called Ultraist criticized Lugones, and yet Lugones was always a presence for us. I remember, when I was with González Lanuza, with my cousin Guillermo Juan, with Norah Lange, we couldn't look at a sunset without reciting, 'And the eternal sun dies like a tiger'. And the moon would lead us to continual allusions to *Sentimental Calendar*. And we all proclaimed that aesthetic, the aesthetic of metaphor. Now, Lugones points out in the prologue to *Sentimental Calendar* that language is made up of metaphors, since every abstract word is a metaphor. Starting with the word 'metaphor', which means, if I'm not mistaken, 'transference' in Greek.

FERRARI. Of course.

BORGES. Similarly, Emerson said that language is fossil poetry. But we should say that, in order to understand one another, it helps to forget the etymology of words. Ortega y Gasset said that in order to understand something, one had to understand its etymology, but I would say, rather, that in order to understand one another, it's better to forget the etymology of words. An example of this would be the word 'style'. A stylus was a small tool that was used in ancient times to write, in wax I think. But if I talk now about baroque style, it isn't helpful to think about that small tool, or that baroque is one of the names for a syllogism. Because if I think: A tool comparable to a syllogism, I'm clearly departing from the concept of style.

FERRARI. Of course.

BORGES. So that in order to understand one another, we have to forget the metaphorical origins of words.

FERRARI. Now, in the case of the Latin etymology of 'metaphor', you will recall: *meta-fero* ('beyond the intention'). That's important because, as Murena observes, to take something beyond intention would imply that one is going beyond the purpose of the person who is trying to do the thing . . .

BORGES. That would be right then, since I think that, if what one writes expresses exactly what one wants it to, it loses its value—it's better to go beyond that. And it's what happens with every book from the past—one reads it beyond its intention. And literature consists, anyway, not of writing exactly what one proposes but of writing, mysteriously or prophetically, beyond whatever one's intention happens to be.

FERRARI. When one talks about metaphor, one inevitably thinks of Plato. In *The Symposium*, Alcibiades says, I am going to praise Socrates using similes because the aim of the simile is truth.

BORGES. Well, I completely agree with Alcibiades. Besides, we can't express ourselves any other way. On the other hand, what one says indirectly is more powerful than what one says directly. I don't know if we've talked about this before, but if I say 'So-and-So died,' I'm saying something concrete. But if I use a biblical metaphor and say 'So-and-So sleeps with his fathers,' it's more effective.

FERRARI. Much more effective.

BORGES. Besides, it points indirectly to the idea that all people die and return to their fathers. Or, as they say less attractively in English, 'Join the majority.' And as there are more dead than living people, it means that someone has died, since the living are a minority, and a provisional minority.

FERRARI. Of course.

BORGES. At some stage we'll join the majority, the dead.

FERRARI. We'll have company (*laughs*).

BORGES (*laughs*). We'll have a lot of company, yes.

FERRARI. You've said that perhaps a single line of verse without metaphor would be enough to refute the theory that metaphor is an essential element of literature.

BORGES. Yes, I must have been talking about Japanese literature which isn't concerned with metaphor, and where it would perhaps be easy to find examples of lines that don't include any metaphors. Unless one thinks that every word is a metaphor. But I think not, let's say, if one hears or if one uses the phrase 'the *via lactea*', it's better not to think about a milky way, I think. Fritz Mauthner points out that the Chinese call the *via lactea* 'the silver river' and says that, to us, it seems poetic. Just as, doubtless, to a Chinese person, it will seem poetic to talk about the *via lactea*, about the milky way for the galaxy. Galaxy, the Greek word for *via lactea*.

FERRARI. In Greece, as I think you've recalled, Aristotle bases metaphor on things, and not on language.

BORGES. I think he says that someone who can perceive resemblances can create their own metaphors. Someone who perceives resemblances which aren't immediately apparent. And metaphor would consist of expressing the secret connections between things.

FERRARI. Of course, you sometimes mention metaphors gathered by Snorri Sturluson from Icelandic poetry.

BORGES. Ah, yes, but those metaphors were what we would now call functional, that is, they don't involve poetic intuition—they were rational, perhaps overly rational. Because if I say of a warrior that he is 'the helmet post', that metaphor is fairly unremarkable—it has no beauty, don't you think?

FERRARI. No, not in 'the helmet post', no.

BORGES. Perhaps the mistake of the ancient Germanic—Saxon or Scandinavian—metaphors is that they were reasonable.

FERRARI. They're less poetic.

BORGES. They're less poetic. Now, of course, in the case of 'whale's way' for the sea.

FERRARI. That isn't bad.

BORGES. No, I think that there's beauty there, but I don't know if they realized that, possibly not. Of course, 'whale's way' is good for the sea, because the vastness of the whale seems to match the vastness of the sea. In Anglo-Saxon poetry, the metaphor 'meeting of spears' for battle is fairly unremarkable. I think there's an essential difference between Germanic metaphors which make rational sense and, let's say, Oriental, Persian or Arabic metaphors which have an emotional justification. For example, when one compares a prince or a princess to the moon, one is clearly not thinking about the moon's shape— one is thinking about the brightness or the poetry of the moon, no?

FERRARI. About its radiance.

BORGES. About its radiance. And I think that it's more effective, and that's how things are justified. Because if I call the sun 'day's eye', I don't know if it's more beautiful. That metaphor gives us the English daisy, because when one draws a daisy it looks like a sun, that is, it looks like the 'day's eye'. And then an expression that I've come across, I think that the Kabbalists use it: 'left eye of heaven'. The left eye of heaven is the moon. I suppose that the right eye would be the sun, or it would be because the word 'left' in some way denotes a certain inferiority, or perhaps something base. . . . Well, the word 'sinister' means left, yes.

FERRARI. Well, it's strange that, in spite of your poetic temperament, which seems to associate you naturally with metaphor, you haven't agreed with Lugones or with Ultraism in your assessment.

BORGES. I don't know if Lugones was always faithful to that idea. Lugones knew that the rhythm, that the music of language is very important—he must have known that. I don't know if I've quoted those lines from Lugones: 'The garden with its intimate retreats / will give to your winged reverie a ready cage.' Well, that could be reduced to a sort of equation that says: 'Fantasy is a bird whose cage is the garden,' but, put like that, the poetry evaporates.

FERRARI. It dissolves.

BORGES. It disappears, so that there, although there's a metaphor— and a new metaphor, perhaps, although it's not very interesting—we immediately feel that the poetry is in the rhythm. And in particular, 'will give to your winged reverie a ready cage' works immediately, one feels it as poetry. And then one can find a logical justification for it by saying that the fantasy is a bird, and that the cage of the fantasy is a garden. But to find a justification for it like that is almost to destroy it, in fact.

FERRARI. Of course, the justification is alien to poetry.

BORGES. It's alien to poetry . . . In general, I think that one feels the beauty of a phrase, and then, if one wants to, one can find a justification for it or not. At the same time one has to feel that the phrase isn't arbitrary.

FERRARI. That the justification is inherent, in some way.

BORGES. Yes, in some way, although one may not be aware of it.

87

Edgar Allan Poe

●

OSVALDO FERRARI. Some time ago, Borges, you told me that you would have loved to have been different literary figures. In fact, each of the writers or poets you talked about was characterized by an unfortunate, difficult and almost tormented life. One of them, an American who was translated and admired in Europe in his time, was Edgar Allan Poe.

JORGE LUIS BORGES. Yes, Poe was unquestionably a genius, but one has that conviction, not when reading specific passages by him but when one remembers his work as a whole. I have a story about a man who decides to draw the world. So, he sits in front of a blank wall— there's nothing to prevent us from thinking that the wall is infinite— and the man starts to draw all sorts of things: he draws anchors, he draws compasses, he draws towers, he draws swords, he draws staffs. And he carries on drawing like that for an indefinite period, because he would have reached old age. And he's filled that long wall with drawings. The moment of his death arrives, and he's given a vision—

I don't really know how—of all his work in one glimpse, and he realizes that what he's drawn is a portrait of his own face. Now, I think that parable or fable of mine could be applied to writers. That is, a writer thinks he's writing about lots of subjects, but really what he leaves behind, if he's lucky, is an image of himself. And in Poe's case, we see that image—a fairly concrete vision of a man of genius, of an extremely unfortunate man. . . . And that is aside, well, from the poems which I think are mediocre. Poe at his best was like a minor Tennyson, although Tennyson's poetry is lovely, of course.

FERRARI. But his stories are a different matter.

BORGES. His stories, perhaps more the memory of the stories than their reading . . . well, he produced so many unforgettable things. He had the fortune to be read by Baudelaire. Baudelaire didn't know English very well and couldn't spot Poe's technical faults but he was astounded by the imagination of Poe, who was read by Mallarmé as well. And now, oddly, he's a much more important poet in France than in the United States.

FERRARI. But, how odd that is.

BORGES. Yes, I was in the United States, I was talking about Poe, like all foreigners, and they looked at me with surprise . . . I had to remind them that he'd given rise to Baudelaire, who gave rise to the symbolists, that symbolism would be impossible without Poe. And *modernismo* as well, since *modernismo* which appeared here, in America, was produced in the shadow of Hugo, of Verlaine and of Poe.

FERRARI. So in the shadow of symbolism.

BORGES. Yes, and that lovely book by Lugones, which is so unjustly forgotten, *Strange Forces*, is clearly written under the influence of Poe. A proof of that, if further proof were needed, is the fact that at the end there's a 'Cosmogony in Ten Lessons'. Which is amusing, no? And that 'Cosmogony' is a sort of echo of Poe's 'Eureka', which is also a sort of philosophy of the world, and has some relation to Schopenhauer's work, *The World as Will and Representation*. Besides, Poe wrote those three stories, 'The Murders in the Rue Morgue', 'The Purloined Letter', which is perhaps the best of them, the idea that something obvious can be invisible, the idea that Chesterton used for his story 'The Invisible Man'. And then, yes, 'The Mystery of Marie Rogêt' which is the pinnacle of the detective story, in the sense that there's no physical action—there's simply the presentation of a crime, a discussion about its circumstances and then a solution. Exactly the opposite of American crime novels today, which aren't crime novels but, well, accounts of crime and sex. What Poe couldn't predict was that he'd created a genre with those stories. And also with 'The Gold-Bug'. That genre is the well-known detective genre which shouldn't be disparaged, since it has gained the attention of Wilkie Collins, of Dickens, of Chesterton, of writers of detective fiction throughout the world. And all of them come from those stories by Poe.

FERRARI. Many things start with Poe.

BORGES. Many things start with Poe. . . . Now, I had an argument with Roger Caillois, to whom I owe so much, since he forgot about that argument and voted for me in the Formentor Prize, and he published a book of mine in French. And I owe, well, my fame to that publication. I owe it in large part to that publication which Roger Caillois produced of some of my stories in French.

FERRARI. And also in large part to the Formentor Prize.

BORGES. Yes, undoubtedly. So Poe sketched, left his image in his stories. Or we could say that he posthumously cast a long shadow—a glowing shadow one would have to say, so that the word isn't too gloomy. On the other hand, there are his stories which are very different from one another. Because if you take, for example, the story about the maelstrom, the story 'The Man of the Crowd', 'The Pit and the Pendulum', 'The Masque of the Red Death' and 'The Cask of Amontillado'—they are very different.

FERRARI. But the terror is always there.

BORGES. The terror is always there . . . Poe was accused of being a follower of the Germans. He replied with a lovely remark, he said, 'Yes, but terror is not of Germany but of the soul.'

FERRARI. Ah, how wonderful.

BORGES. Yes, it comes from the soul. He felt that terror. Of course, if he hadn't felt it that way, he couldn't have conveyed it as he did. Now, I think that if I had to choose one text by Poe—and there's no reason to choose just one—I'd choose 'The Narrative of Arthur Gordon Pym'.

FERRARI. I thought so.

BORGES. Yes, the name, of course, is clearly a variation on Edgar Allan Poe, because Arthur and Edgar are English, then Allan and Gordon are Scottish, and Pym is clearly Poe. But I'd say that the final pages of that story are particularly remarkable. In them, a really strange idea stands out—the idea of thinking about the colour white, of perceiving the colour white as something terrible. At the same time, that's the basis of a justly famous novel, *Moby Dick, The White Whale* by Melville. There's a chapter in that book called 'The Whiteness of the Whale', and there Melville talks about the colour white as something terrible. And that's what one finds in the last pages of Poe's story, and Melville must have known it. I don't say that to criticize Melville, since why assume that if poets are interested in everything, the books they've read shouldn't also interest them. Emerson said that poetry is born of poetry . . .

FERRARI. And in Poe's case, Borges, what literary influences do you see?

BORGES. Not in his stories, but one sees in his poetry that, well, Tennyson was very important at that time. I remember that they held a dinner for Walt Whitman, and towards the end of it Whitman said: 'I toast the master of us all, Tennyson.' On the other hand, they asked Tennyson what he thought about Whitman, and he said, 'I am aware of Whitman,' that is, I think about Whitman as one might think about a great whale, in an ocean, and he added, 'but no, sir, I do not think about Whitman.' That means that Tennyson felt that Whitman's poetry (free verse) was a challenge in some way, that this new type of poetry was destroying the poetry he wrote. And so he preferred not to think about Whitman, because it was something so strange . . .

FERRARI. And dangerous in a way.

BORGES. And dangerous, inconceivable, so he preferred not to think about it. In fact, it's impossible to think about modern literature without those great American poets, Whitman and Poe. Now, Whitman wasn't very generous with Poe—when Poe died, Whitman wrote a piece on him, and said (I almost feel ashamed to repeat it) that in Poe's work there was no trace of American democracy. I don't think that Poe ever thought about American democracy.

FERRARI. No, Poe thought about the aristocracy, as Baudelaire says.

BORGES. . . . Yes, but that always happens—that a poet is reproached for not having done what they never set out to do, no?

FERRARI. Of course, and Poe was completely removed from that type of intention.

BORGES. Of course, Whitman might have done it to draw attention indirectly to Poe. Otherwise, one can't explain it.

FERRARI. As you know, I always associate you with, let's say, the speculative genre. With having turned speculation into a literary genre.

BORGES. In any case, I feel more speculative than affirmative or negative. I'd like to be affirmative—being negative upsets me. I stick with the perhaps, with the maybe, which is perhaps the wisest course.

FERRARI. On the other hand, I think about fate as Poe's own, personal literary genre—we see it in the 'Nevermore' of 'The Raven'.

BORGES. Yes, and that's a fairly common feeling, and one which can also offer consolation, eh? Because if one doesn't believe in free will, like myself, then one doesn't feel guilty—if I've acted badly, I've been compelled to act badly.

FERRARI. By fate.

BORGES. That's why I don't believe in justice, because justice presupposes free will—and if there's no free will, then nobody can be punished, or rewarded. And that brings us again to those lines that I always quote from Almafuerte, who I've quoted each time we've talked: 'Only ask for justice, but better not to ask for anything'— because to ask for justice is already asking too much.

FERRARI. I hope, Borges, that we've dealt justly with Poe.

BORGES. I think so.

88

Paul Groussac

●

OSVALDO FERRARI. There's a writer among us, Borges, who you value for his style in particular. I think that you see him as fundamentally a stylist, the style that, as you say, taught Alfonso Reyes how to write . . .

JORGE LUIS BORGES. Groussac.

FERRARI. Paul Groussac.

BORGES. . . . Yes, Groussac merits, certainly, a biography, a biography that dispenses with encomium, with hyperbole, with everything apart from reading him, and perhaps with the excess of proper names and with dates, which is one of the faults of biography as a genre. Groussac's was a strange fate, and it would merit, as I've said, a biography that was sensitive to that fate. Groussac would have loved to be a famous French writer, I don't know what circumstances brought him to this country. He started off as a Hispanist, and he was a friend of Alphonse Daudet. Now, when one talks about Daudet, one tends to think about minor works like *Letters from My Mill, Tartarin of Tarascon,* or *Jack*, but one forgets the great novelist of *The Immortal*, for example, and other works. And, besides, Daudet was a friend of Flaubert, they shared more or less the same aesthetic. Well, I don't think that biography of Groussac will ever be written. In any case, I don't think it will be written in the Argentine Republic, because the sin of being French isn't easily forgiven, and it won't be written in France because as I've confirmed, not without sadness, Groussac is unknown.

FERRARI. Unjustly . . .

BORGES. Unjustly, and that's only to be expected, because in France they look for the specifically, or the professionally, or the typically Argentine. And Groussac certainly wasn't that. Groussac would have loved to be famous in France, but it was his fate to be famous here, and as he said, 'To be famous in South America is not to relinquish being unknown,' which was true then. Now it isn't, now there's been that commercial Latin American boom and a South American can be famous. For example, I've been one of the beneficiaries. But in Groussac's time, no. And it's only natural that it should be like that, since, well, we owe so much, we owe almost everything to France. France, on the other hand, can do without 'Argentine culture'. Groussac didn't know that his fate was not to be a famous French writer, but something quite different—to be a missionary, let's put it like that, for French culture, and in particular for French style, for economy, for sobriety, for the elegance of French. And he laid the foundations of that economy, that sobriety, that French elegance, at a time when Spanish prose was havering between what Groussac himself called 'after-dinner prose', or the archaisms of people who think they're imitating Cervantes by imitating his style which is the least important part of his work. Well, Groussac wanted to write with economy, and that still isn't understood in France, since now the main criteria is statistical: one tends to accumulate the greatest number of words, and proof of that is the latest edition of the Academy dictionary which comprises two volumes. But there was a time when the French language struggled between two possibilities: between an abundance of words, and an abundance of expression or the expressive possibility, and it chose the latter. That is, it chose, let's say, Boileau rather than Rabelais. Now the idea of judging a language by the number of words it contains is a mistake, and this example serves to demonstrate it. Let's suppose a system of numeration that consists of two figures, as in Leibniz, a binary system. We would first have one, then zero—one-zero, which would count for two rather than ten. And then three would be one-zero-one. That is, the series of natural numbers, which is infinite, could be expressed with two symbols. And that's not normally taken into consideration, but in Groussac it is—he wrote with precision, and with that type of irony, of wit which is in itself French. Because when one talks about wit in Spain, one understands something different. We can see it in Gracián's case, who wrote his *Acuity and Art of Wit*, but in saying 'wit' he was thinking specifically about wordplay. He refers, for example, to *alígero* Dante. Of course, 'Dante Alighieri' lends itself to the wordplay of *alígero*. And Groussac certainly didn't take that approach. Groussac's work is not only interesting for its style but also for its variety of subjects, since he was interested in many things. In *The Intellectual Journey* there's a chapter on dreams.

FERRARI. That's right.

BORGES. He was very interested in the psychology of dreams—he noted that it was strange that we were more or less reasonable despite having passed the best part of the night in the fantastical, irrational world of dreams. 'How strange,' he said, 'that we wake up sane, after having passed through that region of shadow . . . '.

FERRARI. Of intermittent madness, he says.

BORGES. Ah, yes, the intermittent madness of dreams. He also venerated the classics and French literature, but, no doubt under the influence of Victor Hugo, he perhaps excessively venerated Shakespeare, who for him was the greatest poet. He was interested in so many things . . . such as Argentine history, he has that book, *Essays on Argentine History*, which is a lovely read, where there's no cult of the great man, since he judges them in an impartial way. I remember that my father would say, 'The catechism has been replaced in this country by Argentine history' (that is, by the cult of the great man). The truth is that we have such a brief history, and yet we're so overwhelmed with anniversaries and equestrian statues . . .

FERRARI. Groussac criticized Cervantes on the same grounds.

BORGES. Yes, his two talks on Cervantes are perhaps the most perceptive things that have been written about Cervantes, and all that in the short space of two talks. Then, the essays on French Romanticism, well, what he said about Mariano Moreno, his opinions on Argentine literature—he believed that Argentine literature didn't exist organically, he thought that those four volumes by Ricardo Rojas were absurd, pompously titled *History of Argentine Literature* and written in the style, well, let's put it politely, of an after-dinner toast, no? Rather than in a critical style, since it's assumed that one should try to praise each author, to lessen their defects, to exaggerate or invent their virtues, because the book is written with that aim.

FERRARI. Yes. Now, Borges, you seem to have identified with Groussac over the years. There's a passage of yours where you say, 'Groussac or Borges, I don't know which of them is writing this page.'

BORGES. Well, yes, but that's down to the fact that I was made director of the National Library in 1955 and that same year I discovered that I was surrounded by 900,000 volumes—we would always say that there were a million, but there weren't actually that many (*laughs*)—and the impossibility of reading them all. And I wrote that poem about God, 'who with magnificent irony / gave me both books and night.' And then I thought that Groussac must have felt the same, but he was braver than me and he didn't write the poem. Yes, our fates are similar to a certain extent. According to some people, that poem, 'Poem about Gifts', is one of the best that I've written. And its theme is that blindness can also be a gift, that I've thought that, and that possibly Groussac would have thought that as well, and in the same place. That is, in some way, if only for an instant, I have been Groussac, and I must be thankful for that fate. For a few instants I have been Groussac, since I've thought the same thing and I've experienced the same environment, and doubtless at that same desk that was his desk. And to have been Groussac, if only for a moment, is something that one must be thankful for, and that I must be thankful for. And once that poem was written, I understood that it was a triple dynasty, since there was another director of the library, Mármol, who was also blind. Mármol is now forgotten as a writer. Yet, when we say, and we say it a lot in conversation, especially now, thinking about contemporary events, 'the time of Rosas', the image that those words conjure for us is the image of the novel *Amalia*, by Mármol. That is, people can forget the name of José Mármol, or they can think that he was a minor writer, but each time that we say 'the time of Rosas' we don't think about the historical time of Rosas, nor even the lovely volumes of Ramos Mejía's *Rosas and His Time*, but those wonderfully moving and indiscrete pages of *Amalia* by Mármol.

FERRARI. Like that marvellous chapter, 'Scenes from a Dance', for example.

BORGES. That's right, and the characters' conversations, and their indiscretions as well. For example, when that woman appears, Doña Marcelina, who was a brothel madam, and she talks about the three unities of classical tragedy, 'which my client and friend Doctor Juan Crisóstomo Lafinur taught me' (*laughs*). So that through her we learn about the habits of that Romantic poet. Well, Ernesto Palacio told me that a test of someone's literary sensitivity was whether they valued Groussac. That is, if a person had literary sensitivity, they would be drawn to Groussac. If they were insensitive to literature, they would feel indifference or aversion. And I think that Ernesto Palacio was right. I've taught four courses on Argentine literature, that literature which doesn't exist, according to Groussac, in four universities in the United States: Austin, Harvard, East Lansing and Bloomington. Well, each time I've taught Argentine literature, I've talked about Groussac, and I've invited my students—since I don't believe in compulsory literature—to find any book by Groussac and to read it, because I know that once one starts on Groussac's work, one becomes ensnared, fortunately ensnared by it. And here we could think about his essays . . . I would choose the book *Literary Criticism* if I had to choose one, but why choose one, when we have the two volumes of *The Intellectual Journey*.

FERRARI. And *From the River Plate to the Niagara*.

BORGES. Yes, now I don't know why in *From the River Plate to the Niagara* he's so inexplicably blind to the great virtues of North American literature, I can't understand it—it seems strange that he wrote so thoughtlessly, and made such superficial and unjust criticisms of great writers like Emerson, for example. He said of Emerson that he was a pale imitation of Carlyle. Well, Emerson considered himself a follower of Carlyle, but their work is completely different. More than anything, the first difference would be that Carlyle was an unhappy man, that Carlyle was one of the forefathers, one of the sad forefathers of Nazism, but Emerson wasn't, Emerson was a happy man, and a man of great curiosity. I have here a book I'm reading by Emerson, about Asia, and there's a lovely essay in it that made me study Persian literature, Persian poetry. And that other book of his, *Representative Men*, which led me to the study of a man he characterizes as a mystic: Swedenborg, about whom I'm thinking of writing a book at some stage, although it's a vast subject and the time I have left is short. But I got to find out about Swedenborg through Emerson.

FERRARI. Of course. According to your essay, Borges, Groussac was a humanist, a historian, a Hispanist, a critic, a traveller and an educator.

BORGES. Yes, and an educator, of course, that is, his mission—something he couldn't know—was to be a teacher of French culture and, in particular, of the habits of French prose in this country.

FERRARI. Which benefited Argentine literature.

BORGES. Yes, he's one of our benefactors, and a rather neglected benefactor at times. And yet, in the library magazine he published a poem by Almafuerte, at a time when Almafuerte was rather disparaged by the critics. He also published a story by Lugones.

FERRARI. Which means that he also appreciated our better things.

BORGES. Yes, of course.

89

Shakespeare

●

OSVALDO FERRARI. In other interviews we've talked about the classics, Borges, and also about your favourites among the classics, but we haven't talked about the figure who inspired your story, 'Everything and Nothing'.

JORGE LUIS BORGES. Shakespeare.

FERRARI. For whom you say the plot is of secondary importance, for example.

BORGES. I think so, but besides, for commercial reasons, he was looking for plots that were already well known. For example, in the case of *Macbeth*, when there was a Scottish king on the British throne, who'd written a treatise on demonology, and who was also a descendant of one of the figures in the action, Banquo. And all that was useful. Now, Banquo, according to Holinshed's *Chronicles* which Shakespeare had read, was a rather sorry figure but Shakespeare had to turn him into a hero so as not to displease the king. So he changed the plot. And Macbeth seems to have been a fairly good king, but he had to turn him into a tyrant. And he ruled for I think nine or ten years, but it suited Shakespeare to compress all that action, and in fact *Macbeth* is Shakespeare's fastest-paced drama, that is, let's say, it hits the ground running, with the witches' scene: 'When shall we three meet again? / In thunder, lightning, or in rain?' Bioy Casares and I made a translation of *Macbeth*, and we translated that as 'Cuando bajo el fulgor del trueno' (a deliberate confusion of thunder and lightning) 'otra vez seremos una sola cosa las tres?' Which is good, I think, no?

FERRARI. It's very good.

BORGES. Well, it's not a literal translation, but that's only fitting . . . well, Shakespeare would have approved, no?

FERRARI. Most probably.

BORGES. We translated three or four scenes, and then I don't know why—one never knows why these things happen—we stopped, we put it aside, and I don't know if we'll take it up again.

FERRARI. Later they were gathered by Victoria Ocampo for the *Sur* issue on Shakespeare, in which you write a short piece about him.

BORGES. I didn't know that—was there a *Sur* issue on Shakespeare?

FERRARI. Dedicated entirely to Shakespeare, yes.

BORGES. . . . I think that you're making up the past.

FERRARI (*laughs*). No, no, it's true.

BORGES. Talking about Shakespeare, one always thinks that one hasn't said enough, no? That one should have said more. How strange, it's as if Shakespeare were infinite. And I've sometimes used that name, and not another poet's, because I've sensed that connotation of infinite variety that's there in his name, and which isn't there with other poets who perhaps aren't inferior to him. For example, if I say John Donne, well, I mention a great name, but it's not a great name for the reader's imagination. On the other hand, if I say Shakespeare, it is. Hugo has also contributed to giving Shakespeare's name a connotation of infinity.

FERRARI. Talking about the infinite in relation to Shakespeare's name, we're also talking about the infinite richness of the English language.

BORGES. That as well, yes. Well, the English language, as I've said before, has an advantage over other Western languages. Statistically, there are more words of Latin derivation than Saxon derivation in English—the essential words are Saxon, that is, Germanic. And the atmosphere, let's say, of each word, is a little different. That doesn't matter if we're translating a book on logic, for example, or philosophy. But if we're translating a poem, perhaps the rhythm and the atmosphere of the words are more important than the meaning. So that a literal translation would be the least faithful. And so, for each notion in English there are always two words: one of Saxon derivation, which is usually short, and another of Latin derivation, which is usually longer and more abstract. Of all the languages I know, English is the most physical. Spanish is a relatively abstract language, as is Latin. But English is a very physical language, and that's an extremely important quality for poetry. And then, the play between Saxon and Latin words . . . One sees that in what would become the classic book of English literature, which is the translation that was made in the time of King James I, the author of the treatise on demonology and the contemporary of Macbeth, yes—*The King James Bible*. There those two sources of the English language are in constant play: the Saxon source and the Latin source, and one notes the interplay of both elements. On the other hand, in Germany, they've taken the Latin words and they've translated them. For example, 'Vaterland' is an exact translation of 'patria', and they've taken it because the Germans didn't have that idea of the importance of the 'land of the fathers'. They would simply think in terms of their loyalty to this or that chief, for example, but not about having been born in a specific place, which is natural among people who were constantly moving from one place to another.

FERRARI. In the case of Shakespeare, you see the English language as something mysterious, you talk about the 'mysterious English language', referring to Shakespeare.

BORGES. Well, yes, because he used words from both sources. . . . At that time, English was perhaps even more flexible than it is now— one could constantly use neologisms, and they were accepted by listeners. On the other hand, now compound words can be used naturally in German while in English they're rather artificial. Although Joyce has devoted himself to coining words. But he's made a literary work that's incomprehensible to most people, no? He's devoted himself to that, and I think that in *Finnegans Wake*, apart from the conjunctions, and the prepositions and articles, each word is a neologism and a compound word. And that applies not only to the nouns but also to the adjectives and verbs too. Joyce invents verbs. Of course,

English has that capacity—that a word, without changing its form, can be an adjective, a noun, or a verb, one simply has to use it in whichever way. For example, in Spanish we have 'vals' and 'valsear' but in English 'waltz' is both things, and it can be used as an adjective but the form doesn't change.

FERRARI. Yes, perhaps it's the most functional language possible.

BORGES. Yes, in that sense, yes. On the other hand, I'm trying to learn some Japanese, and I discovered with horror that adjectives are conjugated. That is, the adjective changes according to whether it refers to a current event, a past event or a future event. Not only does the noun or the verb change but also the adjective. And a Japanese child learns that without realizing that they're learning something very, very complex. It's the same as what I told you about numbers that change according to what is being counted. So that there are two different types of words for four instruments, for four small animals, for four big animals, for four abstract ideas, for four people, for four long, cylindrical objects. The system changes.

FERRARI. There are many languages in the one language.

BORGES. Yes, there are many in one, but it seems that for a child that doesn't present a major difficulty, since every language is easy for a child.

FERRARI. Indeed.

BORGES. That's why some English poet said, 'Wax to receive and marble to retain,' which was later applied to the lover, who readily receives an impression of the woman he loves, and who holds on to it for ever. But it was first applied to children, who receive easily and retain for ever.

FERRARI. Of course. Now, returning to Shakespeare, to Shakespeare's personal life, you tell us that once he'd achieved economic well-being the theatrical manager and author stopped writing . . .

BORGES. Yes.

FERRARI. And that would be an extraordinary example of the way that the muse sometimes chooses to express itself momentarily through a man.

BORGES. One could think that, or one might also think that he needed that stimulus, the stimulus of having to work, well, for a particular group of actors, in such and such a theatre, and that without that he had no inspiration. That can happen . . . we would have a minor example in the case of our own Hilario Ascasubi, who wrote lovely poetry in the Civil Wars because he needed that stimulus of conflict and he wanted to inspire the gauchos, the soldiers. And then, later on in Paris, when he tried to recreate all that, he wrote that lengthy rhymed novel called *Santos Vega or The Twins of La Flor*. It contains few memorable passages because he didn't have that stimulus.

FERRARI. Ah, of course.

BORGES. It seems that Shakespeare needed that stimulus, well, the commitment of having to write a theatrical piece for his actors which had to be performed on such and such a date. And then, once he had attained financial comfort, he no longer had that stimulus. It seems that in his last years he didn't write anything, apart from his epitaph or will which was deliberately prosaic, yes. And he died, as Groussac recounts in an admirable book of literary criticism, after a big meal with actors who'd visited him from London. He died shortly after that. He'd also devoted himself to legal disputes. Legal affairs always interested him, and that can be seen in the abundance of legal metaphors in his poems—there are lots of metaphors taken from, well, the legal statutes. He makes use of legal metaphors that wouldn't be common in colloquial language either. But Shakespeare was interested in that, and it interested him so much that his old age was filled with niggardly legal disputes. He was also a moneylender, I'm sorry to say. That is, he forgot that he was a great poet and preferred to be a moneylender and a litigator. In the end, he chose a curious fate. For me, it's quite incomprehensible.

FERRARI. But he never entirely abandoned metaphor.

BORGES. No.

FERRARI. Now, towards the end of your story, Borges, towards the end of your story about Shakespeare, 'Everything and Nothing', it says that Shakespeare spoke to God, telling him, 'I who in vain have been so many men, wish to be one.'

BORGES. Yes, it means that he would have liked to be Shakespeare, and then it reveals, of course . . . the parallel was necessary for literary reasons—that God doesn't know very well who he is either, no?

FERRARI. Yes, that emerges in God's reply to Shakespeare, which I'm going to read.

BORGES. Of course, it's a way of comparing Shakespeare to God. Which would be the highest praise, no? To compare a man to the divinity.

FERRARI. God's reply to Shakespeare is, 'I too am not. I dreamt the world as you dreamt your work, my Shakespeare.'

BORGES. On the other hand, according to the Holy Scriptures, God said, 'I Am that I Am.' But I think that the power of that passage is in 'my Shakespeare', because it implies a sort of personal affection of God towards Shakespeare, no? And, besides, Shakespeare is one of his creations, and he acknowledges him among the thousands of his creations . . .

FERRARI. It also implies your personal affection, Borges' affection towards Shakespeare.

BORGES. I, or the muse, we got it right with that 'my' which was the essential word for that line to be at all effective, to have any power.

90

New Dialogue on *The Conspirators*

•

OSVALDO FERRARI. Regarding your latest book of poems, *The Conspirators*, I maintained, Borges, that it brings you towards a form of cosmogony, or a foundation . . .

JORGE LUIS BORGES. I hadn't thought about that. Now, they told me at La Pampa that they'd spotted a sadness in that book that isn't there in my earlier books.

FERRARI. Ah, I didn't think of that.

BORGES. I hadn't thought about it either, and they told me that the only book of mine in which there's happiness or joy is the series of milongas that are called *For the Six Strings*, that there's happiness there. And I told them, 'Perhaps that's because it's an anonymous book, a book that's been written by my elders, or by everyone.' On the other hand, the other books, as they are personal, may be sad. Now, what you've said about cosmogony, I didn't know that, but it could be true, since if a writer writes what he sets out to write, he hasn't written anything—he should write something more than what he's set out to write. That is, the work should exceed the writer's intention.

FERRARI. And each work should be a new beginning.

BORGES. Ah, yes.

FERRARI. If it's a beginning, it's cosmogonical.

BORGES. I think that if one writes something to suit a particular book, one is simply writing to fill up space. One must write each piece thinking about the composition of that piece. The fact that it becomes part of a book later on is insignificant.

FERRARI. Accidental.

BORGES. Yes, irrelevant, as they would say in English.

FERRARI. What is beyond doubt is that your book has an oneiric inspiration.

BORGES. Well, I hope so.

FERRARI. Almost all the poems . . .

BORGES. Generally, if I compare my dreams to my waking hours, I regret many things. For example, I regret my nightmares, which can be terrible.

FERRARI. One of your distinctive features appears in the book—enumeration.

BORGES. Yes, it's assumed that Walt Whitman invented it, but I think that the Psalms had already invented it. And, besides, enumeration is a natural form, a mental activity, no?

FERRARI. Yes . . .

BORGES. If time is successive, well, enumeration is successive, and it takes place in time.

FERRARI. And it occurs in poetry.

BORGES. And it occurs in poetry. Now, I talked to Bioy Casares about this. He thinks that one starts to sense enumeration after the number four. That is, if you list three things, the reader doesn't experience it as an enumeration, but if there are four or five things, one senses them as an enumeration, and perhaps one senses them as something mechanical. Yet, in Walt Whitman's case, we have strange enumerations, in the Psalms of David as well. One doesn't sense that they're mechanical—one senses that they're inevitable.

FERRARI. Of course.

BORGES. Or in any case, one appreciates them, one doesn't criticize them. No, I don't think that enumeration is a prohibited figure. No figure is prohibited—if things turn out well then they are good (*laughs*).

FERRARI. Silvina Ocampo talks in a poem about a long enumerative joy . . .

BORGES. Ah, how lovely. And her book is called *Enumeration of the Patria*, no?

FERRARI. Precisely.

BORGES. The idea of counting isn't an anti-poetic idea. The proof is in . . . well, in English, you have 'tale' and 'tell', but 'tell' applies to a story and to the consecutive beads of the rosary, or the consecutive peals of a church bell, since the words 'tale' and 'tell' must share the same origin, no? 'Toll' which is applied to bells, and 'tell' which is applied to stories, to counting, must be the same thing.

FERRARI. Now, I would say that enumeration . . .

BORGES. No, I think that enumeration is licit.

FERRARI. And in your case . . .

BORGES. . . . If it turns out well. As for chaotic enumeration, perhaps it's impossible, since if there's a universe, all things are part of that united whole, and chaotic enumeration could serve to make us feel not chaos but the cosmos or the secret cosmos behind the world, no?

FERRARI. Ah, that's quite clear.

BORGES. Yes, when Walt Whitman says, 'And of the threads that connect the stars, and of wombs and of the father-stuff . . . ,' one feels that those things are so dissimilar, yet, they resemble one another. Otherwise, the enumeration would be irrational and unjustifiable.

FERRARI. There's order in it.

BORGES. Yes, it has an order, and a, well, secret and therefore mysterious order. Now, I don't know if I've perhaps been guilty of the abuse of enumeration in that book.

FERRARI. No, I think that it has to do with your desire to be faithful to all those symbols that have seemed essential or permanent to you.

BORGES. Well, I've written about that recently, as a matter of fact, and I listed them and I wondered why I've chosen those particular ones. And then I came to the conclusion that I've been chosen by them. Because I wouldn't have any trouble, for example, doing without labyrinths and talking about cathedrals or mosques; doing without tigers and talking about panthers or jaguars; doing without mirrors and talking, well, about echoes, which are like auditory mirrors. Yet, I feel that if I worked like that, the reader would spot immediately that I'd lightly disguised myself (*both laugh*), and I would be exposed, that is, if I said 'the leopard', the reader would think about a tiger; if I said 'cathedrals', the reader would think about labyrinths, because the reader already knows my habits. And perhaps expects them, and perhaps . . . well, they're resigned to them, and they're resigned to such an extent that if I don't repeat those symbols, I disappoint them in some way.

FERRARI. Or you disappoint yourself (*laughs*).

BORGES. Or I disappoint myself, and I disappoint my readers, who expect that of me, and not something else. That is, perhaps any tic, any habit can be turned into a tradition.

FERRARI. If it's firmly established, of course.

BORGES. Yes, all things tend towards tradition. So that what in the beginning was arbitrary and exceptional, ends up being traditional, expected, accepted and approved.

FERRARI. Of course, but, in your case, it could also be a matter of something like paying your debt of knowledge to the world . . .

BORGES. That's right . . .

FERRARI. Returning each of the elements of your knowledge to it.

BORGES. Well, that's a very generous interpretation, I'm grateful for it and I adopt it forthwith. I will plagiarize it, I promise you (*laughs*).

FERRARI (*laughs*). It's an idea, but it could also be to counteract the nightmare of an excess of memories of the world.

BORGES. Yes, well, Jean Cocteau said that all style is a series of tics, and he's right.

FERRARI. Of habits, of course.

BORGES. Of course. There the word 'tics' is used pejoratively or, rather, as a joke, no?

FERRARI. Yes, but, in this case, the poems of *The Conspirators* reveal both love and affection for the world, for those symbols taken from the world.

BORGES. And, I hope to feel that way. In that passage that I dictated recently, I'm astonished by the singularly limited number of my symbols, since, let's suppose that we call an indefinite series of things 'world', it means that I'm not very sensitive, since only a few have made such an impression on me that they become my habits, eh? For example, I talk so much about tigers. Why don't I talk about fish, which are much stranger? Yet, I don't know why tigers have made a greater impression on me than fish, although now, on reflection, I realize that fish are much stranger.

FERRARI. In any case, Borges, what I do see is that you need to stay faithful to your habitual symbols.

BORGES. . . . Yes, it's that if I don't, I feel that I'm committing a fraud.

FERRARI. Of course.

BORGES. And, besides, well, a sort of decline, a form of exhaustion, or perhaps knowing that if those symbols have chosen me, it must be for some reason, that I have no right to change—I've been chosen by tigers, by mirrors, by knives, by labyrinths, by masks, and I have no right to other things. Although each one of those things presupposes the universe, which is made up of infinite things, of indefinite things. We just don't know.

FERRARI. Yet in the poems of *The Conspirators*, we encounter many more symbols than you've mentioned.

BORGES. Ah, yes? There will be one or two more.

FERRARI. For example, in the poem 'Someone Dreams' . . .

BORGES. I don't remember that.

FERRARI. That poem in which you wonder, 'What will Time have dreamt up until now?'

BORGES. Ah, yes, yes.

FERRARI. And you reply with, let's say, all the primordial elements that continually inform your poetry, and some other elements.

BORGES. Are there any other elements? Well, thank you very much, perhaps you're right.

FERRARI. I would like to read a section of the poem as demonstration.

BORGES. Well, I've forgotten it. I know that it's enumerative, like almost everything I write, yes, let's see.

FERRARI. 'What will Time have dreamt up until now, which is, like all the nows, the apex? It has dreamt the sword, whose proper home is verse' . . .

BORGES. Well, there I'm condemning the sword, of course. I say it in a reticent, but sufficient way, no? 'Whose proper home is verse,' that is, rather than the hand of man.

FERRARI. But it lives on in verse.

BORGES. Yes.

FERRARI. 'It has dreamt and worked the judgement, which can feign wisdom' . . .

BORGES. And, it's a good line, eh? Although it's also a judgement— 'which can feign wisdom,' of course, we can feign wisdom.

FERRARI. With a judgement.

BORGES. Of course.

FERRARI. 'It has dreamt faith, it has dreamt the barbarous Crusades' . . .

BORGES. Well, 'the barbarous Crusades,' yes, because the Crusades have always been praised, and yet they were terrible affairs.

FERRARI. 'It has dreamt the Greeks who discovered dialogue and doubt. It has dreamt the destruction of Carthage by fire and salt. It has dreamt the word, that clumsy, rigid symbol. It has dreamt' . . .

BORGES. It was Stevenson who insisted that the word was clumsy. Yes, of course, the word is clumsy.